MW00575031

IQ84

Mike Dickenson

IQ84
Copyright © 2017 Mike Dickenson
ISBN 978-0-9908983-1-3

All rights reserved. No part of this publication may be reproduced, distributed, or transmitted in any form or by any means, including photocopying, recording, or other electronic or mechanical methods, without the prior written permission of the publisher, except in the case of brief quotations embodied in critical reviews and certain others noncommercial uses permitted by copyright law.

This is a work of fiction. All names, characters, and events are either products of the author's imagination or used fictitiously. Any resemblance to actual persons, living or dead, events or locations, are entirely coincidental.

Published by Commonlink Productions

www.mikedickenson.com

Reader Beware!

This book will make you think. If you find yourself hovering around the IQ of 84, you may want to put it down now. In fact, go watch some TV. Stay safe out there.

If you're still with me *don't worry* — there isn't any Advanced Calculus or references to Nietzsche that you'll need to deconstruct in the footnotes. But there *are* some questions that *you will* have to think about. Some of these questions may include: "What would *I* do if *my* head blew up?" and "If freedom isn't free then where can I buy some?" These are big questions that every American must ask at least once in their lifetime.

Another thing. The characters in this book are not the brightest. Thus, some of the language is not appropriate for various grandmothers and your occasional zealous church-goer. *Oh!* And about those zealous church-goers...if you happen to be one of them you *might* get offended. While some of the humor you are about to read is *fucking hilarious* (if I say so myself), the subject matter takes a few unconventional turns.

So please, enjoy this book with *caution*! This is a work of satire, which by its nature scrutinizes the long-held beliefs of the status quo and sometimes this can get messy, especially when brains are involved. If you find yourself laughing uncontrollably, then please take a break. Read the news, grab some take-out, go to Walmart - do anything that will give your brain a rest. Then come back.

Chapter 1: David Dingle

It was a typical rainy day in Seattle, when the virus literally exploded on the population and the first person's brain burst into bits, but we'll get to that.

David Dingle looked up from his phone and swerved his car out of the oncoming traffic lane. He was simultaneously sending a text to his mother, checking his HeartMatch.com responses, and wrapping up level seventeen of Zombie Gophers.

"Wow, you're cute!" he said to a profile image of Maria Valdersmart from Ohio as he cruised down Denny Way. He considered this his third and favorite draft: "You have a great smile on your face." David hit send.

"Turn left here," his phone said in a friendly Australian accent and David obliged without needing to think and turned onto 5th Avenue. His phone followed the most efficient route among David's nearly two dozen stops. "Accelerate lightly to reach optimal speed limit," his phone said. His car passed effortlessly through the perfectly timed lights of 5th Avenue. The engine of his BMW Limited Edition hummed like a purring cheetah. It was undoubtedly the nicest car David had ever driven. It was a work vehicle and he appreciated the perk. Too bad his job didn't pay enough for him to actually afford a car of his own. Though he had been thinking of finding employment elsewhere, he wondered if he was qualified for much other than pizza delivery.

His phone rang and he brought it to his ear as he sped down the road. "Hello?"

"David. This is your father, Martin Dingle." (A typical hello from his father.)

"Hi Dad. How are you?"

"Can't sleep. Found a tree snake on the back porch. Out of bullets. Listen, I got your message."

"Are you still in...?"

"Guam. That's right. Now what's this I hear about you quitting your job?"

David hesitated. He hadn't been looking forward to this conversation. His father was not exactly easy going, but David needed some advice. "I haven't quit yet, Dad. It's just, maybe - I don't know. I've been doing the same thing for almost ten years. I was thinking I should see if I'm capable of doing *other* things. It's a big world out there, apparently."

"That's where thinking will get you, David. Now listen to me, I got you this job because I knew it was something you could do."

"Dad, I drive around Seattle and collect signatures from rich white guys and unknown bureaucrats. I'm pretty sure just about anyone could do this job. In fact, I saw this Youtube video the other day about a dog that had been trained to drive one of those Smart Cars. The dog had trouble reaching the gas pedal, but still... Maybe I should get a dog..."

"Stick with me here, David," his father said, accustomed to his son's tangents. "I really don't want you to quit. Remember, your job is important. It's a government job and the government is about the best boss you could ask for because they've already got it all figured out. Now granted, your work may not be as glamorous as fighting on the front lines, but we both know you're too much of a pacifist to ever join the military. You're *certainly* not fit for politics, and you're no good with numbers so accounting's out. Hell, you're barely capable of delivering the mail. In fact you might just be-"

"Dad..."

"My point being, this job is perfect for someone like you."

"Gee thanks," he said, and scrolled through his Facebook feed.

"I mean it. While the true heroes are kicking ass and taking names, you're doing the monotonous groundwork that is still essential to protecting our freedoms. A lot of people died for those freedoms, David. I sure as shit didn't shoot all those people in 'Nam just for you and all your non-contributing millennial drinking buddies to pass back the baton to the communists in the eleventh hour."

"Dad, I don't even drink," he said and began level 18 of Gopher Zombies. This level was important because if he got a kill streak of ten he could buy a titanium mallet.

"The point is," his father continued, "just because the War on Terror is over doesn't mean we still don't have to fight for our freedoms. Remember, the signatures you collect are keeping our nation at peace."

"But how?" David asked for the second time in his life.

"What do you mean *how?*" his father thundered. "Because the government says so, that's how! Listen, you have one job to do and only you can do it, David. Think you can handle that?"

David bit his hangnail. He loved his father but these conversations were growing increasingly difficult to endure. He always felt like he didn't have a choice when he talked to his dad. Still, Martin Dingle was a patriot in the truest sense, apart from the fact that he moved to Guam and married a communist. "I guess," David said.

"Good lad. Don't screw this up. America is counting on you to keep us free."

"Sure, Dad. Tell Matryoshka I said hello," David said and they both hung up.

He shot a glance at the clock. Right on time. He parked his car on the side of the street and trotted into the WestLake Center, white envelope in hand. He jogged up the two flights of stairs and exited the stairwell into a comfortable office building. He liked this spot. There were reclining seats, plenty of freshly brewed coffee, and an excellent wifi signal. David smiled to a rather large woman named Bernice who took his envelope and told him to take a seat.

David sat down in a dark leather couch and disappeared into his phone. He was able to check the weather, synchronize the rest of his route, order lunch, knock out another three rounds of Gopher Zombies, and check to see if Maria Valdersmart had replied yet. (She hadn't.) Five minutes later Bernice returned with his white envelope.

David looked up and smiled. "Thanks!" he said cheerfully and walked out to his car. If everything went smoothly he could finish work an hour early. He stopped at a stoplight and banged out two more levels of Gopher Zombies while he simultaneously watched a video about unhappy cats taking baths.

The light changed and David took a quick right and disappeared into the garage of Bank of America. He drove down to the 12th basement floor, parked his car near the front, grabbed his briefcase and his phone and got out. This was his final stop. He hated this stop. David walked to the underground elevator and pushed the down button. The doors opened and a surly man with a briefcase looked at him impatiently from inside the elevator. David stepped inside.

"Hi," David said in a friendly tone.

"Grm," the man replied. David pulled out his phone.

No Signal.

David shuddered. Luckily, he had come here enough times to know he had to manage his distractions offline. He pulled up a trial version of Zombie Meerkats and set to it. At some point the surly man got out.

David let out a long measured breath as the elevator descended to floor Integer 33. Unexpectedly, just as he was about to smash a monstrous zombie meerkat on its decayed hairless head, the screen on his phone darkened and tall thin important looking words read: LOW BATTERY – POWERING DOWN. David stared at his phone as if it were his mother who had just gone into a coma.

The elevator doors opened with an ominous *DING*! Tiny beads of sweat had already begun to accumulate on his brow. His hands had gone cold and clammy. This was, without a doubt, the worst place in the entire world for his phone to die.

David stepped out of the elevator and into the long boring hallway. At the far end of the hallway, an eternity away, was a solitary brown door. It was the only door between here and there. The ceiling tiles were light brown. The floor was brown with brown stains which had likely been left by dirty brown shoes. David walked quickly towards the brown door much like someone who desperately needs to use the toilet.

He did not knock on the boring brown door at the end of the boring hallway, but rather rushed through the door into the expectedly boring office hoping to get this miserable stop over with as soon as humanly possible. The walls of the office were the same off-brown as the walls in the hallway. The floor was brown and dirty. There was a large desk that likely came from China, had been bought in IKEA, and assembled in this very spot by a guy named Jon. It really didn't get much more exciting than this.

Behind the desk was Gary. Gary was equally as boring as his desk. It was unlikely that Gary had any hobby other than going home at the end of each day. Gary did not look particularly smart. Rather, he looked particularly fat. David didn't dislike Gary, but he sensed quite accurately that Gary disliked him.

"Hey, Gary!" David smiled.

"Mmm," Gary hummed and pushed one of his pudgy fingers onto the keyboard, waited a moment, pushed another key, waited and so-on.

David set his briefcase on the desk and opened it up. Inside were exactly ten 8x11 folders. One of them, however, was different from the others.

"Got something special for you today, Gary," David said with a friendly smile. "I've been working this job for almost ten years and I have *never* seen a folder like *this* one."

Gary looked up. It was the first time he had visually acknowledged David in the last eight months. "Mmm?"

"It's a *manilla* folder," he said and waved it playfully in the air.

Gary looked at the manilla folder for a moment. After a strange and awkward silence Gary shifted his vision and made eye contact with David. David felt as if he were looking into the eyes of a glazed donut.

Gary half-groaned, half-sighed and leaned over and picked up the phone beside him. After a moment's pause he said, "Dale is here."

"David," David corrected with a smile. (There was a one in two chance that this conversation took place every day.) "I'll just wait over there," he said in conclusion after another awkward moment and took a seat in one of the two brown boring chairs. David stared at his comatose phone in tragic denial, poking the power button as one might prod a sleeping gerbil. He regretfully accepted that his phone would not save him today.

The door clicked open and Deborah stepped out. Deborah was a boring-looking woman in her mid-forties who was usually just as excited to see David as Gary was. She was wearing her usual brown skirt. David gave her a big smile and held out the envelope.

"*Manilla* envelope *today*," David said awkwardly, hoping to win a smile from her boring face.

Debora raised an eyebrow. "Neat," she said and took the envelope. "I'll be..."

"Right back," David said, timing his words with hers.

"Mmm hmm," she said.

"I'll take a seat," he smiled, knowing that is what she usually told him to do.

The door closed behind her and David sighed and slumped into his seat again. With Deborah gone, so began the worst part of his day: sitting in this miserable sensory deprivation chamber without a phone.

He tapped his foot nervously.

He tore off a nail.

He pulled a string out of his sleeve and ruined his shirt.

There had to be something to keep his attention.

He stared at the only exciting thing in the room — the clock. David could swear it was ticking backwards.

His eyes lit up with hope — the documents! Maybe *they* would help propel him out of this bored madness. He clicked open his briefcase and pulled one of the envelopes out at random.

He opened the envelope and saw a stack of papers. The top one had a very important looking seal stamped on it which had been left by someone at David's previous stop. Every day he made twenty-four stops at twenty-four different buildings throughout Seattle where he collected signatures which were mailed off in bulk for transport to Washington D.C.

Below the very important looking stamp the document read – Federal Peace and Freedoms Act. A long spread of legalese ensued. It was compelling at first with such provocative terms like Liberty and Emancipation, but eventually all those ten dollar words just ran together and everything became indiscernible. David struggled to stay focused. He reached for another envelope. The Administration of Economic Growth Independence. "*Grrraaaa,*" he sighed. "How can anyone *read* about this stuff?" he wondered. "Isn't there a translation app for this?"

He looked at the clock. Already five minutes had gone by. Deborah should be back by now. It wasn't like her to dilly dally. She was part of the government and the government was a well-oiled machine. *He* was a part of that machine.

Eight minutes.

David coughed. "Excuse me," he said to Gary. His voice reeked of panic. "But don't you think Deborah should be back by now?"

"Mmm," Gary mumbled and shook his head simultaneously up and down and left to right.

David tapped his foot on the floor. Nothing to do. Nothing at all. "Family?" David asked Gary suddenly.

Gary paused for an instant and then resumed typing.

"Just noticed you don't have any photos of family," David began a rapid jolting ramble. "Was wondering if that was allowed or if the room is designed this way, to, you know, keep you from...enjoying yourself maybe." Gary lowered his head. "*I* have family," David began. "A Mom. And a Dad..." he said. "But they're gone now."

Gary blinked, now understanding that this stranger was about to share his life with him. "Sorry?" Gary said, looking at his reflection in the computer.

"Oh gosh," David said, "Not like that. They're alive I mean. Just gone. You know...awaaaay."

Now *Gary* was tapping his foot nervously.

"Overseas, that is. My mom is in New Zealand. Dad's in Guam. Married a Russian Communist, actually. She looks really sweet in the photos he sent. I've only been to California."

Gary's breathing was becoming visibly labored.

"Dad's a pretty grounded guy, actually. Now *mom* on the other hand..."

Suddenly his mind drifted back to the last time he had seen his mother in the flesh. It was the day David had graduated from high school and found his mother was packing her bags. She was wearing a long gray pointy hat that bent behind her waist and her ever present walking staff was resting against the open door of the house.

"Mom?" David asked in surprise.

"David!" she exclaimed. "Oh. Well. Hello then," she said, bowing awkwardly.

"What are you doing?"

David's mother looked at the bags at her feet. "Nothing." She smiled. "Did you just graduate?"

David nodded. "Yeah. Were you there? I didn't see you." He looked at her bags. "Are you um, going somewhere?" he asked.

She sighed. "David, I'm not going to lie. I have been waiting for this moment for eighteen years. I have done everything in my power to raise you to the best of my ability. I have mothered you, *fathered* you — no good dirty father," she mumbled to herself. "I have even exposed you to the greatest literary works of our time, despite the fact that you have *refused* to re-read them."

"Mom, please, not again."

"I'm sorry," Ginny Dingle said, adjusting her hat. "You know how I feel about the Great Trilogy. It has become a part of who I am. You, unexpectedly, I might add, interrupted my plans for adventures of my own. Since you were born I have bided my time. And, well, the moment has come for me to follow my dreams. David, I'm leaving."

"*Leaving?* But where?"

She looked at him for a moment and sucked in a nervous chestful of air. "I am going on the Tolkien Trail."

"The *what?*"

"It's in New Zealand. Since the trilogy's debut on the silver screen I knew I had to see Middle-Earth for myself. And so I shall, I leave in about five minutes."

"*Now?* You're leaving *now?*"

"Well, my plane leaves in three hours, but I still have to catch a ride to Sea-Tac and get through security," she said. "I'm concerned about my Gandalf staff."

David shook his head. "Mom, were you even going to tell me or did you just expect me to come home to an empty house?"

She gave him her best insulted look. "Of course not! Look – I wrote you a note," she said and handed him the back of a used envelope which read: "Going away. Last night's spaghetti is in the freezer. Out of salt."

David's mother took her son in her arms and hugged him. "It's *your* house now, my son, my Frodo. You are a special boy," she said gently. "I am lucky to be your mother. You have gifts that others do not."

"Oh yeah?" he said, pulling away. "Like what?"

"Like, well," she fidgeted with her hat again. "You seem to know a lot about television. Always took a real shine to reality TV," she said proudly.

"That's because no one's around when I get home. You're always off on your role-playing quests."

"Wizard gatherings," she corrected. "You know, it wouldn't hurt you to read a book every now and then. That TV will make you stupid. And *weird*," she said with a raised eyebrow.

"Oh, Mom, not again."

"OK, OK. Sorry." She picked up her bags and stuffed her staff under her arm. "You have a good heart, David. Put it to use, someday." A car honked outside. "Oh, there's my taxi!" she exclaimed and patted his shoulder.

"Am I going to see you again?"

She turned around, set down her bag and grabbed her staff. " 'Don't adventures ever have an end? I suppose not. Someone else always has to carry on the story . . .' Goodbye my son!" He shuddered, knowing that she was quoting The Hobbit.

Back at the office Gary's face was buried in his hands. "Why are you *telling* me all this?" he asked desperately.

"Sorry," David blurted, stealing another glance at the clock. He had been here for twenty minutes! "It's just, well, I suffer from acute anxiety syndrome. Do you have a magazine or something I can look at while I wait?"

Gary seemed to push his face into the computer, perhaps hoping it would absorb him.

Another ten minutes had passed and still no Deborah. A small pile of fingernails lay between his feet. He began taking in long deep breaths and then switched to quick shallow breaths. Even hyperventilation was more exciting than this room. This was sooo boring. He stood up and began pacing the room. He pursed his lips together and broke out into a melodic outburst of *row row row your boat* as he walked back and forth.

David was on his eighteenth round of *row row row your boat* when Gary realized that if he didn't do something, David was going to be the cause of his latest, and likely final, heart attack. "Dale," Gary said. "You have *got* to sit down. Deborah will be back any minute."

"She's *never* taken this long before, Gary," David said hopelessly. "Could you at least call her or something? *Please.* I've really, *really* got to get going."

Gary sighed. He was only supposed to use the phone for protocol and emergencies, but the way he saw it, this was kind of an emergency. David looked like he was about to self-combust. Gary picked up the phone and waited. After an uncomfortable pause Gary said into the phone, "Sir, our courier is still waiting. Is Deborah on her way?" There was a long moment of silence. Gary looked up at David who was staring at him like a dog waiting to be let out to do its business. Gary looked away and put his hand over the mouthpiece.

After three excruciating minutes of boredom, David watched Gary set the phone back onto its cradle. The desk jockey looked shaky; a thin trickle of sweat ran down his forehead. "I'm sorry," he said carefully, "but it appears Deborah cannot come out. You will have to come back. Tomorrow."

David crumpled his brow. "*Tomorrow?*" he asked. "This is very unusual. Did they give you a reason?"

Gary shifted in his seat. "I'm s-sorry," he stuttered and resumed typing. David couldn't help but notice that Gary's hands were slightly trembling.

"What about my envelope?" David asked.

Gary flinched noticeably but said nothing.

David had *no* idea what was going on. In all his years this had never happened before. Had the circumstances been different, had David not been on the verge of a total nervous breakdown, he may have stayed an extra thirty-seconds to inquire further. Instead, he shot out of the office, screamed down the hallway, and punched the elevator buttons in a hopeless code of panic until the door finally opened up.

It was a long excruciating sensation-less 45 seconds inside that boring elevator without a cellphone, and when the doors finally opened David burst out into the lobby of Bank of America like a drowning person finally returning to air. He felt like he had been lost at sea for the last eight years. A strange psychotic smile spread across his face as David looked upon the cosmopolitan world once again — the shiny marble floor, the hundreds of people bustling about, the smell of Starbucks coffee, ahh, it felt good to be back in reality. He found an outlet and plugged in his phone. Moments later it came to life. He studied the screen like a surgeon. He swiped the screen a few times. "Wow, new evidence suggests earthquakes are caused by earthworms? That's incredible!" he said and clicked share.

A green light on the touchscreen flashed and beeped.

"Crap!" he said and stood up. His final timer had gone off. Normally he was early to his drop-off-mail-location, but the waiting had thrown off his schedule. He only had five minutes to drop off the contents of his briefcase. This did not concern him too much as his drop-off point was only two blocks away. What *did* concern him was the fact that he was missing his final folder. In all his years he had never failed to turn everything in. He decided he would just write a note explaining the circumstances and place it inside the briefcase. After-all, they couldn't fire him for something that wasn't his fault.

His drop-off was in the mail slot of a building across from Pioneer Square, and David usually took the alley to save time. He had just stepped into the alley when he heard a metallic scrape and watched dumbstruck as a manhole cover moved out of place. Two boring-looking hands appeared and a woman in a brown skirt crawled out. Her hair was dirty and disheveled and her once impeccable outfit was covered in grime. It was Deborah, and in her hand was David's manilla envelope! Very quickly she brushed herself off and started running away in the other direction.

"Deborah!" David cried, but she didn't hear him. She had taken off at a near sprint.

David couldn't let that envelope get out of his sight so he ran after her as fast as he could. Her running was panicked, it seemed. She reached a sidewalk and zig-zagged through crowds of people, bumping into angry strangers along the way. David was closing the distance between them. She was only meters ahead of him as they crossed Second Avenue and into Pioneer Square.

A gathering of sorts was taking place. Hundreds of people crowded together under a long white banner that read: COMPUTER NERDS EXTRAVAGANZA. Indeed, hundreds of pimply-faced people had converged upon the plaza like money on Bill Gates. Tall ones, skinny ones, fat ones — many with pocket protectors, a few without. Several wore white t-shirts reading, "Have you tried turning it off and on again?" or "My floppy disk is bigger than your hard drive." Semi-circles of pale-faced geeks crowded around short-haired girls with tattoos of Macintosh apples on their forearms. It was indeed a nerd social free-for-all, and Deborah was running right into the middle of it.

She was halfway through the plaza when David finally caught her. He clamped his hand down on her wrist and pulled her to a stop. When she saw him she gasped.

"David! Oh my God!"

Now it was David's turn to be surprised. She knew his name!

Deborah grabbed his other hand and looked up at him like a frightened deer. David noticed for the first time that tears were streaming down her face. She looked like she had just seen a ghost.

"It's OK, it's OK," he said trying to calm her down. "Just tell me what's happening."

"Oh, David! I came here *looking* for you," she said. "I know that this is where you take your envelopes. I came to give this to you," she said, holding out the manilla envelope to him. Her hand was shaking like a leaf.

"Wow, you really take your job seriously," he said with a sense of awe. Gently, he took the manilla envelope from her. He squinted his eyes. "Is that...*blood* on the envelope?" he asked.

Deborah pulled at her hair. "Oh, David," she said, her eyes reliving some terrible moment. "I can't even begin to explain what just happened."

"Start from the beginning," he encouraged.

Her eyes raced with emotion. "Well, as soon as I went into the Organizer's office I could tell right away that it was going to take longer than usual. Normally the Organizer, oh my God, I shouldn't even be *telling* you this," she said looking around, as if someone might hear her.

"It's OK. Just keep going."

"Well, the Organizer sits at the head of a long black table that is usually covered with piles and piles of paperwork. I hand him the envelope, he opens it, reads it, and then stamps it. But today, there were no piles of paperwork and instead there were other people in the room. Twelve, I'd say. They all looked really important, and I know an important person when I see one. I mean, *everyone* in our building is important. Except you, of course — sorry!" she blurted. "It's not that you're not important. What I mean is that you're just a courier. You don't really *do* anything. You just take papers from one building to another, drop them off, get them back — all day long! Even in this electronic age. I mean, really, what a *stupid* job. You'd have to be mentally handicapped to get excited about something like this-"

"Why don't you go back to the people at the table?" David interrupted.

"Oh, right. Sorry. Anyway, the Organizer asked me to give him this envelope which I did and he opened it and began to look over the paperwork, like he normally does. Only this time, he was reading it *very* carefully. After a few minutes the Organizer put the document back in the envelope and handed it to the next man at the table, who read it carefully, and then passed it to the next man. This went on for almost twenty minutes until finally, all of the men had read the contents. None of them, however, stamped anything. They just had this look about them, but I couldn't tell what it was. Eventually, the Organizer handed me back the envelope with the document inside, but when he did so a little plastic case fell out, big enough to hold a memory card for a camera or a phone. At first the little case seemed empty to me. But one of the men opened it and a tiny amount of water-like liquid spilled onto the table. I watched as one of the men reached out with his finger and dipped it into the liquid and brought it under his nose to smell it. And then...his head...*exploded*!"

Deborah was sobbing now and her arms were wrapped around David's shoulders as she cried uncontrollably. "It was like his head had been shot with a *bazooka* or something. And then...oh, David, *all* of their heads started to explode. One by one. I screamed hysterically and ran out of the room with the envelope still in my hand. I didn't know what else to do. The elevator wouldn't work because Gary has to authorize it, but I sure as hell wasn't going back in the room to make the call. All I knew was that I had to get out of there. I pushed a ceiling tile out of the way and found a room with a ladder. I must have climbed over a thousand feet. Thank God it led me to that man-hole cover."

"But why on earth did you come looking for *me*?" David asked, the weight of her story fully dawning on him.

She looked up at him with big sad deer eyes. She looked a lot less boring in this moment, he thought. "B-because moments before the first head exploded I glanced at the paperwork which was resting between my thumb and the envelope. On the first page there was a long detailed description and a picture of...you!"

"Of *me*?" he cried. It felt like the air had been knocked out of him. "But why?"

"I don't know, David. It could have something to do with what happened down there. In fact..." She took back the envelope from David and opened it and began reading the contents. Her eyes scanned the document frantically as she read it. Finally, she looked up at him. Her eyes were full of panicked understanding. "Oh my God, of course!"

"What?" David yelled. "What is it?"

"David, this whole thing revolves around you."

"*What* revolves around me? How come?"

"It's so obvious. This is happening because you are the-"

KABOOM!!!

Deborah's head exploded like a watermelon shot by a canon. David had her in his arms until she fell to the ground like a sack of dead boring. The blast had been so loud that everyone in the plaza took notice. Very slowly, people started to walk toward the epicenter of the blast. There was a long moment of silence like the kind right before a lightning strike. And then a girl started to scream. Then another girl started to scream. And then another, and another, until every nerd had realized what had happened and had begun to scream.

And then, just like that, it *really* happened. A tidal wave of exploding heads swept through the plaza like a red tsunami. The blast was so loud that car alarms were set off blocks away. The COMPUTER NERDS EXTRAVAGANZA banner was splattered with blood. Everyone in the plaza was dead. Everyone, that is, except for David Dingle.

Chapter 2: Jerry Burger

David ran the four miles home because he completely forgot that he had driven to work. His brain was not functioning properly. All he hoped was that the sound of exploding heads would stop by the time he got home. In his hand he still carried the manilla envelope.

When David burst through the front door his roommate Jerry was taking his third bong rip of the hour from his four foot glass water bong.

"*Holy shit!*" Jerry yelled and kicked the bong across the table and into the wall. Immediately, he scampered over and stamped out the burning weed coals that were singeing the carpet. "You scared the — living — crap — out of me, dude," he said in-between coughs. Now confident that disaster had been averted, Jerry shook his head sadly. "That poor bong thought it was gonna be just another normal day when it woke up this morning."

Jerry looked at David and his eyes brightened. "Man. I didn't think you'd *ever* get home," he said. "Look what finally came." Palpable excitement danced within the irises of his bloodshot eyes.

"One Shot Ten Kills?" David asked, reading the video game box.

"Best. Game. Ever," Jerry announced and quickly sat down again. Steadying his X-Box remote he said, "I'm gonna need your help spotting all the little fuckers that keep sneaking up on me. Goddamn thirteen-year-olds have nothing better to do than play video games," he shook his head. "They're like video game *ninjas*. I just can't keep up. Come on, sit down."

David collapsed on the couch and wiped the dripping sweat off his face. His eyes stared sullenly into the wall. "I haven't run that hard since I got chased around the cafeteria by Marcus Holtsbreath in eighth grade," he said in a daze.

Jerry surveyed David. "You OK, man? You don't look so good." David turned and faced him. Jerry thought David's expression resembled the terrified look of a noob looking down the barrel of his sniper rifle in One Shot Ten Kills. Jerry noticed that David's hands were trembling. David noticed that there were bits of Doritos in Jerry's beard.

"I don't even know where to begin," David said. "I just keep reliving it, over and over again."

"Reliving *what?*"

"Maybe I should have joined the army like my dad wanted," he said to himself. "If I were in the military then maybe all those dead bodies wouldn't have affected me that much."

Jerry nodded, barely hearing a word. "Well, you're gonna have to get used to it if you're gonna play with me. I pile up bodies by the minute," he said and fiddled with the menu options.

"I just hate violence," David said absently. "Even football makes me cringe. Some of the commercials are fun, though."

Jerry gave him a suspicious look. "Listen man," Jerry said. "You've never been much of a comedian, but you gotta admit you're acting sorta funny."

"Jerry, it's because I just saw-"

"Now, I've never liked being an enabler," he interrupted, "but today's the day that you should start smoking pot. You stay here. I'll be back."

"Hey," David said half-heartedly. "Whatever it is I don't want it."

Jerry re-appeared ten-seconds later with a brand new fully loaded bong.

"Did you load that just now?" David asked as Jerry sat down and handed the piece to him.

He gave him a perplexed look. "Of course. Who'd you think loaded it, the refrigerator? Hurry up. We need to start this next game. I've got a reputation to establish."

David held the bong in front of him absently and stared at the TV screen like an opium addict. It was all still like a dream to him. Nothing seemed real. The only thing that David could figure was that at any moment he would wake up and things would be back to normal. In all likelihood news stations would announce that the explosion had actually been a test of some kind and that the test had been a success. In fact, he pondered, the whole thing was probably such a non-issue that the media probably wanted to report on it just to let everyone know what a non-issue it was.

"I need to turn on the TV," he said with the faintest inflection of hope.

Jerry pulled the remote off the couch velcro. "Go ahead."

David turned the channel to the SmartNews report. A beautiful female reporter was standing in the middle of Pioneer Square with piles of dead headless bodies behind her. It was a strange oxymoron. David watched in awed terror.

"Mark," the reporter began, "I have just arrived in downtown Seattle at a terrible scene and reports are still coming in. We have no way of knowing anything for certain, but simple observation tells us that we are at the epicenter of a mass suicide. Gamers and programmers from all over the city undoubtedly gathered here today under the guise of celebration, but instead were set on making a larger point."

"And Stacy, can you elaborate on what that point may have been?"

"One can only guess, Mark, which I am prepared to do. Seattle is well known as a technological hub in America – the home of computer giants such as Paul Allen and Bill Gates, as well as the source of the 2000 dot com economic boom. While so much has been gained through this technology, so much has been lost as well. Countless people have lost their lives to Facebook and Twitter. No doubt these young activists felt they had done all they could to make people aware of the pitfalls of social media."

"Now Stacy, when I hear the term 'mass suicide' I think of incidents involving Jim Jones or Marshal Applewhite. Is there any chance this is just some sort of kooky Hale Bopp incident, or are these people in fact today's modern extremists, techno-terrorists, if you will?"

"No one can say for certain, Mark, as this incident just happened, so again, all we can do right now is assume things we don't know for certain."

"Were there any eye witnesses to the event?"

"There was one, Mark. A man by the name of Joe Weebins who is here with me right now. Joe, would you mind explaining what you saw?"

Joe, still in the blue streak of his high, was talking a mile a minute and not making one goddam ounce of sense. It was a TV anchor's dream come true.

Joe took the mic and stared into the camera at the floating dragon that drifted over the lens like a pink ribbon. "Boy I tell you," he began, "Weebin's sittin' down on that bench smokin' o'r there when I done heard me ten maybe twenty booms like a bomb. I'm not a clean man nor a priest but I tell you that when I heard it I messed myself good front and back. I didn't know if it was a nuclear ex-pa-lotion or Osama bin Laden comin' back from the dead to finish us off. All I knew was four things for certain. One, I knew it was trouble, two, I knew it was clean, and five, I knew I done smoked my last good rock. Good God almighty and that right there is the honest truth."

"Joe, do you have any idea how many people were involved?"

"Two hunerd? A million, maybe. Hard to say from that side of the street. All I know was that jess about every body good and holy was blowed up like a Mexican piñata. All except two. Me and this other fella. He was just standin' there holding this poor lady in one arm and a manilla envelope in the other."

"Can you say what he looked like?"

"Yes, 'em. He was tall, he was white, he was skinny and he had long hair. Why, heck. Now that I think about it, it was 'prolly Jesus Christ hisself trying to catch the bus out to Renton."

David fumbled with the remote until he had shut off the TV.

Jerry stared blankly at the wall. "Whoa man, that's some heavy shit. I just...can't imagine." He stood up and walked out the room, obviously troubled. After a few minutes he returned with a quart of ice cream and sat down again. "You mind turning that back to my game?" he asked.

"Jerry, I was there!" David shrieked. "I was that guy! I'm the guy that Joe Weebin's was talking about."

Jerry squinted at him. "You know, you *do* kind of look like Jesus," he said curiously. "I think it's the blue eyes." He studied him for a few more seconds. "Maybe the ponytail too. Yeah, it's definitely the pony tail."

David shook his head absently as he stared at the manilla envelope that he held on his lap.

"What's that?" Jerry asked.

"This is the envelope they were talking about."

"Well, what's in it?"

"I am."

"*You* are? Well, open it already! What's it say?"

"I can't, Jerry. Otherwise my head will explode."

Jerry cocked his head. "I don't get it."

"It's OK," David said. "Neither do I."

There was a knock on the door.

"Who *iiiis* it?" Jerry called out playfully.

"FBI. Open up."

"Holy *shit!*" Jerry said, and kicked his bong into the wall. "It's the fucking feds. Quick, you gotta help me flush this grass."

"Jerry, this is Washington State. It's legal here now."

"Those idiots don't know that. They just want to crack some skulls."

"I think they're here for me."

Jerry looked at him. "Oh man," he said now with a look of understanding. "Because of the Hale-Bopp thing?"

"Yes, *no.* Crap!" he said and pulled his hair and scanned the room in a state of panic. "What am I going to do, Jerry?"

"Don't let them know you're here."

"We can hear you inside, Mr. Dingle. We know you're in there. Open the door."

"OK," Jerry whispered. "I've dealt with this kind of stuff before. Let me handle this."

"I really don't think you should-"

But Jerry was already opening the door and a small cloud of marijuana smoke poured out of the house like a fog machine. Standing outside were two white men wearing identical black suits. They were of course, not smiling. Instead, they were pointing their guns at David.

Jerry cleared his throat as he realized he had just entered the coolest moment of his life. "May I help you gentlemen?"

One of the men gave Jerry a strong shove. "Under normal circumstances you'd both be on your stomachs by now," he said and flipped open a billfold revealing himself as an FBI agent. He looked over Jerry's shoulder at David who was peering back at him from over the couch. "David Dingle?" he said.

Jerry shook his head at David like he was trying to get a rock out of his head. "Nope. Just me and Marshal Applewhite here, talking about how great America is and how much we love cherry cobbler," he nodded.

David's mouth had become as dry as a stone. He knew that if he played this wrong he could go to prison for the rest of his life. "Uh, David Dingle is only a name that I usually go by. It's not what I...want to be called...in this moment."

The second agent handed the first agent a series of 8x10 photos. "Don't touch him," he whispered to his partner. The first agent dipped his chin in agreement and passed the photos to Jerry to hand over to David. Jerry looked at them briefly but did not react. However, as he passed the photos on to David he widened his eyes in panic and silently mouthed, "You're *fucked!*"

David took the photos which looked like they had been taken from a security camera somewhere in Pioneer Square. In them, David could be seen from multiple angles, clear as day, in the center of hundreds of headless bodies and holding a headless woman in his arms. In his hand he was holding the manilla envelope.

"What were you doing in Pioneer Square, Mr. Dingle?" the first agent asked.

"You don't have to answer them, man," Jerry ordered. "They're trying to entrap you. Mind your business, square," Jerry said. "David's got the right to remain silent. You didn't even *read* him his rights. Free to go!" Jerry declared and grabbed a napkin and a broken pencil off the couch. "Came in door, did not read rights. I got it all on record, bro," he beamed in support to David.

The FBI agent ignored Jerry so perfectly that David had no doubt in his mind that ignoring people like Jerry had been a part of his FBI training. "Mr. Dingle, we just came from the epicenter of the attack. We are certain that you were there and that you were involved in what has become a triage incident. We believe that the envelope you were holding contains the information of everyone involved. You have no choice but to-"

"If you're so sure he's a terrorist, why didn't you bust the door down and kill us *one shot ten kills?*" Jerry asked.

"It doesn't work like that," the agent said impatiently. "We are here on special orders from some very high profile individuals who want this taken care of quietly. Mr. Dingle, you're going to have to come with us."

"Don't go with them, David!" Jerry said. "*I'll* go. *I'll* represent you," he said and quickly tucked his shirt into his oversized pants.

The agent stepped past Jerry and extended a gloved hand out toward David. "Give me the envelope, Mr. Dingle."

David never was one for arguing. "OK."

"*OK?*" Jerry cried. "Jesus, David. You're giving them what they want. As soon as you give them the envelope they'll take you into an alley and shoot you with a Spencer P22. It's a gun with a silencer," he added knowledgeably.

David stepped back. "Really?"

"Yeah, totally. It's a really amazing gun, fashioned for getting the job *done*," he said with proud emphasis. "I'm a colt .45 kind of guy, myself. But everybody has their own preference. I know from my own experience playing Tom Clancy's Rainbow Six that-"

"Would you *shut up!*" the agent said, breaking his training and acknowledging Jerry for the first time. "Your friend is involved in the worst terrorist attack since 9/11 and our job is to find out why. We are not going to kill him, but we *are* going to confiscate that envelope, take him downtown, ask him some questions and proceed from there. I assure you that if you continue disrupting any process of this litigation then you will be put under arrest. Is that clear?"

Jerry stood still for a long moment. Finally, seriously, he asked, "What's a litigation?"

"*Give me the envelope!*" the man demanded.

It was a difficult decision but David couldn't help but wonder if maybe the man could help decipher what it said. In fact, maybe the envelope cleared him of everything. Maybe Deborah had misunderstood its meaning.

With a heavy sigh he handed over the manilla folder. The corner of the man's mouth went up half a degree and he walked over to where the other agent was standing. He opened the folder, pulled out the paperwork, and the two agents read the contents carefully. After several paragraphs both of the men crumpled their brows in confusion. "Oh my *God*," one of them said quietly.

"What? What is it?" Jerry asked and stepped forward.

"This doesn't make sense," the other said and then looked at David. "How could *he*..."

"*What?* What is it?" Jerry asked, looking back and forth between the man like a little kid trying to figure out who had the key to the candy store. "I wanna see it," he said.

"Say, turn it over," the second agent said. "There's more on the back."

They lowered their black glasses simultaneously.

"Of course!"

"Dear God, we've got to tell someone," the first agent exclaimed. "This is a concern of national security. This is powerful information." He looked at David and his eyes widened. "Everything makes sense now..."

KABOOM!!!

Their heads exploded all over Jerry and covered his shirt and face with skull and brains. Jerry screamed. "What the fuck happened!?!"

David backed into the wall in horror. He felt like he was trapped in déjà vu. "Their heads just exploded, Jerry! Just like everyone else's."

"Are you telling me you saw this happen to *hundreds of people*?" Jerry asked.

David's head bobbed in agreement. It was all it could do.

"Cooooool," he said with widening eyes.

Very slowly David walked over to the two headless men. Their bodies were slumped together on the floor. In between them was the envelope. He bent over and picked it up and walked back to the couch. On the coffee table was Jerry's lighter which David picked up, flicked on, and held the flame under the envelope.

"Stop!" Jerry cried. "What are you *doing*?"

"What do you think I'm doing?" David said. "I'm going to burn this thing."

"What? Why?"

"Because it's making people's heads explode, that's why!"

"But whatever it says has got to be important, otherwise those agents wouldn't have wanted it so bad."

"Whatever it says has got to be destroyed," David responded. "You *heard* the man, Jerry. It's a matter of national security." The tiny flame danced below the paper, but when a phone rang David stopped. David looked at Jerry and Jerry looked at David. "Do you have a new ringtone?" David asked.

"Oh my God," Jerry said. "I think it's the FBI agent's phone." He walked over and stared at the blue light beneath the fabric of his pants. He grimaced. "Is it weird that I want to grab the phone out of his pocket even though he doesn't have a head?"

"Don't do it," David peered from behind the couch.

"It's like eating broccoli," Jerry asserted and reached into the agent's pants. "Just gotta do it quick." Seconds later his hand emerged with a small black ringing cellphone.

"Jerry," David pleaded. "Put that down."

But Jerry had already flicked open the phone. He held out his hand toward David and nodded his head assuredly. "I got this," he whispered. "Hello?" he said in a deep and authoritative voice.

"*Jerry!*" David hissed.

Jerry, listened carefully to the other man on the line. "Uh, yes," he said. "We have him. He is alone."

"*Alone?*" David whispered angrily.

Jerry put his hand over the mouthpiece. "I don't want to get involved.

Shh. Hold on." Jerry spoke back into the phone. "To be honest, he doesn't appear to be the man we are looking for," he said. "He doesn't fit the profile. *How*? Oh, well," he said, looking at David. "He's just not, um, not the mastermind we thought he was. Nope nope. We checked the bathroom and there were no strange photos of women hanging over the tub or anything like that, Sir. He appears to be absolutely, one hundred percent normal. A law abiding citizen, no doubt about it. I was actually just planning on going and grabbing a beer, seeing as how our work is all done," he said, nodding his head.

David was pacing back and forth in front of the couch. He couldn't believe Jerry was doing this. There was no way they were going to believe him. Now Jerry was listening attentively and his expression was so perplexed that David stopped pacing and stared at him. After a few more minutes Jerry said, "Yes, Sir, right away, Sir. You can count on me." He hung up.

"Well?" David asked.

"You are not going to believe what they told me," Jerry said. "Those guys sure are official. Everything is cut and dry with them. No messing around, no tom-foolery or small talk. It's all, 'this is the way things are going to be, goddammit!' I'll tell you. I think I'd end up *killing* myself if I worked for the U.S. Government. Bunch of people who take themselves waaay too seriously. I mean, lighten up. You get *Columbus* Day off, for Christ's sake!"

"Jerry!" David screamed. "What did they tell you?"

"Oh, yeah, that," he said, gently setting the phone down on the dead agent's leg. "They want me to take you to Las Vegas."

"Vegas?" David asked, scratching his head. "Are you sure?"

Jerry's eyes widened. "Vegas, baby! We...are going...to Vegaaaas!" He ejected a sound that might have come from a drunk frat boy after getting laid.

"But why?" David asked and began pacing again.

"Because Vegas is the shit, that's why! He said that it was very important that I get you to the Caesar's Palace Casino."

"And you said yes?" he asked in disbelief.

"Dude. Have you ever *been* to Caesar's Palace? It's *awesome*. Marble floors, talking statues, six foot tall drinks, you've *gotta* check it out. Besides, we can't stay here. They're obviously after you. You were at the scene of the crime. Long enough to get some pretty nice 8x10's, I might add."

David looked at the blank television. "But I'm all over the news. They're saying things about me that aren't even true. Why would they do that?"

"Because you got something they want."

"What's that?"

Jerry's eyes widened as if David should know. "*Information*," he said, spreading his fingers for effect.

"I don't understand."

Jerry looked down and his eyes landed on the envelope which rested against the leg of the dead FBI agent.

"Ohhhh no!" David said and put up his hands. "No way. I don't want anything to do with that."

"*What?* Why not? You *gotta* wanna know what it says. It's obviously important, otherwise, you wouldn't have been wherever you thought you might have shoulda been."

David hesitated. "I don't...know if that makes any sense." He sighed and looked up at the ceiling. As much as he hated to admit it, Jerry was right. He *did* want to know what it said inside the envelope, but he was too afraid to look at it. He liked having a head and he didn't want to risk having it explode. "I just want to clear my name," he said finally. "I'm not a terrorist, Jerry. I work for the U.S. Government. How could *I* be a terrorist?"

"Maybe the envelope proves you're *not* a terrorist," Jerry suggested. "Maybe instead it says that you're important somehow."

"Hmm," David thought. "I do have an important job, that's for sure. I mean, I work for some of the smartest people in the country. I collect their signatures," he nodded gravely. "Maybe terrorists are trying to use *my* signature to oppose a peace plan or something."

"Or to smuggle cocaine into Oregon!" Jerry nodded back.

"Whatever it is has got to be big," he said, "otherwise everyone's heads wouldn't have exploded when they looked at it. Maybe it's just really hard to understand," he mused. "If only I could find someone smart enough to explain it to me."

"Well it just so happens that I'm supposed to take you to a medical convention when we get to Vegas."

"Really? Why?" he asked.

Jerry shrugged. "Who knows? But one thing you can count on is that doctors know what they're talking about. Otherwise they wouldn't wear those official-looking white coats. Never disagree with a man in a white coat," he shook his head. "Trust me. I think this is all working out. They don't know that you're not in police custody. You're in *my* custody, buddy, which is about as lucky as you can get."

David smiled nervously.

"All we gotta do is crash that little party of theirs, get someone to clear your name, and have a doctor write me a couple prescriptions."

"Mmm, I don't know," David said. "Getting to Vegas isn't going to be easy. I'm a wanted man, Jerry. In their eyes I've already killed hundreds of people. It's not like we're hiding from some Seattle cop. This is the *government* we're talking about here."

Jerry waved his hand in front of his face. "Take it from me, Dave. Those guys in Washington don't know they're asses from their sunglasses."

Chapter 3: President Benjamin Alan

"Son-of-a-gun, now *that* was a good speech," President Benjamin Alan said under his breath as he walked off stage. He raised his hand up again and throngs of people screamed in applause.

"Great speech, Mr. President," Mary Buckingload, his personal assistant, said to him as she began to escort him back to his ride.

"I know," he agreed. "They just ate it out of my hand. The trick is to remain calm yet energized, eloquent but not *overly* arrogant. It can be hard," he said. "Good thing *you* don't have to worry about stuff like this, eh Mary? Must be nice only having to worry about minor logistics for the President." Mary clenched her jaw. "I guarantee you this speech is going to dramatically boost my popularity. I'd like you to watch the polls, Mary. People came from all over the country for this event. It's not only important for you and me. Heck, it's important for this entire *nation*."

The crowds were still screaming and cheering like maniacs as Benjamin Alan disappeared out of sight under the wide yellow banner which read: NASCAR Fans of Freedom celebrate NASCAR.

The President shook hands as he walked out the door. People were still screaming for his attention. Expectedly, President Alan stopped near the exit and raised his hand into the air and swept it backwards over his head and then threw a thumbs up into the air — his *signature* goodbye. (It had taken him most of his time as Governor to perfect his salute. He liked to think of it as lassoing a tornado.)

"Take a seat, Mr. President," Mary said as they got to his ride. "You've got another engagement shortly."

President Alan ducked into his limousine. "Phew!" he said, and crashed backwards into the seat. "What a speech!" He sat up and opened his mini fridge and pulled out a Dr. Pepper. "And what a day!" he said after a satisfying gulp. First there had been the cutting of the ribbon at Mother Mary's Church of the Saved. Then he had been rushed over to the East side where he had shaken hands with several dignitaries from various African nations appealing for aid. Luckily, Mary had been there to help him pronounce the names of those African nations and remind him when to say country instead of continent. After that was the luncheon at the children's hospital with the press and half a dozen cancer survivors, which would have been somewhat of a downer had the food not been *absolutely* stupendous.

With such a busy schedule the President relished these moments of solace.

His phone rang. "Blast it," he muttered and pulled his phone out of his breast pocket. "Hello, this is the President," he said for the twentieth time today.

"Mr. President, I have just been informed that we are going to have to cancel your eight thirty. It looks like a meeting with your cabinet was just added to your line-up about an hour ago."

The President shook his head in frustration. "But Carlson, my eight-thirty is very important. Are you sure this is necessary?"

"One hundred percent, Sir. I've been told it relates to a level five security order."

President Alan rolled his eyes. "They usually just let me play golf during that kind of stuff."

"Not this time, Sir."

He sighed like a punctured fuel container on a million dollar yacht. "I would like you to reschedule my eight-thirty as soon as possible," he said with a tone of disapproval.

"Right away, Sir. I'm sure your barber will be able to fit you in tomorrow morning."

"Good," he said and hung up. President Alan looked out the door as he sipped his Dr. Pepper. He didn't like the unexpected. Whatever this was had better not take too long.

Thirty minutes later President Alan walked into the Cabinet Room and everyone looked up as the President strode in. The conversation died down; to say they looked tense would have been an understatement. Someone suggested they open a window. Twenty-five men and women looked at him expectantly from around the oval table.

The President sat down at the center of the table and looked at each of his cabinet members. "Good afternoon," he said. The group nodded back to him, waiting for him to say more. He felt an impatience. "I apologize for my delay," he said. "I've been in the bathroom – Mary," he said and looked over his shoulder, "have the FDA shut down the cafeteria at the Children's Hospital." He faced the group again. "Anyway, I received the documents. They looked very important and I'm beginning to think that I should have read them while I was on the pot."

The Director of Homeland Securities, Lou Donahue, signaled the doorman who left and closed the door behind him. "Mr. President," Donahue said with an edge that could have cut through a bank safe. "There has been an attack. Two hours ago a biological weapon was released in the heart of downtown Seattle. Over one hundred casualties were reported at the epicenter."

Beads of sweat began to form on the President's brow. "One...hundred?"

"Yes, Sir."

The room was quiet. "What's the population of Seattle?" he asked.

Donahue furled his brow and did a quick google search. "Almost seven hundred thousand."

Benjamin Alan gritted his teeth. "We can only pray they weren't all registered voters."

"I am afraid the initial attack was only the beginning," Donahue said. "By seven o'clock there were nine hundred casualties. By eight o'clock, over eight thousand. Dead. We have received a report that the virus has already spread to Tacoma, Portland, Spokane, and Boise, Idaho. We are still gathering data, but the numbers are looking grim."

"What are the estimates?" the President asked.

"It's hard to say for certain. Two hundred thousand. A half a million, maybe?"

Nervous faces stared at the leader of the free world. All eyes were on him now, awaiting his reaction.

The President took in a deep breath. "Would someone get me a Dr. Pepper, please?"

Mary opened the lightweight refrigerated bag filled with chilled sodas that she carried with her wherever the President went. She quickly passed him his favorite drink which the President drank down in two choking gulps.

"Now," he said, laying his hands on the table, "I am well aware that everyone here *knows* that I have never been to Seattle before, which would make this a pretty easy prank to pull off. So you might as well come clean. Come on now, who is it? Jenkins? Was this *your* idea?" he pointed playfully at the Director of the ATF. "aJenkins looked at his hands and shook his head.

Donahue eyed the President with measured concern. "Sir, this was a terrorist attack."

The President burped loudly in surprise. "A *terrorist* attack?" he said more to himself than to anyone else. "But the War on Terror is *over*. We brought freedom to the Middle East *years* ago and blasted all the terrorists to kingdom come. Those towel-heads, forgive my Arabic, deserve what they got (may they rest in God's arms)," he said, and then crossed himself. Many in the cabinet followed suit.

"I just don't understand it," he said. "Those countries are democratic beacons of the world now. Why, we standardized their way of living, or we *better* have what with all the money we've been sending them," he muttered under his breath. "Do you have *any* idea how many American school books my wife has sent to Samoa?"

"You mean Afghanistan?" the Director of Education asked.

"*That's* the one!" he snapped. "The point is they have *infrastructure* now. More roads. Less camels. How many McDonalds are in Libya now? Becky, what's your latest count?"

"Well over a hundred, Sir."

He shook his head in amazement. "We've left nothing but opportunity there. We brought them freedom and they drank it down like a tall smooth glass of Scotch," he said and closed his eyes with an expression of suppressed nostalgia. "No. Something tells me that we need to look at this differently." He looked across the desk. No one spoke. No one knew what to say. Suddenly, his eyes widened and President Alan looked at Donahue. "General Donahue, you mentioned it was a biological attack. Is that correct?"

"Yes. Most certainly."

Alan grimaced. "I was afraid of that. Now it's been a long time since I took Biology One at Yale, but I remember a tremendous amount," he said tapping his head with his finger. "Biology is the science of living things. Birds, rocks, monkeys, it's all biology, got it? Now who here has seen the movie *Outbreak*?" he asked. "You know, the one with the monkeys?"

A handful of people raised their hands slowly.

"Great. So the way I see it, we're likely looking at the wrong culprits. While we were busy killing jihadists in the Middle East, the real terrorists have been plotting to take back all the land we've been encroaching on."

"You mean monkeys, Sir?"

He shrugged. "Maybe. I'm talking more about your local flora and fauns. Bears, bobcats, mountain lions, your occasional porcupine. We'll definitely need to watch out for *them*. Porcupines can shoot quills like a trained soldier shoots a rifle."

"Sir?"

"I'm saying they're *infected* quills," he said angrily. "Like in *Outbreak?* Am I the only one paying attention, here?" The President stared across the table and scanned the eyes of his advisors until they landed on those of the Administrator of Environmental Protection.

"Liz?" he asked. Elizabeth Munsfield's eyes widened with a strange look of panic. "How long since you've received information on an animal attack?"

"Um…" Ms. Munsfield said, "Well, they come in every day."

He snapped his fingers. "And I'd be willing to bet that it's been getting worse."

"Well, what with increasing urban-wildland interface, that would be true."

"Haha!" he yelled in triumph. "Mary," he called over his shoulder. "Get Ms. Munsfield a Dr. Pepper!" Mary handed her a soda. An alarm on her phone prompted her to leave the room. "OK," he clapped his hands. "Now we're getting somewhere. I want everyone to be focused on large game animals. Bears, bighorn sheep," he said, counting off his fingers. "Skip the birds for now but keep a watch on them."

"What about rodents?" the Vice President asked.

"If they come across your path just step on them and move on."

"Mr. President," Lou Donahue said as carefully as possible, "though you pose a convincing theory, I fear the story is a bit more complex." He passed a yellow folder across the table. "For the last two months we have been observing a budding terrorist cell that popped up outside Midland, Texas. It was small, only five men in total, but all of them had previous connections with both Al Kabob and Al Kabib. After the fall of the Taliban, we felt certain that all terrorist organizations below them would fall like dominos, which they did. All but *that* one," he said, pointing at the folder in the President's hands. "Halam Hakbar was just seen last week in Seattle along with three of his men. Hakbar was a chemist in Iran for fifteen years before he legally entered the U.S. sixteen months ago. He has become quite adept at social media. What bothers us is that his ratio of jihad-like rants to kitty memes is practically a thousand to one. He has been quite vocal about his distaste for American international politics and has vowed on multiple occasions to make the U.S. government pay for the slaughter of innocent women and children. His family was killed years ago in a drone attack though we still have not confirmed if his wife was indeed a terrorist or a preschool teacher."

Donahue paused. "There is also another man," he said and swiveled his chair and flicked a switch. A wide screen lowered from the ceiling. A young man in his late twenties was standing in the center of a plaza of dead people. "This is David Dingle," he said. "This man was the last person at the scene of the crime. We believe he is working for Halam Hakbar."

The door opened and Mary walked into the Cabinet room carrying a large television. She walked laboriously over to the far end of the table and set the television down with a loud *clunk*. She walked over and presented Alan with a remote control.

"Mary?" The President asked. "What is this?"

Mary tilted her head, indicating that he should turn on the TV.

President Alan pressed the on button. The TV screen flickered and hummed to life and a granulated picture wavered into focus. In front of them a short over-weight Jewish man in his late sixties stared back at them. He wore thin-rimmed glasses, though the President could not see the bags under his eyes, because the man's entire face was covered with an industrial gas mask.

"Mr. President, can you hear me?" the man said.

"Melech!" the President exclaimed, recognizing the voice. "Hell, I didn't even realize that you weren't here. Where the hell are you?"

"Hello, Benjamin," Melech said morosely. "I apologize for my absence. I'm in…Seattle."

Everyone at the table collectively gasped.

The President leaned forward. "What on earth are you doing in Seattle, man? Don't you know there's been an animal attack?"

"For the time being I am safe, thank you." A thin line wavered through the transmission. "I'm underground, Mr. President, in bunker unit B-683."

"So you've heard then?" the President said.

"Heard?" Melech said with a grim smile. "I'm at ground zero. I was here when it happened, in this very room. My colleagues and I were finishing up the last of our business when an envelope came in," he said. "You see, the virus that was released onto the populace had been inserted into this envelope without our knowledge. Senator Macklemuck inadvertently triggered the device and within moments everyone in the room had become infected. I knew what it was the instant I saw it on the table, the weapon, I mean. Luckily this room is equipped with hazard masks and hand grenades."

"How did they die?" the President asked softly.

All emotion left Melech's voice. "Their heads exploded."

President Alan shook his head in disbelief. "My God - I can only imagine. I've only seen that happen in cartoons," the President said quietly. "I'm so sorry, Melech. That must have been horrible." Melech was a dear friend of the President's and it felt horrible knowing how much Melech must be suffering. Melech was his go-to man, had helped him get elected, in fact. Melech was probably one of the smartest people President Alan knew, which was saying a lot, considering that the President surrounded himself with brilliant men.

"Have you had to drink your own urine yet?" the Vice President asked.

"Are you planning on using the grenades to blast yourself out?" Donahue inquired.

"Can you show us the tag on your gas mask so we know what kind to get?" the Secretary of the Interior asked.

"Gentleman, gentlemen," the President said, raising his hand. "Please, not all at once. Let me handle this. Melech," he said with a tone serious enough to stop the charge of a sugar-crazed four year old in his tracks. "We've got to handle this disaster with diligent care. If we screw this up our chances of a second term are shot. Elections are less than a year away! If more people's heads explode then Senators Guiles's spin-masters are going to have a field day with this." He put his hands on the desk and leaned forward. "Do you think there's any chance we can wrap this up before the primaries in four months?"

Melech sighed. "Sir, forgive me if I sound trite, but this might just be more important than getting re-elected."

The President coughed. More important than *re-elections*? Benjamin Alan straightened his tie as he tried to collect his thoughts. "What about the economy?" he asked. "Surely this is going to be detrimental to the economy."

Melech shifted uncomfortably. "I agree, Mr. President. No doubt the economy is going to suffer. But right now we're going to have to set that aside."

"But Melech!" the President said. "You've always taught me that the economy is the life-blood of this great nation. Without it, why, we just wouldn't be America."

Melech nodded. "You are correct, Sir. That is why you have to do exactly as I say."

"What do you suggest we do then, Melech?"

"Shut down all commercial flights and impose a quarantine on the Western states."

"You're talking about taking away people's freedom of travel! No, I don't like the sound of that one bit. I am the President of the United States of America, Melech. I *give* freedoms. I don't take them away."

"A quarantine on Westerns states is only the beginning, I'm afraid," he said. "You are going to have to close the Canadian and Mexican borders after that. It is imperative that you do everything in your power to prevent this from spreading beyond our borders. If this were to cross into other countries then we are talking about a global pandemic."

Benjamin Alan involuntarily crushed the empty Dr. Pepper can in his hand. "Are you suggesting that we isolate ourselves off from the rest of the world?"

Melech's words were slow and steady. "For now."

"But the world *needs* us, Melech. We're like a big brother to most countries, ready to beat up shitty countries who make fun of democracy while still giving our younger siblings the occasional but necessary noogie."

"I understand your sentiments, Sir. But if you want to wrap this up quickly, you must do as I say."

"What about the terrorists?" the President asked quietly, afraid of the possibility of getting sucked into another war. "The War on Terror has been over for five whole years. It would be a real bummer if it resurfaced now, during elections and all."

"All terrorists must be apprehended as soon as possible," Melech said. "If this is to end quickly, we must nip this in the bud. I understand your Secretary of Defense has a few leads. Follow them vigorously. Leave no stone unturned. It is imperative that you find David Dingle, Mr. President. We must get to him at once. The American people have the right to see this man behind bars. Get your best men on this assignment. The sooner we find him, the sooner this mess will be over. Just make sure he is apprehended alive. A dead terrorist cannot answer for his crimes."

Chapter 4: Hashim Abaduba

The streets of Midland, Texas were hotter than usual today, which was a lot like saying that the drinking water was exceptionally wet.

Hashim Abaduba adjusted his sunglasses as he walked down the blazing street. So far the oppressive heat was the only thing that reminded him of the scorching deserts of ExxonMobilastan (formerly known as Iraq). Having only been in America for just over a week, Hashim was far from understanding American culture. Born and raised in Iraq before the war, he had never tasted Coca-Cola, never seen an American football game, and only once as a boy had he seen the second half of a movie called *American Pie* which left him with a strange impression of life in America. As far as he was concerned, if freedom was the ability to put your dick in a pie, he didn't want any part of it. The only thing he knew about America for certain was that Allah wanted him to blow some of it up.

Hashim's decision to join "Operation Blow up America" (rough translation) became a reality two years ago. Hashim begged to join Al-Kabob as soon as he heard they were sending a handful of jihadists to the U.S. to destroy the American Dream. It turned out to be a good match. Both Hashim and Al-Kabob detested everything American, though Hashim knew little about the place he hated. His new brothers informed Hashim that the U.S. wanted nothing more than to replace their Korans with iPhones and Islam with reruns of *Family Guy*. Granted, Hashim had no idea what an iPhone was, but he could only assume that one day a drone would eventually drop one on his head if he didn't do something about it. Before he knew it he was speaking English and learning the intricacies of blowing himself up in crowded places.

Then, one day out of the blue, Al Kabob was bombed (not by iPhones but by fire and shrapnel) and the terrorist organization virtually disappeared overnight. Soon after, the independent state of ExxonMobilastan was formed and the U.S. Government announced that the War on Terror was officially over.

A mild stability was brought to the region and the economy normalized again. Although people lived without fear of being bombed, the deep hatred Hashim felt against the U.S. had exploded. He wanted revenge for the death of those he cared about. One day, auspiciously, Hashim bumped into four of his companions who had also been a part of Al Kabob before it was blown to smithereens. Muhammed, Jamir, Muhammed and Muhammed were well versed in the ways of terrorism. They were not wealthy nor particularly smart, but they were loyal and dependable, and loved the idea of the many virgins in heaven awaiting their arrival. To his surprise, the jihadists told Hashim they had recently raised enough money through Kickstarter to fly to the United States and were leaving this Tuesday, would he like to come? And so, just like that, Hashim boarded a plane to America to blow up some infidels.

The five freedom-fighters made base in Midland, Texas. There they formulated their plan which turned out to be rather simple: find a place where a lot of people congregate and *Kaboom!* They felt it was important to spread their efforts rather than all blowing themselves up in Texas. Muhammed and Jamir would fly to Seattle. Muhammed would travel by land to San Francisco, and Muhammed would take the train to New York City. Hashim's job was to stay behind and erase all evidence of their existence. Afterwards, he should find a comfortable place and blow himself up.

Before his brothers left, they stressed the importance of creating a believable disguise. The worst possible thing that could happen for Hashim would be getting recognized as a freedom-fighter before he could accomplish his goal. It was essential, they said, to look and act like a local. They warned him that people in Texas had little sympathy for Middle Eastern-looking men. Hashim shaved his long unkempt beard but left a thick black handlebar mustache beneath his nose. He abandoned his white loose-fitting clothing for tight fitting Wrangler blue jeans and a long-sleeved plaid wool shirt. Reluctantly, he replaced his lucky turban for a baseball cap that read, "*Dios Bendigo Tijuana.*"

Bullets of sweat ran down his face as he approached the site where he would carry out his mission. He adjusted the wires under his shirt and winced as he pulled a few chest hairs that were tangled in the device. He sighed with gratitude, knowing that soon enough he would be free from the hardships of this world.

Hashim had spent the prior week scouting locations. He had considered blowing himself up in a number of places, but none of them had the consistency he needed. The churches were only open on Sundays and they weren't always full. The parks were rarely visited because of the oppressive heat. But *this* place was *always* packed with infidels.

He walked quickly through the parking lot as the heat from the asphalt crawled up his pant legs like rattlesnakes. Looking around he couldn't see a single empty parking place. People were flooding in and out of the building like ants. Allah had prepared everything *just so.*

A cool blast of air hit Hashim's face as he walked through the sliding doors of the store. "After-noon, Sir. Welcome to Wal-Mart," an octogenarian said with a smile.

Hashim feigned a smile and continued onward at a brisk pace through the store. It was hard to walk fast, however, as the store was crammed with people. After all, it was Saturday afternoon. Men and women pushed carts full of infidel merchandise while hordes of sugar-fed children rotated around these carts like snot-covered satellites. Babies screamed in the arms of their obese mothers who trudged through the clothing department like buffalo searching for the right patch of grass.

In the distance, Hashim could see the electronics department. It was there that he planned to set off the device. Not only would he blow up hundreds of people, but also that obnoxiously American brand of imperialism – Bruce Springsteen, Jean Claude Van Damme, the Mario Brothers, Jurassic Park, cell phones, cell phone cases, computer chargers, rechargeable batteries, and everything else that this terrible country stood for.

When he came to the department entrance, his way was blocked by two fat women currently debating the pros and cons of Miley Cyrus versus Hanna Montana circa Miley Cyrus. Meanwhile, the women's children were tossing things off the shelves and onto the floor.

"Excuse me," Hashim said as politely as possible. His strange accent brought them out of their argument. They looked at him with dual expressions of annoyance and suspicion.

"Can I *help* you?" the woman with the blue overalls asked rudely.

"Good afternoon?" he offered.

"You lookin' fer somethin'?" she asked.

"Just the electronics."

"Well yer here, buckaroo," she said and took a micro-step back, affording Hashim just enough room to squeeze between the two women if he held his breath.

He walked to the back of the aisle where ten televisions played ten different things — sports, news, movies, pop-culture. This was definitely the place to make a stand for a cause.

Hashim stood with his back to the screens and looked at all of the infidels milling about, their infidel faces intent upon their capitalistic endeavors. Hashim sucked in a deep gulp of air and reached into his pocket and pulled out the trigger device. All he had to do was release the safety and press the button.

"Oye!" a man said from out of nowhere.

Scared shitless, Hashim tossed the trigger device into the air and fumbled in a panic to catch it before it hit the ground. Got it! Hashim stared wide-eyed at the man who had spoken beside him. The man was slightly shorter than Hashim, but they looked nearly identical apart from the man's broad-rimmed cowboy hat caked in grime. "Could this also be another terrorist in disguise?" Hashim wondered.

"Disculpe. ¿Pero tú eres de Tijuana?" the man asked, pointing at Hashim's hat.

"Um," Hashim said.

"Porque yo también soy de Tijuana. Me encanta pero lo extraño mucho. Allí están mis hijos y esposa. Yo quiero viajar para Tijuana pero aquí me quedo para trabajar. ¿De que parte de Tijuana eres?"

Hashim had no clue what this man was saying to him or why he had suddenly struck up a conversation. The man however, seemed completely oblivious that Hashim was about to blow them all to kingdom come.

"Mira, también yo quiero un gorro así. Es muy bonito, creo. ¿Como te llamas? Yo soy Jorge."

"OK?" Hashim said. He realized that the man was evidently a Mexican and was speaking Spanish. He began thinking of all the signs and stores he had seen in Midland that were written in Spanish, hoping that perhaps if he could speak just a few words this guy would leave him alone.

"Um...*restaurante*?"

"¿Te llamas Restaurante?" the man asked in confusion.

"Uh, *sí. Tacos. Mecánico.* Uh...*Casa de Miguel. Restaurante,*" he said again, nodding his head with persuasion.

"Mira, tú eres loco," the man said, and walked away.

Hashim let out a sigh of relief. That was close! He wrapped his fingers around the trigger device again and prepared to flip off the safety.

"Holy shit!" someone screamed.

Again, Hashim nearly dropped the trigger. Convinced that a mob of angry people were about to tackle him, Hashim held one arm at length while he desperately attempted to unravel the magic of turning off this motherfucking safety. But with a quick glance up, Hashim realized that people were not actually focused on him at all. Instead, they were now all staring at the television.

"Turn it up," someone said.

The sound of the television penetrated every corner of the electronic department and Hashim looked up to see a white man in a suit standing in front of a camera with a microphone.

"There's no doubt about it, Bill. San Francisco has been hit hard. Estimates are still coming in, but the number of dead continues to rise. The virus has finally made its way into California and the repercussions have been horrendous. Undoubtedly, this will spread east through the country until everyone and everything has been infected." Hashim watched in shock as the man's eyes twitched involuntarily. The news anchor opened his mouth to speak again, but before he could say a word, his head, on live television, *exploded*!

The electronics department erupted into hysteria. Panic was beginning to spread like wildfire. Now people were flooding out of the store in waves, grabbing DVDs and iPods as they ran. Hashim didn't have a moment to lose. He found the safety, flipped it off, and held the trigger high into the air. "Allahu Akbar!" he cried. Hashim closed his eyes as his thumb pressed down on the button.

An electrical burn singed his chest and he cried out in pain. Hashim opened his eyes and lifted his shirt to see an exposed wire flicker sparks and then pitter out. All that was left was a patch of black hair and melted plastic. He hung his head and cursed himself softly. "I'm not a terrorist," he said pathetically. "I'm a failure." But looking around he realized it didn't matter. Everyone in the store was already gone.

Chapter 5: Special Agent Jon Boring

The black suburban rolled to a stop. Special Agent Jon Boring and his partner Bob Fleckle surveyed the Seattle neighborhood. It was dark and it was quiet. *Too* quiet for Agent Boring. 4026 Pickle St. was not exactly South Compton, but Boring wasn't about to take chances. Chances were what killed you in this line of work. He pulled the vehicle behind a rainbow colored Vanagon and killed the engine. It had been thirty hours since the attack in Pioneer Square. Both Boring and Fleckle were wearing masks over their faces. While Boring surveyed the scene, Agent Fleckle scribbled down some notes.

"This is it," Fleckle said without emotion.

Boring exhaled nervously. "You really think Dingle shot them?" Boring asked.

"It's more than likely. I'm getting a signal from Agent Barker's phone. It's directly behind the front door," he said gravely and turned to his partner.

Boring's hands were slick with sweat. "Wow. Two top agents taken down by a serial killer."

"Terrorist," Fleckle corrected.

Boring's eyes widened. "The sonofabitch could still be in there," he said, allowing his fingers to pet the cool metal of his gun.

"Unlikely," Fleckle said. "They're probably long gone by now." His words came out slow and without inflection. His voice reminded Boring of his eighth grade history teacher.

"I disagree," Boring said with a condescending tone. "If *I* were a terrorist, I'd wait until the best guys came after me, and when they found me I'd put them in a headlock, pound their faces into raw hamburger and then I'd blow them up. I'll betcha a million dollars he's in there waiting for *us*."

"We are *not* the best," Fleckle said.

Boring gave him a look. "Speak for yourself, *Fleckle*. *I* got the phone call from Benjamin Alan, and he told me aaaall *sorts* of things," he bragged.

"Like what?"

Boring gave a duck face and looked away. "Right now, Fleckle, you're on a need-to-know basis, so that's all I'm gonna tell ya." Holding the duck face to build tension he mentioned, "President Alan said he wanted this thing taken care of quietly. Said it's real important that we do this job right. *That's* why he called *me*, Fleckle, because he knows I'm the best."

"I'm having a really hard time understanding you with that mask on," Fleckle said.

Boring lifted the mask over his eyes and glared at Fleckle. "I said I'm the best. Geez, *Fleckle*," he said, rolling his eyes. "Your job is to kill terrorists, not the mood."

"I really think you should put your mask back on."

Boring rolled his eyes yet again. "You're *killing* me, Fleckle. Why's it always gotta be protocol with you? I've got fifteen years on the job and here you are telling me to put on a stupid gas mask. Let me tell you, I've picked up a few tricks since I started here. Protocol will get your ass killed in this business. Protocol would have us politely knocking on Akmed's door so he could blow us up. Not today. No Miranda rights, no 'hey how's your jihad?' The plan is if these guys give us any shit, we kill them. And then we get Arby's. Got it?" He tossed his gas mask in the back seat.

"We're not supposed to kill anyone."

"Geez, Fleckle. Don't they teach you noobs anything?"

"I've been an agent for ten years," he said evenly.

Boring ignored him. "I'm gonna aim for his hands so he can't trigger whatever bomb is strapped to his body. Didn't you ever watch *Speed?* It was mandatory material when *I* was learning the ropes. Anyway, that should shock him long enough for us to tackle him and begin to beat the living shit out of him, or them — there could be *multiple* bogies, you know?" His eyes became soft. "God," he said with a strange look of nostalgia. "It's like Occupy Wall Street all over again."

Fleckle shook his head.

"OK. You ready? Let's *do* this," Boring said and stepped out of the vehicle. "Hey!" he whispered. "Pass me the megaphone."

"I thought you said we were supposed to take care of this quietly."

"I'm pretty sure the President meant that metaphorically. Now gimme!"

Fleckle sighed and passed Boring the megaphone and then got out of the suburban.

Boring held it up to his mouth. "Terrorists!" he yelled. *God* it felt good to say it like that. This had to be one of the coolest assignments he had *ever* been on. It was like finding Osama bin Laden hiding out in a cave in suburbia making meth with Timothy McVeigh. "We have the place surrounded! Come out with your hands up and we won't shoot you." He looked at Fleckle and winked. "Much," he whispered and grinned. Fleckle gestured that Boring shouldn't say stuff like that into the megaphone.

Twenty-five seconds went by. No one responded.

"OK, Fleckle. It's pretty clear they're gonna stay inside. We're gonna have to break in. It's important that we're prepared for anything they throw at us. They could have explosives, rusty knives, panthers, there's really no telling. Lead the way."

Fleckle didn't budge. "I don't really want to be the first person-"

"You *have* to do what I say, Fleckle, because I have seniority."

Fleckle shook his head and said something indiscernible into his gas mask but began walking toward the house.

"I'll cover you," Boring said from behind the suburban and pointed his gun at the front door. He wanted to take a photo of the house blowing up sooo bad, but he knew his phone was just about out of battery. If only he had parked the suburban differently the dash cam would have caught it. "Fleckle, you're about to become a hero," Boring whispered to himself.

Fleckle knocked on the door and waited. After a moment he turned around. "I'm *telling* you, Boring. No one's in there."

"After all that talk about knocking," Boring muttered angrily. "OK, moment of truth." Agent Boring took a few steps, leaped and slid across the hood of the suburban, and then ran top speed to the front door. He just *knew* the terrorists were on the other side waiting for them, but if he could surprise them he'd have the upper hand.

Tucking his head, Boring crashed full bore like a linebacker into the front door which broke off its hinges and fell inward. Boring had a history of crashing into doors, and actually, had gotten pretty good at it over the years. Some of his co-workers had even started calling him 'Doorbell.'

Boring groaned, rolled over, and in one motion transformed the door into a shield and started shooting off rounds into the living room. When he finally emptied his clip he looked behind him for Fleckle.

"Did I get them?" he asked with adrenalized excitement. But Fleckle had become frozen. "Fleckle!" he screamed. "How many bad guys did I kill?"

All Fleckle could do was point and Boring followed his sight. On the floor were two dead FBI agents. And they were missing their heads.

"Holy *shit*!" Boring yelled as he saw them. He scampered to his feet and grabbed the side of the couch for support. The sight of the bloody scene complete with brains hanging from the living room ceiling fan sent Agent Boring into a dizzy spiral.

"Agent Boring, are you OK?" Fleckle asked.

"I think I'm...gonna..."

Boring lurched over and proceeded to throw up over most of the forensic evidence. When he was finally finished he stared at the bodies and then looked at his gun. "This baby's *powerful*," he said with a look of awe.

"You didn't do that," Fleckle said through his mask. "They've been infected."

"How can you tell?" Boring asked.

"Are you testing me, Agent Boring?"

Boring shook his head. "Testing is for idiots."

Fleckle scratched his cranium. "I don't understand. *How* did you get on this assignment?"

"A *lot* of reasons," he quipped. "None of which concerns you. Now," he said and brushed off his pants, "why do you think they're infected? Is it because of the box of Kleenexes over there?" he asked.

Fleckle sighed. "We better get going, Boring. Our boy is long gone and your friend the President is going to want to know where he went."

Chapter 6: Courtney Spears

Courtney Spears carried a tray of empty glasses down an aisle of slot machines as she made her way to the back bar. People ignored her as she passed, their eyes locked on the diamonds and cherries that spun in front of them like hamsters in seizure. Somewhere in the distance a crowd of anonymous gamblers cheered. Almost a year had passed before Courtney realized it was actually a recording the casino played eight times a day through the sound system.

"Two beers, jack and coke, and a shot of tequila," she said as she set her tray on the bar.

Steve slicked his hair back and smiled. "All for you?" he asked.

She gave him a practiced smile. "Come on, Steve. I could use some help."

Steve nodded. He glanced up at her occasionally as he poured the drinks. "You should take a shot with me," he grinned. "Gotta get on the level with the people you're serving, you know? Helps the time pass."

"I don't drink."

"You're kidding!" he said.

Courtney rolled her eyes. "Only tell you every day, Steve. Don't gamble, neither."

"OK, now I *know* you're crazy. Crazy hot, I mean," Steve said and pushed a shot of vodka across the bar to her.

She smiled. Steve was a sleazeball, but at least he talked to her. Most people barely gave her the time of day. They sure hadn't in Hollywood.

"Seriously, you've been here for two years now, Courtney. Don't you want to mix things up a little? Try something different! Have a few drinks, sleep around a bit? Lots of pills in Las Vegas. I could getcha some, you know?"

She held up the shot and toasted the air in his direction and set the shot back down on the counter.

"Sounds fun," she lied.

"Totally," he agreed.

She stared at the television behind Steve. Reporters were still talking about the epidemic in Washington State and from what she could tell it was spreading fast.

Steve followed her gaze. "Holy shit!" he said suddenly and grabbed a remote control. "Game's been on for thirty minutes!" he said, changing the channel. "Arg! Stupid commercials. I just wanna see the score. If the Raiders win then they'll be in 14th place. That's big news these days," he shook his head sadly. "Stupid Dallas Cowboys."

Courtney's eyes glossed over as she looked at the television. A man and woman were laughing. Apparently the tube of toothpaste they were holding was making them happy. She wished she could be that happy, but working here she'd have to brush her teeth with that toothpaste every moment of the day.

"You OK?" Steve asked. "You don't look as hot right now for some reason. Are you a Cowboys fan? Did I offend you?"

"No, it ain't that, Steve. It's just sometimes I wish I could meet someone who really wanted to be somebody."

"Hey, I wanna be somebody," he proclaimed.

"Oh yeah? Who?"

He thought about it. "I dunno. A punter, maybe?"

She smiled politely. "I guess I'm looking for someone who wants to make the world a better place. Someone who cares about the direction we're all headed in, you know? What with global warming, and the destruction of the natural environment and this big pandemic, it's hard for me to not get depressed sometimes."

"Well, why don't *you* do something about it instead of judging other people's dreams?" he said, realizing that he could never be the kind of punter the Raiders needed him to be.

"I *do*!" she said. "Or at least I try." She looked at him sheepishly. "I like to sing."

"*Sing?*" he scoffed.

"I believe music can change the world," she smiled. "The right song can change the course of history. Just look at everything Britney Spears has been able to accomplish," she said.

"Yeah, but you're no Britney Spears. You're just Courtney."

"Thanks a lot, Steve."

"No. What I mean is, Britney Spears has been famous ever since she had that thing with Mickey Mouse. If you wanna get big you gotta start sleeping around. No records label producer will ever want to jump your bones if you haven't even made it with the people you work with."

"Eww," she said. "I would never sleep with someone to get what I want, unless it was a good night's sleep."

"Well then how the hell do you expect to ever make it? The music biz is a hard knock life. They don't take just anybody."

She looked at him and the corners of her mouth rose into an awkward and excited smile. She looked around and leaned forward. "Can I tell you something?" she said almost in whisper.

"What is it?"

"I got a gig!" she gushed. "I *finally* got a gig!"

"Really? That's great! Where?"

"I just got a spot at Harold's. I'm goin' on Tuesday tonight."

"Really?" he asked, impressed. "They've got some good acts. You gonna be singing?"

Her smile was enormous - dorky, but cute. "I've been pestering Michael the owner for months now and he finally decided to take a chance on me. I go on at 8:00."

He looked at her. "I think that's when they have open mic."

She shook her head. "No. I think it's just a bunch of different acts that are only supposed to last for five minutes."

"Hey, whatever floats your boat!" he said and grinned. "Well go on then, sing me something."

"*Really?*" she beamed. "You wanna hear a song?"

"Yeah, why not? Give me the best part."

She smiled and curled her hair with her finger. "Gosh, there's just so many. I could sing the one about puppies or the one about mountain sunsets in Arkansas...Oh! I know! I've got the perfect one. This one is real special to me because it's about my family. Here goes..." she said and cleared her throat and looked out into empty space. "Daddy is my world but my world is unemployed. Mommy is my rock but my rock has diabetes. I'm in the West but the West ain't got the best 'cause this family lives in the South. Naa na na. Naa na na."

Steve grimaced. Her pitch was worse than that of a one-fingered baseball pitcher. It was without a doubt the worst song he had ever heard, and working as a bartender in Las Vegas at Caesar's Palace, that was saying a lot. He reached over and plucked up the shot he had poured for Courtney and threw it down his throat. "Ugh," he said.

"Wait, I'm not even done."

"Even better," he said and looked around.

She looked like she had been punched in the stomach. "I've got another one, if you'd like."

"God no!" he practically shouted. "Listen, singing might not be your thing. But its obvious that you like music. Why don't you go pass out those drinks and when you come back we'll record a song on the skin flute."

"OK," she said, trying to be cheerful, wondering what a skin flute could be. "Be right back!"

She fell into a slump of depression as she walked along with her tray of drinks. Steve's critique of her singing had been about the politest constructive criticism she had ever received. No one, besides her family, appreciated her artistic ability. She thought of them often...

She handed over the last of her drinks, walked down an empty hallway and popped a quarter in the only remaining pay phone in Las Vegas. (There was talk that it might become a National Monument.) Courtney did her best to communicate with her family as often as possible but it was hard working this job while simultaneously building her singing and acting career, but she promised herself she would call today because today was a special day.

"Hello?" a voice on the other end said.

"Happy fifteenth birthday, Tatum!" Courtney squealed.

"Courtney? Is that you?"

"'Course it's me, you *goof*. I called to say how much I love you an' miss you." Her accent always thickened when she spoke with her family.

"Momma's sick," Tatum said.

Her heart sank. "Momma?"

"Came down with the sneezes 'bout a week ago an' hasn't stopped coughin'. Pa thinks she's got the virus."

"No way, Tatum. Ain't nothin' can kill momma. She's like a polar bear in a bullet proof vest."

"I keep sayin' the same thing, but Pa's worried. When you commin' home?"

"Tatum, stop. I can't, you know that. I'm *workin'*."

"You still in L.A.?" he asked.

A slot machine went off nearby and she covered the speaker. "Yeah," she lied. "I been *suuuper* busy. Last week Jodi Foster asked me if I'd be in a movie with her. She seems real nice and everythin' but I really had to think about it 'cause I jess did *not* like that *Silence of the Lambs* movie. I mean, it wasn't even *about* a farm."

"There's work in Arkansas, you know?" he said.

Courtney groaned. They had this conversation nearly every time she called. Her family lived in a small, rural, conservative town where everyone believed that the best way to help the economy was get a job in the energy industry. "Tatum, you know how I feel about that kinda stuff. I ain't gonna work in no nuclear power plant or do somethin' with natural gas. What next, mountain-top removal? No. I'm doin' what I'm *doin'* 'cause it's fer me an' no one else."

There was a pause on the other end. "You ain't hookin', are you?"

"*Tatum!*" she yelled. "'Course I'm not hookin'. What kind of girl you think I am. I'm an *honest* girl makin' an *honest* livin' with Jodi Foster."

"I got the money you sent us," Tatum said quietly. "I appreciate it. I understand that it ain't easy doin' what yer doin'. I just want you to know that I'm workin' on some stuff on *this* end so that we can all be free from our collective slavery. I been talkin' to a *lot* a folks around here. People are startin' to see what I been talkin' about all these years."

"You mean that Illuminati stuff?" she asked doubtfully.

"*Goddamit*, that shit's real!" he yelled. "Just take a look at the TV. The damned Illuminati are trying to kill us like rats."

Courtney sighed. "Yeah, well, I'd agree that whatever's goin' on sure is scary. I heard that the virus has started comin' into California."

"Courtney, it's just like I always said. When the shit goes down it ain't gonna go down nice and quiet. Most people are too stupid to know what to do. They ain't got no concept 'bout things like preppin' and stuff. I tell ya. There was a line outside the gun store that went halfway around the block this mornin'. Owner kept sayin', 'I done sold outta bullets,' but no one had the brains to believe him. Ya'll laughed at me when I spent all our money on guns, and bullets, and flashlights, and dehydrated Tex-Mex, but *now* who's laughin'?" he said with a chuckle. "Did you know there's already been word of a revolution against the Illuminati?"

"Revolution? Really?" she asked.

"Yep. Heard it on the news this morning. It's basically a big group of armed vigilantes. Said they're gonna march on Washington D.C. to destroy it. American heroes..." his voice trailed off.

Courtney put her hand to her head. "It's all so scary, Tatum. Do you really think it's going to get that bad? I mean, the President has put roadblocks on the Nevada border already. I been watchin' the TV as much as I can, but you know, I think I'm the only one who cares. Everybody else around here is...well, drunk."

"You gonna be just fine, Courtney. I'm pretty sure Jodi Foster ain't Illuminati, but if you end up workin' with Madonna, you turn and run, you hear me?"

"I hear ya, Tatum."

"I'll tell ya one thing," he said. "That roadblock ain't gonna do shit. Illuminati's gonna slip right on through. It's only gonna take away more of our rights. But you know what, you could be immune and not even know it yet. Like the Indians who survived cancer and stuff. It was in their blood to not die. Maybe you got special blood, too."

"I hope so, Tatum," Courtney said. "I hope so."

Chapter 7: Jacob Timpson

Across the border, in Hildale, Utah, Bishop Jacob Timpson was getting ready for church. The night before, he had had the most inauspicious dream that could only have come from God. He dreamt he was drowning in a lake of strawberry JELL-O. The JELL-O pulled him under like quicksand and the only way he could stay afloat was to eat more JELL-O. When he could eat no more, and was certain death would take him, the Lord Jesus Christ appeared on the shore and walked across the JELL-O, leaned down, and pulled Bishop Jacob out.

"Thank you, Lord for saving a sinner like me from the gelatinous strawberry muck," Jacob had said.

"You betcha!" Jesus replied. "Now come on! Let's grab a cup of decaf together."

But when Jesus let go of Jacob's hand, Jacob immediately sank back into the JELL-O and drowned.

The dream left quite an impression on him.

Normally, Jacob was an optimist, a firm believer that there was a silver lining to every cloud. The Lord Jesus Christ was his savior and captain of the greatest team on heaven and earth, and Jacob was the quarterback of that team. And so, despite the strange dream, Jacob did his best to cheer himself up. Looking in the mirror he adjusted his collar and combed his hair. He smiled dimly as he observed the thin silvery wisps protruding out of his handsome brown part. "Lord, you can keep givin' me wisdom, but you'll never take away my good looks," he chuckled to himself. He lifted his shirt and applied a heavy application of deodorant. He always doubled down on deodorant for preaching day.

Jacob trotted down the stairs at a healthy pace to be greeted by the familiar sounds of babies crying. In the living room his older sons, Jeremiah and Bartholomew were reading to themselves. On the floor in front of them were Mary, Ruth, and Constantine engaged in a heated game of The Settlers of Zarahemlia. His wife Alma sat with the children and played along. She looked up at her husband and smiled.

Jacob returned her smile, but patted his stomach. Alma gave a knowing grin and motioned with her chin toward the kitchen. "Something in there for you, I do believe," she said lovingly.

Jacob allowed the sounds of crying to guide his way. When he entered the kitchen, he saw his other wife, Sariha, holding his youngest son Samuel. Seth and Jenedy sat in their highchairs, happily eating breakfast, while his third and fourth wife finished preparing their husband's breakfast. "Where are Lehi, Noah, and Adam?" he asked.

"Outside, playing," Neleh said with a smile.

"And Alma?" he asked.

"Why on the floor with the children. Didn't you see her?"

"No, the *other* Alma," he said, referring to his fifth wife.

"Oh, silly me. She went out to get some more bread for the children."

"I do hope she hurries," Jacob said. "The service begins in just under two hours."

"Of course she will make it. Hasn't she always?"

Jacob smiled. "I suppose you are right. I apologize for seeming rushed or nervous. I confess that I barely slept a wink last night."

"Was it the JELL-O dream again?" Neleh asked.

"Yes," he said. "I'm afraid so."

"Perhaps our Lord is trying to tell you something," she suggested.

"Always is, always has been," he smiled.

He looked up when he heard the sound of the front door close. Alma walked into the room with two loaves of bread under her arms. Her eyes were wide and excited.

"What on earth is it?" Neleh asked. "You look like you just saw Nimrod having lunch with Abraham." The other wives and children gathered in the kitchen, overtaken by the strange wind which carried her.

"I was at the store buying the bread," she said with wide and disbelieving eyes. "The owner Jonathan had the television turned on, as usual, and there must have been twenty people watching it."

"Well, what on earth was it saying?" the other Alma asked.

Her eyes switched back and forth between Alma and Jacob. "It's just...so hard to believe."

"*What?*" they said.

"I'm terribly afraid to say it out loud, on accounts of what it could mean. But I think...the Apocalypse is coming!" she said and smiled as if Jesus Christ himself could be standing there in the kitchen. "The end of the world has finally come!" She ran and embraced Jacob tightly. "Isn't this exciting!"

Jacob gently pulled her away. "I don't understand, my love. What do you mean?"

"Oh, it's just *wonderful!*" she said, clapping her hands together. "The Lord God has brought a great plague to our wicked nation. People all over the country are dying by the thousands, *millions,* they say. It's all over the news. Nothing can stop it. Judgement Day is truly here."

There was a strong silence in the kitchen. Even the babies had stopped crying.

Neleh broke the silence first. "Hooray!" she shouted.

"Praise God!" Mary said.

"Hallelujah!" Ruth chimed in.

"Judgement Day!" Jeremiah yelled in excitement.

"Oh, Jacob, don't you believe that the Lord has finally come to save us?" Alma said looking up at him. "I feel that He is cleansing the world of all its wickedness."

"Has the plague come into Utah?" Neleh asked hopefully.

"Not yet," she said with disappointment. "But they say it's likely on its way. They've tried to put barricades up to keep people from passing through, but no one can stop Jehovah's will."

"But what about us?" little Ruth asked. "Is the plague going to kill us?"

"Oh heavens no!" Alma said and scooped her up like a sweater-vested terrier. "Our God is a compassionate God, and he cares a whole bunch about good Christians like us. He is a wonderful *loving* God, a wise God who will smite every single man and woman who hasn't accepted Jesus as their personal savior. The rapture is truly upon us, my darlings," she said.

Jacob's wives hugged each other. "Praise God!" they said. "Praise God!"

"Oh your sermon is going to be *so* good today!" Alma said.

Jacob's heart skipped a beat. The sermon! What in heavens name would he say now? He had planned on giving a talk about the sins of premarital fornication. But all of that would have to be scratched now. Surely he must talk about the plague. But how could he? Why he didn't even know the full story. His eyes jerked down to his watch. If only he had a little more time to prepare!

"What will you tell them?" Jeremiah asked.

"Uh, umm..." Jacob stammered. "Well, there will be lots to talk about, certainly."

"People are going to have *so many* questions," Sarah said.

His eyes widened. "You're right! I should really get going."

"Not before you eat. I've already prepared breakfast," Joanna said and opened the stove and quickly placed a heaping plate of food in front of Jacob. "You will need strength today," she said.

Jacob stared at the plate, but his apprehension could not compete with his appetite and he sat down and dug in. "I juth hope The Great Thpirit will work through me," Jacob said in between mouthfuls of steak and potatoes.

"Doesn't He always?" Alma asked.

"How long do you think it will take until the rapture hits Hildale?" Neleh asked.

He thought about it. "It's hard to say. Only the Great God in heaven knows for sure. Why it might take months or it could happen at any minute, I suppose."

"Well," she said softly, "wouldn't it be a blessing to bring in another child, right before He reins on Earth?"

Jacob looked up from his food and at his wife. She fluttered her eyelids at him. "Oh!" he said, suddenly overcome by all the memories of having lain naked with a woman before. All thirteen times. "Are you willing to bear the fruit of a new soul in such a time of change?" he asked.

Neleh did her best to cover her excitement. "You're gol darn right I am!"

"Hey, no fair!" Joanna said. "Neleh already *has* two babies."

"So do you," countered Neleh.

"You can't count the miscarriage," she said defensively. "I have one *live* one to your two. Sarah has born three as well as Alma. It's *my* turn."

"You *do* have two living babies," Joanna declared. "It's just that one of 'em is living in heaven, that's all," she muttered.

Joanna crossed her arms. "*Jacob!*" she pleaded for support.

"Now now, wives. Only the good Lord will know for certain who should be the next mother. Let us pray." They all bowed their heads. "Dear Lord," Jacob began. "Please give us the guidance and the wisdom, open our hearts to Your will, but close our minds to the will of man, for man knoweth nothing, only You are wise. Amen."

"Amen," they said in unison.

"Nice one, Dad," Jeremiah said.

"OK," Jacob said, wiping his mouth. "I must be off. You know how I like to spend an hour alone before I preach." The bishop stood up and kissed his many wives and children (which took a considerable amount of time) and walked out the door.

As he left the house a gust of wind blasted him in the chest. In the distance dark clouds were gathering over the western hills; a storm was clearly on its way. Nevertheless, Jacob walked with resolve into the powerful winds toward his temple. Neither the wind, nor anything else, would stop the bishop when his flock needed him most.

Jacob crossed himself as he approached the temple. He was surprised to see nearly two dozen children waiting at the front steps.

"Why, what in Brigham's name brings you all here? Don't you know that service doesn't begin for more than an hour?"

"My daddy said the end of the world was a-comin'," one of the younger ones said.

"We're scared, Bishop Jacob."

"Now now," Jacob said. "There isn't a thing to be afraid of, unless you're a sinner." The little one's confidence seemed to recover some. "Now you children aren't sinners, are ya?"

"No, Sir."

"Maybe a little?" he asked with a playful smile.

"A little, Sir," they agreed.

"That's right. We're *all* sinners. Born that way, gonna die that way. But we got the big J C lookin' out for us. And you know what? He's a-comin' to town."

"You know so, Sir?" they asked.

Jacob cocked his head as if trying to multiply fractions for the first time since high school. He smiled awkwardly and made a quick retreat inside the temple. Inside his quarters, Jacob shut the door firmly behind him and exhaled a long nervous chestful of air. The bishop's chamber was simple and small. A thick wooden desk, a filing cabinet, a couple of chairs, and a mirror. Normally, Jacob would rummage through the cabinet and pull out his weekly notes. He was an organized man and he usually prepared his sermons months in advance. But not today. Today was the day that only one man could prepare for.

The bishop pulled a trembling hand out of his pocket and opened it. Sitting on his palm was the magic key he had grabbed before leaving his home. Good Grace had come and reminded him of its existence. He held the tiny silver key in two fingers and lowered it to the bottom drawer of his desk. He had only opened this drawer once before in his life, and now he was about to take out what he had once put in.

Jacob placed the key in the lock, held his breath, and turned it.

The key was jammed. He tried again. It budged a little but the lock wouldn't open. Already nervous, he began breathing like a pregnant woman going into labor. "It's OK, It's OK," he assured himself. "Lord, I ask your guidance."

Nothing.

"Here we go," he said with hopeful panic. "Open sesame." He jiggled the lock and tried again.

Nada.

"Goddamit!" he blurted then immediately crossed himself. "All are sinners," he mumbled and slicked down his tousled hair. "Jehovah, you have *got* to let me in that drawer. My flock depends on it."

Alas, the Lord's locksmith was unavailable forcing Jacob to dash out of the room and return with a crowbar. He was so flustered by the whole ordeal, terrified that somehow the contents inside the drawer had been raptured by God Himself, that he did not hesitate to strike the drawer with everything he had. Splinters of woods dashed against the wall and the desk groaned like a walloped manatee. Again and again he hit the drawer until it looked like the desk had been the target on a hillbilly gun range. Jacob stared at the gaping hole as he panted to catch his breath. Never before had he broken into something, but gol' darnit, it felt kind of good.

Gently, he set the crowbar down and opened the drawer. Inside was a white envelope. It was plain to the naked eye, although Bishop Jacob knew that the words "Top Secret" were written across the front in Holy Water. Never before, however, had he read the contents.

He opened the envelope and Jacob's eyes scanned the documents like a boy looking at porn for the first time. There were papers that had been signed John Barlow himself. It was like holding the golden tablets passed down from Angel Moroni. Jacob squinted his eyes and read the front page.

Instructions for the end of the world. Jacob's mouth salivated with anticipation.

Jacob was a fast reader, but it still took him over an hour to read the full document. He was stunned by the amount of protocol that John Barlow had laid out. There seemed to be a ritual or ceremony for everything. Never before had Jacob considered the importance of covering the temple floor in purple tassels while sacrificing a chicken as everyone sang Father is a Friend of Mine, but who was *he* to question anything?

He rummaged frantically through the papers, searching for what he hoped was there, but by the time he had reached the end of the document, it was clear that the information he needed was not inside. Nowhere in the top secret document did it tell him what to tell his people. Panic had arrived and was about to buy some real estate.

He looked at his watch. There was little time! Jacob dashed over to his filing cabinet and pulled out his notes for today's sermon. Hopefully there was something in there, an anecdote of some kind, an analogy, a parable, a metaphor — *anything* that he could use to calm the hearts of his people. He read the top of the folder – Sunday, March 3rd – The fellowship of Byron Handerfore and the papers of ownership for livestock and third wives. Panic had not only taken up residence, it had built an outhouse.

Jacob slumped into his chair. "What am I going to do, Lord?" he asked. "I don't even know the full story of the coming Rapture. How can I speak of it?" Bishop Jacob Timpson was not a quick thinker nor was he a man for impromptu speeches. He was a well-trained man who could deliver carefully crafted prose. Men and their women came from miles around just to hear his sermons. Sure, many of them could have just as easily traveled down to Colorado City to hear Bishop Mathew nasal away about the same issues that concerned members of the Fundamentalist Church of Jesus Christ of Latter-day Saints, but Bishop Timpson didn't have the poise or passion that Jacob had. Jacob's was a *practiced* passion.

The windowpane rattled violently and Jacob stood up and looked outside. The sky was ominous, black almost. The storm would arrive at any moment. There was no rain yet, but the wind, however, howled like the dogs of hell. His watch timer went off sending a cascade of sweat down his back. Fifteen minutes until curtain call. He could hear his sheep beginning to flock inside. Jacob Timpson pulled out some paper and began jotting down words and phrases, anything at all that came to him, anything that might save him in this dark afternoon of the soul. Jesus. Abraham. BYU. God. God is a man. Faith. Dinosaurs.

There was a knock on the door and Sarah, the church Treasurer, poked her head in. She looked beyond excited. Her smile couldn't have been stretched farther with wires. "They're ready for you, Bishop."

He nodded and mumbled and accidentally called Sarah, Mary Joseph. The Bishop's steps were slow and uncertain and by the time he got to the pulpit the auditorium had become as silent as a raptured orphanage. Jesus Christ, it was *packed!* Jacob didn't recognize half of the people in the congregation. A good deal didn't even look Christian, but that secret was between them and God, he figured.

The bishop cleared his throat. "Good afternoon," he said. "My, what a day. What a week!" he offered with a nervous laugh. He set his papers on the pulpit. "It may not be a well-known fact," he said, doing his best to sound confident, "that goats and sheep are considered property of the third wife and not her spouse." He paused. Someone in the back row coughed.

"Oh Jesus, help me now," he said quietly.

Gary Sorenson in the front row was tapping his foot like a broken metronome.

"I apologize," the bishop said. "I am sure that many of you have come today because you are looking for answers. Aren't we all, my friends? I too, am waiting, *stalling* even, for a sign." Not only was his pause pregnant, but it could have given birth twice.

"Come on!" someone in the back shouted. "Tell us what's going on!"

"Yeah," another contributed. "When's the rapture?"

"Should we buy more flour?"

"Were dinosaurs *real*??"

"Friends, Friends!" he shouted over the commotion. "You *must* remain calm. Even in the face of such powerful circumstances, the Lord demands your respect and humility. Let us not forget what Ruth said when her husband passed off one of her goats for his own — 'Know thy flock to be thy own.'" He paused and looked out. "'Know thy flock to be thy own,' " he repeated in solemn reverence.

No one, however, had one fucking clue what he was talking about.

"Tell us about the disease!"

"Yeah!" someone else yelled.

"Yes yes," he said, scrambling through his paperwork. There *had* to be something here about the rapture. But it was useless. There was no material. He would have to ad lib. God help him.

"The disease is...an abomination!" he shouted with a tinge of hopefulness.

"Amen!" someone said.

"You and I, we and she, her and these kids right over there...well, Jesus cares. And you know what? He cares...a bunch!"

"Amen!" came a voice, this one not as confident.

If he wasn't careful he would lose them all. He had to think about everything he'd ever talked about and somehow draw out something relevant that actually mattered. "Let me tell you about Jehovah," he said, giving a pause for emphasis. "Jehovah is a good God, and somehow, paradoxically, a wrathful God. It's kind of weird, I'll admit. But the fact of the matter remains. God sent us his only Son to save us from ourselves. And you know what? He's a-comin' back! There may be a thing or two I'm not one hundred percent sure about, but one thing is for certain, if there *is* a pandemic, which my wife Alma tells me that there is, then I have no doubt that Jesus Christ himself is a-walkin' this Earth. He cares about you, and *you*!" he pointed at Gary Sorenson. "And it's because you've chosen the true path. The path of a good Christian. Not just any Christian, but a member of the FLDS church. The Lord does not open his door to all faiths. Not to the Muslims, or the Hindus..."

"Or those stupid Jehovah's Witnesses," someone shouted.

"Amen!" someone yelled.

"But friends, those Jehovah's Witnesses, and Muslims, and Hindus are people too and they still have time to know Christ. I would give anything to see Christ face to face, wouldn't you?"

"They've had enough time to figure it out!" someone yelled.

"Yeah, like 6,000 years!" someone else chimed in.

"What I'm trying to say is that we must still pray for them."

"But what about *us*?" someone yelled. "What's going to happen to *us*? How do I know if I'm worthy or not of Christ's love?"

Bishop Jacob paused, beginning to wonder if *he* was worthy of Christ's love. He felt that he was a good person, but he *did* sin every now and then. If this were truly the end of the world, every sin counted. He couldn't tell his flock what to do or what any of this meant because, well, he didn't know himself. Many people were becoming impatient and several were already standing up to leave. He *had* to do something.

"People!" he shouted, surprising even himself. "I empathize with your need to understand. I have spent my whole life trying to learn about the Word of

God."

"*Trying to learn?*" Melissa Cargie bellowed. "Cheese and Rice! You've been *teaching* it to us. We've been *listening* to you because we *believe* in you. I sure as sugar hope you've been doing more than just *trying* to learn. Don't think we don't remember you're from the East Coast. We know all about the 'political influence' that goes on there. If you've been lying to us..."

He held up his hands in dismay. "Stop!" he said. "I am *only* who I am. I believe that Jesus Christ is alive today and will find each and every one of us and tell us if we are worthy or not. If you came here today to ask me if *you* are worthy or not, then I can only tell you the truth..."

The silence was so thick that not even a miracle could break it.

"I don't...know," he said.

A throng of mixed emotions passed through the crowd like a ten foot wave. Fourteen people fainted. Multiple men stood and shook their fists at him. Women were shouting at their counter-wives. Children were crying despite having no concept of what an apocalypse actually was. The congregation looked more like a rock concert for the devil than the Hildale Seventh Heaven Temple. No one was in his seat, people were shouting and yelling, and not a single person gave a *single* gol' darn about a third wife's ownership of livestock.

A bald fat man about Jacob's age, Marshal Leavenworth, marched up to the pulpit. He shoved himself in front of the microphone and said, "This man *cannot* be our leader! A leader is someone who tells it like it is. This man does not listen to the Word of God. Lord Jesus is coming, brothers and sisters. He's preparing us for His rapture and He would like us to know about it. Well, I for one am well aware of the rapture. My family and I have been preparing for it for three generations and I think it's about high time that we organize now that the moment has come. Our species has not been on this planet for six thousand years to miss the whole point of existence — the apocalypse!"

Suddenly the temple ceiling began to creak. The walls shuddered and groaned. It almost felt like the building was moving; the whole church became silent. Then, one by one, the stained-glass windows began to explode and the congregation descended into panic.

"Stay calm, stay calm!" Marshal Leavenworth said into the microphone. "It's *Jesus!* He's trying to come in!" His words struck the crowd silent and they watched the breaking windows from the center of the church with wonder and fascination. That is, until the roof of the church lifted off the foundation like the top of a cupcake and an angry tornado began to suck people out two and three at a time.

Martial Leavenworth covered the microphone and leaned over to Bishop Jacob Timpson. "Way to go, dumbass," he whispered. "You done it now."

Chapter 8: The Blockade

"Getting close, baby!" Jerry announced as they zipped past a sign which read: Las Vegas - 20 miles.

David looked up from his phone for the first time in a hundred miles. He had just recently killed the Zombie Prince so he was hesitant to look away. In truth though, and he was almost consciously aware of this, David was using the game to avoid facing his situation. He could still barely believe that just yesterday afternoon he was finishing up his last delivery and today he was the key suspect in the worst biological terrorism attack on American soil. He couldn't help but wonder if it had anything to do with forgetting to file his taxes.

"So you really haven't been to Vegas before?" Jerry asked and slugged down another Red Zone Mountain Dew. David shook his head no for the twentieth time. "Well, if I haven't mentioned it yet, I want to assure you that Vegas is pretty fucking great. I like to think of it as the good kind of Alcatraz, not that I've ever been to L.A," his said, lifting his fingers off the steering wheel.

David nodded and looked at the skyline of Vegas for another eight-seconds before he glanced back down at his phone.

"You know," Jerry said, "I was thinking you should put that thing away. Considering our situation, and everything."

"Oh!" he said looking up with stark realization. "Do you think I could be getting roaming charges?"

"Hmm," Jerry mused. "Hadn't thought about that. No, what I was thinking was that the government might be tracking you. It wouldn't surprise me if they were sending satellite beams down to scramble your thoughts."

"Really?" David asked in wonder.

"Absolutely. You of all people should know that."

"I should? Why?"

"You're the one with the fancy Milky Way Phone, capable of sending texts to the farthest reaches of the galaxy." David gazed at his phone in admiration. Jerry continued, "We have technology that can do anything these days. Technology could probably turn a piece of your own poop into something that grows food. It's *that* insane. Don't think for a minute that the government isn't using super-evolved technology for evil reasons. I think we should be very concerned about the beams that they're sending into your brain."

"Why's that?" David asked.

Jerry blinked. "Well, that's like, something you can't defend against." They thought about this in silence as they drove down the road.

David looked down at his envelope which was lying on his lap. "Well, I know they've got their reasons to be worried. If the War on Terrorism taught us anything it's that some people believe they have to kill thousands of people just to make a single point. America has been the most powerful nation in the world for so long that it's only natural that certain people are going to rebel against it. I just don't understand why they have to kill innocent people along the way. The world's a complicated place," he said and looked out the window. "That's why I try not to engage with it. It makes my head hurt."

Jerry sighed as he looked down the road. "Dude. Harsh mellow."

David sat up. "But it's OK," he said cheerfully. "I'm sure that we can take this envelope in and get it all looked at and fix everything right up. I'll bet we can even get back to Seattle by Monday."

"What happens Monday?" Jerry asked.

"I have to be back at work."

"Duuude," Jerry said and shook his head. "Work has been *cancelled*."

His words felt like daggers. "So...*next* Monday?" David said softly.

"*Wake up*, man! Your life is *fucked*! The old David is as dead as Blockbuster video. You got a *lot* of bigger things to worry about than work. The way I see it is you had better start learning how to make tacos and soon."

"What? Why?"

"Because I'm taking you to *Mexico*, that's why! You're a terrorist now, Dave. You gotta lay low, find a cave to hole up in. I'll do my best to help find you some slum to live in across the border but for the most part you're on your own!"

"But I thought you were taking me to Vegas so we can make things good again?"

Jerry gave him a look. "Listen, I'm gonna shoot straight with you here, David. You're my best friend and I want you to be safe and stay out of trouble. More importantly, I want you to *feel* safe, which is why I've gotta be honest with you. There is a *damn* good chance you're gonna wind up in Guantanamo Bay with a bronze medal in the water-boarding endurance challenge. I'm serious. It's not lookin' too good."

"What!?" he cried.

"Relax," Jerry said soothingly and patted his leg. "I'll try not to let that happen. You know why? Because I'm your partner and I play smart."

"Oh God!" David said and slumped back in his chair and looked up at the stained car ceiling. "I don't want to go to Guantanamo," he cried. "I want my old life back. I don't want to be some prison guard's slave. I want to be free and wake up and go to work day after day, collecting signatures from political dynamos who likely override the democratic system for corporate interests and...and to ensure that President Alan makes informed decisions. I help make that happen! President Alan *needs* me. I can't go to prison. What about my car? And my *phone?*" he said, the panic rising in his voice. "There's no *way* they'll let me have a phone in prison. Why, they'll probably *destroy this one!*" he said in horror. "Which," he added thoughtfully, "would be OK, because after being in prison for 40 years I wouldn't want to get out and be handed an old phone, I'd want a *new* phone but who *knows* if I'd earn much money making stop signs and license plates in prison? Probably not much — not enough to buy a new phone at least. Certainly not with inflation! I wonder if there'll even *be* phones in forty years?" he said and stared at the bleak, desert horizon.

"Can you believe that I've been to jail eight times since I first came to Vegas?" Jerry asked. "Nothing bad," he clarified. "Just stupid stuff like arson and forged zoning permits. I'll tell ya, you meet the *best* people in jail," he smiled. "Who knows, you might just meet another Jerry when you get to Cuba. That'd be cool, huh?" he said, and slugged him playfully in the shoulder.

David chuckled nervously and looked back down at his phone.

"Dude, what did I *just* say? Put down your phone."

"It's OK. I was just pulling up directions to our destination. Little Caesars Temple, right?"

"No no no. It's Caesar's Palace. And I don't need directions there. I know Vegas like level one of Halo 3. Highway 95 is going to take us straight there." Jerry pulled out a little recording device and held it in front of his mouth. "Captain's log. David and Jerry have arrived at the outskirts of Fantasy Island. Status: sober and hoping to spot our first prostitute. Wait! There's one! Hold up, nope — just a broken mile marker. Travel has been smooth and uneventful after the inferno at the last gas stop. Mother's station wagon has been running like gravy despite a persistent yet undoubtedly insignificant clunking noise. ETA 20 minutes." He set the device down. "I've decided I'm going to write a book."

"When did you decide that?"

"About two years ago after I read my first book. I've started reading my second book and I really like it. I realized that my life is pretty interesting and that people would enjoy reading about everything I've learned. I've easily learned a butt-load since I started the practice of reading."

"Really?" David asked and sat up. "Like what?"

"Like never punch a rattlesnake in the face. Always chew with your mouth closed in Indian country. I've got all the best ones written down somewhere. It's important to always have a log. The voice recorder helps the world keep up with my brain."

David looked up. "Whoa!" he said. "What's that?"

A line of bumper-to-bumper traffic had formed up ahead and was moving slowly past piles of debris. As they got closer they saw what looked like a makeshift blockade in the middle of the road, what was left of it, at least. Mangled chunks of cement blocks littered the road as if they had been picked up and dropped from the sky. Bits of yellow caution tape tailed in the wind and splinters of wood covered the ground like straw. As they neared David could see an abandoned fire truck and an overturned police car.

Jerry slowed the car and rolled down his window as they came alongside a parked, beat-up blue truck and an overweight middle-aged man and his wife snapping photos of the wreckage. "Hey!" Jerry yelled. "Any idea what happened here?"

"Yeah," the guy said and walked over to Jerry's open window. "Tornado came through here this afternoon. Wrecked the place up good."

"*Tornado?*" Jerry said. "Since when do tornados come through Vegas?"

"Every so often," the man said, still snapping pictures.

"Why all the crap in the road? Hasn't been anything on this highway for years."

The man looked up from his camera. "Buncha fellas came out this morning and started building checkpoints all over the city."

"You mean the police?" Jerry asked.

He shook his head. "No, Sir. Military. Those boys get things done fast. Built this checkpoint within the hour. But then the tornado came in and tore it all down. I guess someone got the bright idea to park a firetruck across the road as a backup. Probably shoulda taken the keys outta the ignition, though. Some traveler musta backed it outta the way." The man shrugged. "Military hasn't been out to remedy the situation. Way I see it, they're more concerned about keeping the interstate secured."

"Why all the blockades?" Jerry said. "They trying to keep people from leaving the casinos?"

"You kidding me?" the guy asked. "There's a huge pandemic sweeping the nation. The President just gave the order to cut off entry into major cities for fear of the virus spreading. Flights are grounded, too. The way I see it, you boys have likely found the only way into the city."

"Do you...work for the government?" Jerry asked.

The man shook his head. "No. I'm just taking pictures for my blog. I run an online prepper site," he said and handed Jerry his card.

"Cooool," Jerry said. "You got like rocket launchers and stuff?"

The man shared a proud grin. "This week's feature column is 'Top ten high assault bunkers for the vacation-minded family.' We do a lot of affiliate marketing," he admitted. The man backed away from the window to take more pictures when he noticed the license plate on Jerry's car. "You guys coming from *Washington?*" he asked in shock. "You can't be driving around! You might be infected with the disease."

"Uh...no," Jerry said quickly and leaned out the window. "We're coming from Reno. We stole this car," he said with a tight-lipped smile and affectionately patted the rusted exterior.

That seemed to throw the man off guard. He looked over at his wife and took a couple steps back. "Well, best that you get back on to Reno. Whole world's about to change."

Jerry flashed a look at David. "My brother is on the verge of crapping his pants," he said to the man and let the car begin to roll forward. "He gets real angry if he soils himself. Can't say I blame him. Up in Reno there's hardly a toilet that doesn't have piss all over it. Thought we'd try our luck and use the commodes at the Luxor. Listen, it has been *great* talking to you," he smiled warmly. "Have a great night."

Jerry pressed the gas pedal and bounced over the rubble and down the road. In the rearview mirror David could see the man jogging after them with both hands waving over his head. What he didn't see when he looked away, was the man's head exploding.

Chapter 9: Melech Amschel Rothschild

A gold plated platinum watch beeped pleasantly and Melech Rothschild stretched his arms after a restful sleep half a mile below the earth's surface. Exactly 19 hours had passed since the event in Pioneer Square, and it was now 12:00 p.m. Pacific time.

"Boy, was that necessary," he said to himself after looking at his watch. Melech had spent practically every waking hour for the last six months making sure his Master Plan went off without a hitch. One does not simply unleash a biological weapon willy nilly.

Melech's underground quarters in no way resembled a typical fall-out shelter. Quite the contrary. Melech Rothschild was a man of fine tastes and it showed. The floors and walls of his suite were lined with Macassar ebony from Indonesia. His kitchen countertops were enameled lava and the majority of his appliances were forged from silver. Turning the silver handle on his faucet, he poured himself a tall cold glass of Chilean glacier water.

Melech took a sip, swallowed, and said, "Television." A large flat screen lowered from the ceiling. "News. Channel twenty-one."

The TV flickered on and a national broadcast began to play. An attractive young woman in a blue halter-top looked gravely into the camera. She spoke. "It is unusual for such large tornados to appear in the southern regions of Nevada and Utah, which have been hit by one of the worst tornado disasters in history."

"Baa!" Melech said angrily. "We're in the midst of the greatest threat to American soil and these idiots are carrying on about a fucking tornado. I don't even know why I bought this fucking station. Channel seven," he said impatiently.

Another attractive woman appeared, this one in a green halter-top. She looked gravely into the camera and spoke. "President Alan has declared a state of emergency and all flights departing or arriving in Western states have been grounded until further notice. The U.S. borders with Canada and Mexico have also been closed in an effort to prevent the spread of the pandemic."

"Good job, Ben," he said with approval and finished his glacial water.

"Already the virus has spread to Colorado and Texas..."

Melech widened his eyes. "Already," he said thoughtfully. "I certainly did not expect it to reach Colorado until sometime next week." He rubbed his chin as he thought about it. "It must be mutating. Good!" he said cheerfully. "The faster this spreads the sooner we can implement Martial Law."

He glanced at his watch again. He had an hour to kill until he was scheduled to travel to D.C. Melech opened a cupboard and pulled out a package of water crackers and then grabbed a jar of beluga caviar from the fridge. Sitting down, he opened his metallic briefcase and began to read some paperwork while he munched on his morning snack. He read quickly through a long list of names, locations, procedures, and potential alternatives. Every detail had been considered.

Melech looked at the empty chair beside him. With a hopeful shrug he leaned over and said into his phone, "Chelsea? Hi. It's Melech. I was wondering if you had a minute? You do? Good."

No more than thirty-seconds had passed when the heavy metal door to his chambers opened with a soft hiss and a beautiful blonde woman in a maroon halter-top entered. The woman was in her mid-thirties and she stood calmly and confidently in the open archway. "Yes, Mr. Rothschild?" Her voice sounded like melting butter.

"Please, Chelsea. Come in. There are a few papers I would like to discuss."

This was not the first time that Melech Rothschild had invited Chelsea over to discuss his paperwork, which was understandable, considering that she was the executive scribe. However, for all the times she had come over, only twice had they discussed paperwork.

"Is everything all right, Mr. Rothschild?" she asked with concern.

"Yes, everything is fine. Please, sit down. And call me Melech. Tell me Chelsea, *how* long have you been working here?" he asked like an old friend.

"Almost a year now."

"And what a year it's been," he said with a sentimental glimmer in his eyes. "I hope we haven't kept you too busy."

She shook her head and smiled politely. "Not at all, Sir. I've actually become quite comfortable with the workload. I *did* work under the Secretary of State for eight years, after all."

"But this kind of work is much different," he said with a nod.

She thought about it. "In a way. In Washington I helped the government lie about what it was doing. Here I just help omit it."

"We value our secrecy," Melech said. "It would be very dangerous if people knew who the real leaders of the country were. The Organization has been underground for hundreds of years steering the course of humanity. We do it as much for humanity as we do it for ourselves," he lied. "It's imperative that people remain in the dark about us."

"I agree," her tone dark and full of understanding. "President Alan has been reacting to the situation in strong accordance," she said, knowing that she was giving Melech a compliment for his puppeteering. "The people must have faith in their leader. Without faith everything would collapse. Everything you have worked so hard for."

He smiled. "It is best to create systems that increase the subjugation of the people. What with the passage of civil liberties these last fifty years," he said and shook his head with disgust, "individuals have come up with ideas of their own. It's really hampered progress," he admitted.

"Well, whatever I can do to help..." Chelsea said with a soft smile and sashayed her finger across the table in front of her. She knew that if she could sleep with Melech Rothschild the rest of her life would be spent on easy street.

"I really admire your commitment to our cause," he said. "It's evident that you care a lot about world domination."

Chelsea smiled dimly. "My father taught me everything he knew." She looked away and Melech could see she was holding back emotion.

"Is everything all right?" he asked.

"His death came as a surprise to me, that's all," she admitted and wiped a tear from her cheek. "He was such a passionate father. Just last week he was sharing his excitement about The Master Plan. He was like a little kid before Christmas," she ruminated, "talking about all the death and carnage and the new and improved internment camps. I just can't believe he passed so suddenly. He was such a good man."

"We lost a lot of good men," Melech said and reached over and placed his hand on hers. "Remember, I was there when it happened."

She looked up at him with big doe eyes. "It must have been so horrible."

"None of us could have expected that the device had been tampered with before we received it. It was a real tragedy. Your father was a paragon, Chelsea. He was a brilliant man with enough brains to splatter against all the bunker walls in all the world," he said and squeezed her hand. "I'm certain that our Lord and Savior Satan had a good reason for taking him so soon."

"I just hope I can live up to his expectations," Chelsea said. "I'm his only child and without children of my own, my father's bloodline will end with me."

"I understand your concern," he said. "It's important to know where you come from and who you are. My family has been in the world domination business since time immemorial," he said and looked nostalgically up at the framed picture of the tyrannosaurus rex on the wall. "Here, have some caviar," he smiled.

Chelsea accepted and slowly began to eat.

"You know," Melech said innocently, "having off-spring is very important in this industry."

Her heart fluttered and she glanced at him. "Do you have children?" she asked.

"Oh, my yes indeed," he said. "Hundreds! Illegitimate, mind you, but enough to fill most of the Senate if need be. I have not, however, raised one myself. It's something I think about more and more as I age. It might be nice to raise a family once the genocide is over. How about you? Have you ever considered children?"

Her eyes brightened. "I would *love* to have kids," she smiled. "Boys," she said quickly to reassure him. "I learned so much from my parents that I think I would make a great mother. I'm not really good with men, though," she frowned. "It's hard for me to find someone to connect with on an intellectual level, you know?" she said, looking into his eyes.

His small heart twitched. "Undoubtedly."

"What about you?" she asked. "Do you think you're father material? Did you have a positive relationship with your father?"

"Um..." he stammered and looked away suddenly. The time his father locked him in a wire cage for a weekend came to his mind. "My father set the bar high. He was a perfectionist and it was difficult to live up to his expectations."

"Of course," she said. "Fathers only want the best for us, but at times their ways can be hard to follow."

"Not that I *minded* being water-boarded as a youth," he said amiably. "I just wasn't ready for it. I always felt that I let him down when it came to pain tolerance."

Chelsea took a bite of her cracker which broke in two and fell to the floor. "Oh!" she said.

"Not a problem," Melech waved his hand. "I have technology to take care of that." He pushed a button and a little machine sputtered out through a doggy door. But halfway to the fallen chip its engine sputtered out of life. Melech pressed the button again. "Move, you *imbecile!*" he shouted at the robot.

Chelsea leaned over and picked up her chip which had landed caviar-side down. She looked at it thoughtfully.

Melech put his hand out. "What are you doing! Stop! There's plenty more. Don't expose yourself to germs."

Chelsea laughed and looked around. "Melech, your room is immaculately clean. Besides, it would be foolish to waste this," she said and raised the chip to her mouth.

"There's more! I have cans full of cans of caviar," he sputtered like the faltering robot, but it was too late. Chelsea had put the cracker into her mouth with a single satisfying bite. But seeing his expression she began to apologize.

Melech closed his eyes and shook his head side to side with a thin smile. "It's quite all right, Chelsea, quite all right. I merely wanted to talk to you about what a good job you've been doing. Keep it up."

"Is that...all?" she asked.

"Yes, that would be all. Keep me updated on your progress if you would," he said.

"OK?" she said standing, obviously confused by his reaction.

Melech crossed his hands at the waist. He grinned and waited until she took the hint and left the bunker. When she was gone he pulled out his phone and pressed a button. "Mason? Please see that Chelsea gets tossed into the incinerator before we depart for D.C. I think her time with the organization should be terminated. Very good. Goodbye."

He shook his head at the single remaining crumb where the cracker had once been. Melech shuddered. "What a loss," he said to himself.

His phone rang to the tune of Mozart's Cosi Fan Tutte. He raised it to his head without looking at the number, thinking it must be Mason calling back to confirm. But instead of the calm and collected voice of Mason came a dark and sinister sound from another realm.

"Master!" Melech exclaimed like a frightened girl. "Is that you?"

"Of course it is me, *boy!* Who did you expect?"

"I *have* been expecting you," he said as confidently as possible, though he feared that he sounded like a truant school boy caught with a backpack of shit and dynamite. "I am glad you rang, in fact. I was about to update you."

"I should not have to call for an update," the voice scratched unpleasantly. "Are you not aware that the country is about to be thrown into turmoil?"

"Of course, Sir, of course!"

"When will you and the others be here?" the Master barked.

"Soon, Master," Melech said, still attempting to steady his voice. "Our transportation is set to leave momentarily."

"Good. I will note the timing of your arrival. I will make nine seats available."

Melech winced. He had not been looking forward to this part. His Master was not known for taking bad news well. "The others will not be coming," he said softly.

"*No?!*" the voice bellowed. "They *defy* me? They are *nothing* without me! I will smite them where they stand! I will slay their whore wives and their whore mothers! I will leave nothing but pestilence for their children's children's children. All your miserable lives are what they are because of me!"

"Of course, Master. We owe everything we have to you. I am afraid that the reason they will not be joining us is because they are all dead, Sir."

There was a long pause on the other end. "Did you kill them?" the Master asked.

"No," he lied.

The silence thickened. "I hope not for your sake," the voice said. "You are going to need all the help you can get to get this country back into alignment. If things do not progress quickly I will suck out your soul with a hollow rusted wire."

"Of course, Master. Yes, always the wire. I assure you, everything is going according to plan. I will be there soon to debrief you with everything I know. My word is your command."

A burbling grumble finished the other line.

Melech slumped into his chair and sighed. He knew he was treading in deep water, but he had done his homework and now everything should fall into place. Before he knew it, Melech would be in charge of everything. "Oh, everything is right on target, Master. Don't you worry about that."

As if choreographed to his words, Melech's gold-plated watch beeped pleasantly and a kind and soothing feminine voice said, "Train to D.C. now boarding."

Melech stood, tucked in his shirt, and picked up a metallic briefcase near the door. He pressed the 15 button combination which he had recently memorized and the heavy metallic door opened with a soft hiss. He walked down the narrow well-lit corridor and smiled pleasantly to various shadow-government agents, then he took a right turn at a door marked Station 36V. A tall good-looking man in his mid-forties wearing a black suit was standing inside when Melech entered. "Hello, Mr. Rothschild," said the man.

"Hello Mason," Melech responded. "I trust everything is prepared?"

"Yes, Sir. I've called our entrance station in D.C. and they are anticipating our arrival." He handed Melech a manila envelope. "Here are the latest updates."

"Very good," he said and sat down in a thick leather train seat. He scanned through the documents. Melech could read at nearly 40,000 words a minute. "Any news on our runaway, Dingle?" he asked calmly.

"Yes. As the document states, Special Agent Jon Boring and Agent Bob Fleckle arrived at Dingle's residence at twenty-three hundred hours to find two headless FBI agents in the home."

Melech pulled out a couple of 8x10 photos from the folder.

"Those were taken at a gas station about an hour south of Reno, Nevada. We suspected they were headed to Las Vegas and these suspicions were confirmed by Mr. Dingle's Facebook account."

Melech read Dingle's update aloud to himself. "Headed to Vegas to fix all the confusion. Hope we'll all be ROFLing soon." He leaned back. "He's willingly going to Vegas? What on earth is he thinking?"

"I suspect he knows nothing about his role in all of this. Audio data from the FBI show that his roommate Jerry Burger learned of the Vegas waypoint in a case of mistaken identity."

"What do we know about Jerry Burger?" Melech asked, scanning through the rest of the document.

"An imbecile, Sir. Our biggest concern is that Burger will kill Dingle by accident somehow. He's run off the road twice and was responsible for blowing up a gas station. The evidence indicates he drove away with the gas nozzle still in the vehicle as he flicked out his cigarette."

Melech set the paperwork down and exhaled in agitation. His mind was racing with ideas. "Do you think he's trying something? Could he have seen the document?"

"It's impossible to say, Sir. He could have it memorized for all we know."

"If he has we're cooked. If he talks about it, and people believe him, it's all over. They wouldn't believe him though, would they? He's an idiot!"

"They're *all* idiots now, Mr. Rothschild," Mason said.

Melech smiled suddenly and widely, as if he had just been told that his warm bath of money was ready for him. "They are now, aren't they?" he mused. "Good point," he said and chuckled dimly. "Well, make sure our agents bring him in to Dr. Macaw as soon as possible. We have to get him cleared before we run our final test."

"Shouldn't be a problem, Mr. Rothschild. The entire city is blockaded at this point. When he comes through, we'll find him, bring him to Dr. Macaw, and then kill him," Mason said and began typing into his phone.

Melech sighed and stretched back into his leather rhino seat with ivory armrests. "This is only a hiccup. Everything is going just as it should," he said. "Your actions and loyalty give me confidence, Mason. You're the only one I can trust these days." He lapsed into a long stare. "In this business enemies are more common than friends. I feel good, though, I do." He pressed a green button and instantly there was a woman's voice coming from the speaker.

"Yes, Mr. Rothschild?"

"I'll have a glass of Penfolds Ampoule, Rebecca," Melech said. "You thirsty?" he asked Mason who shrugged agreeably. "Just bring out the bottle, dear. Thank you." He looked at Mason. "They only made twelve bottles and I own nine of them," he grinned.

"You always understand quality, Sir."

"I'll be honest, Mason. These kinds of matters can be stressful. It's times like these on the edge of global social transformation that I wish I could just stand back and let the other members of the Brotherhood handle it. Sometimes I wish I hadn't killed them all," he mused. "Who am I kidding? Of *course* I should have killed them all." He sighed again. "I probably should have never left my Swiss Chattel after 9/11."

A red light flashed on the wall and a small screen appeared from behind a wooden hatch. The words ACQUIRING SIGNAL appeared on the screen and the image of President Alan came into view. The President looked to be in a state of panic. His hair was damp and disheveled, his collar was crooked, and his words came out sharp and terrified. "Is that you, Melech?"

"Yes, Mr. President. Go ahead."

"Oh, thank *GOD*," Alan said. "You have no idea how long I've been trying to get a hold of you. Everything has been going to hell! People in Washington are horrified by what's been going on. Everyone wants me to address the issue, but I haven't the slightest clue what to say. The Department of Defense is telling me to blame the Arabs, The Secretary of State wants me to make an emergency order of sanitation wipes, and the Vice President has been insisting that I try changing the subject to turtles."

"Turtles?" Melech asked.

"I think he likes the metaphor that turtles have a shell."

"I don't follow."

Alan looked relieved. "OK. Good, me neither. He thinks he's onto something, though. My point is, I need you to do something. Anything! Are you OK? Where are you?"

"Everything is fine, Mr. President," Melech said calmly. "I am en route to D.C. now."

"*Really*? How? I've had everything shut down just like you've told me to."

"I'm riding in an underground railway train. I should be there in less than 90 minutes."

There was a pause. "*Really*? I didn't know we had underground trains."

"There are a lot of things you don't know, Mr. President."

The President was silent for a moment. Finally he said, "Are there aliens down there with you?"

Melech sighed. "Sir, if we can stay on topic I would like to debrief you on our situation. As you know, the virus has taken the trade winds east and is headed your way. I commend you for shutting down interstate transportation. Continue to put up road blocks and whatever else you can to slow its progress. Our focus is on Las Vegas, right now."

"If I may, Melech, I *really* don't like the idea of taking away people's freedoms. I *stand* for freedom."

"I'm afraid we don't have a choice. The sooner we implement Martial Law the better."

"This is such a catastrophe!" the President moaned. "We are going to need a massive clean-up crew and a media blitzkrieg."

"Sir?"

"We've got to do everything we can to spin this incident in a positive light, otherwise our chance for re-election is down the tubes." He paused. "Maybe we can tell people that the virus is targeting felons and pedophiles. Maybe we can actually take *credit* for this whole thing," he said hopefully.

"Do *not* take credit for this, Ben," Melech said sternly.

"Are you sure?" the President asked. "I'm *really* good at taking credit. It comes natural for me."

"Sir, you're going to have to trust me on this one."

"So what am I supposed to do? People are knocking on my door this very moment."

"Well, then answer it, for God's sake!"

"I can't. I've locked myself in the oval closet. My guess is they've turned into zombies by now."

"It's not zombies, it's a virus."

"Same thing."

"Mr. President. I can assure you that no bureaucrat in Washington D.C. will become infected. Trust me. You're safe."

"I doubt it," he whispered, the edge of terror returning to his voice. "I used to get chicken pox quite a bit when I was a kid."

"Like I said, you're going to be fine. Tell them whatever you want to tell them and I'll be there within the hour to help smooth things over."

"What about the other incident?" President Alan asked.

"What other incident?"

"Intelligence received a cable that one of our portable nuclear devices went rogue this morning."

"*Excuse* me?" Melech said and leaned forward.

Alan nodded. "All we have is video, but the image is clear. It looks like some Mexican broke into an unmarked facility and stole our suitcase prototype."

"You don't mean the Mushroom Maker?" Melech said, widening his eyes.

"Yep, that's the one," the President said. "He was able to dismantle the tracking device on it as well. We have no idea where it is. You don't think he's planning on bombing Mexico, do you?" Benjamin Alan asked.

Melech stared into the distance. This was unexpected. "Don't say a word about this. Got it? Just continue to do what you do best until I get there."

President Alan sat up straight and tidied his hair with his fingers. "You can count on me, Melech."

Chapter 10: The Freedom Fighter

Hashim turned to face the approaching vehicle and stuck out his thumb. He was on the shoulder of the highway about forty miles outside of Merkel, Texas, a tiny town in the middle of nowhere. The car sped up as it passed him. He had been hitchhiking for about ten minutes, and he hoped he'd get picked up soon. After all, he was carrying a nuclear bomb in a medium-sized briefcase.

Acquiring the hand-held nuclear bomb had been a miraculous affair, as if Hashim had been *guided* to the bomb by Allah himself. It was pretty clear to Hashim that not only did Allah want Hashim to blow up some infidels, he wanted Hashim to blow up a whole fuckton of them.

After the incident at Walmart, or lack thereof, Hashim figured his days as suicide bomber had come to an end before they had even begun. Afterwards, still suicidal and miserably depressed, Hashim decided to visit the local bar and ordered the first beer of his life. Then he had another. And another. And before he knew it, and much to his surprise, Hashim had become the drinking buddy of some really friendly infidels.

After about five beers, a rock-solid friendship had formed between Hashim and his fellow drunks. The drunks sympathized with Hashim's problems. They listened carefully to his complaints about the American government. They related to his challenges of finding his way through Wal-Mart. And they consoled him about his inner conflict that arose from his finding American women so unbelievably attractive.

After the infidels bought him a shot of Tequila (chosen from their assumption that he was Mexican), Hashim complained to them that he had failed his job because he had never been given the proper training. The amiable infidels convinced him that he should call his boss and tell him what a dickhead he was for not training him properly. They also stressed the importance of saying something insulting about his employer's mother.

Nearly blind drunk, Hashim took their advice and later that night on his stumble home, he made a collect call to ExxonMobilastan and spoke with his trainer Abaduba Muhammed. As he drunkenly tried to read the list of insults off the bar napkin, Abaduba interrupted him with a happy shout of surprise.

"You're alive!" he said. "And not a moment too late. Everyone that went with you to America is gone."

"Killed by the virus?" Hashim slurred.

"No. Deported to Mexico. Anyway, forget whatever it is you have been planning. Our men have hacked the military. A barrage of confidential information has come into our hands. There's some place we need you to go. Now."

And so Hashim found himself sobering up on a two hour bus ride out of town. He got off the bus at his stop and then walked ten miles to the east along a deserted, dirt road until he eventually came to what looked like an abandoned shopping mall surrounded by a twenty foot barbed wire fence — and for whatever reason, the fence gate was *wide* open. Hashim looked up at the cameras and wondered if he was being watched. Knowing he had little to lose, he quickly came up with a cover story about selling invisible tamales and walked through the gate. To his astonishment, no one was there to receive him. From what he could tell, the base was *utterly* vacant. Hashim couldn't help but wonder if Abaduba had sent him on a wild camel-chase.

But then he saw the headless bodies.

Hashim had never given himself a private tour of an abandoned secret military weapons base before, but it turned out to be pretty fun. The place wasn't intriguing in a visual sense, but he thought it was pretty neat running down the empty corridors while listening to the sounds of his echoing sneakers. The more he explored, the more convinced Hashim became of three things: One - everyone who had once worked here was now dead. Two — this was where nuclear weapons were made. Three - the nuclear weapons were this way. He knew this third fact because there were signs that read: Nuclear Weapons This Way.

At last, he found himself in a windowless room that was empty except for a table and a medium-sized metallic briefcase. On the briefcase there was a laminated piece of paper with detailed instructions on how to use the nuclear warhead contained within the briefcase.

Hashim, now curious as a desert hedgehog, opened the briefcase to discover that, sure enough, this was indeed a nuclear device so simple that a child could use it. Though there was an assortment of levers, valves, and wires around its sides, there were only two colored buttons. There was a green button with a smiley face and a red button with a mushroom cloud.

He would need to find a bigger Wal-Mart.

The taillights of a silver pick-up turned red as the speeding truck slowed to a stop down the road from Hashim. Hashim ran up to the passenger window.

"Where ya goin', partner?" a friendly looking Texas man asked.

Hashim hadn't really thought about it. All he cared about was getting out of Merkel, Texas.

"Quiet type, eh? Good, I ain't got much time fer talkin' either. Git in."

Hashim smiled and opened the door. "Go ahead and toss yer briefcase in back," the driver said.

Hashim hesitated. "I think I'd like to hang on to it."

"I ain't askin', I'm tellin'. This ain't no business trip."

Hashim looked at the back of the truck wondering if the nuclear warhead would accidentally go off if they hit a pot hole. He figured that if it did he would at least kill one infidel and one was better than none. After setting the briefcase in the back, Hashim opened the door and got in.

The driver put the truck into first gear and peeled out — within 5 seconds the truck hit 60 miles an hour. "Ford - 450," he grinned. "I like my trucks like I like my wimmin. Big n' fast. I'm headed to Arlington," the man said. "Gotta get there by five. That's the first pitch."

It was then that Hashim noticed the Nolan Ryan bobble-head on the dashboard. Nolan had a mild grin, as if he had accepted that he would never look out the windshield.

"You a Rangers fan?" the man asked. He shook his head. "Let me rephrase that. If you *don't* like the Rangers you can *git out*."

Hashim smiled meekly. "I like the Rangers," he said.

The driver laughed. It was a hard metallic laugh like he had spent his childhood gargling with tinfoil. "'Course you do. *Everybody* likes the Rangers – everybody with a brain in their head that is. I been goin' to these games every week for every year since I was five years old," he said. "Now I'm fifty-five. What do you think about that?"

Hashim took a moment while he did the math. "Fifty years," he said, and then nodded, pleased with the math.

"That's a lotta ballgames, boy," he said and laughed again. "Name's Daryl. What's yours?"

"Uh," Hashim hesitated. "Robert."

"Robert, huh? Sure don't look like a Robert. You sure yer name's not Rodrigo or Hindi somethin' er other?"

"No, Sir. Robert. Smith."

Daryl looked him up and down and smirked. "Listen. I ain't Border Patrol or nothin'. I don't care *where* you're from. Personally, I don't blame the immigrants one damn bit. In fact, I kinda feel *sorry* for the poor bastards. Most of them are in poverty because they have no economy. Their country is so shitty that they can't earn an honest living. God bless the American economy, eh? Only thing greater than the economy might be Mt. Rushmore."

"My country is *not* shitty," Hashim said.

"Aha!" he exclaimed and gave him a look. "Is that so...*Robert*," he scoffed.

Hashim inadvertently smacked himself. "What I mean is..."

"I *said* I don't care," Daryl affirmed. "You got yer business, I got mine. Listen, I don't blame you for wanting to be free in America. That's all anyone wants, isn't it? To be free? I swear to God. America is the greatest country in the world founded by the greatest men ever to have lived. Did you know Benjamin Franklin was the original guy who *discovered* lightning? I'm not making this shit up — this country's friggin' amazing!

"Now I'll admit," he said, leaning back into his seat, "that we've got our problems. Things took a wrong turn somewhere around Richard Nixon and now our politicians have gone a little sideways and are tryin' to take away our rights. They try scaring us with some big thing and then they come in and say, 'OK whoa now, stay calm everybody, the government's here to help you.' " He looked at Hashim from the corner of his eye. "Well, you know what I think? I think it's all baloney. Honest to God, Roberto. I think the only thing our government does well is lie. They'll tell you something so many times that you ain't got no choice but to believe it. Least everyone else does. Not me, though. I look at things thoughtfully. I see things as they are and you know what? I know this is gonna sound crazy but I think this whole pandemic thing is one big *hoax,*" he said, managing to say the word hoax in two syllables. "Me personally, I don't know one single person that's gone and died from that there virus. Not a single one. Now you tell *me* what's real." He paused and reflected. "But if it *is* real, if people really *are* dying, then there's only one explanation. People from Texas are immune."

"How come?" Hashim asked.

Daryl shrugged. "Maybe the virus is allergic to Freedom," he said, saying the word Freedom as if he were referring to Christ Himself. "Maybe we just got so much of it that the virus can't handle it and decided to go up to Oklahoma instead. You see, Roberto, we here in Texas *value* freedom. We all earned it back in the day with that whole Alamo thing. Since then, though, times have changed in America. These days ain't hardly anyone free," he said, shaking his head. "They're workin' some government job, or they only got one leg, or maybe they got some busybody mother-in-law that don't let 'em do what they wanna do. I bet," he said, settling into his theory, "that *no one* in Texas will get infected with that virus. Maybe a few old people and some folks too dumb to cover their mouths when other people sneeze. One cannot discount stupid people, Roberto," he said and shook his head with annoyance.

"They ruin it for everyone," Hashim agreed.

"Boy don't they? Tell you what though, where I'm headin', ain't gonna be nothin' of that. You ever gone to a ballgame?"

Hashim shook his head.

"*NO!*" Daryl sputtered in disbelief. "How is that possible? Why baseball is the icon of America – the *symbol* of this great nation. If baseball were an organ, it would probably be Uncle Sam's dick."

Hashim raised an eyebrow. Daryl certainly seemed to know a lot about America, and if Daryl was saying that baseball was practically the original statue of liberty, then that would be a terrific place to...well...

"How many people go to this game?" he said, thinking of the t-ball games he had seen in Midland.

"Only 'bout 50,000."

Hashim grinned. "I would love to go."

"Brother," Daryl said as he pressed on the gas pedal, "there's nothing that would please me more than to take you."

Chapter 11: The Convention

Jerry finally parked the car in the Caesar's Palace garage. (He had gotten lost four times.)

David was a nervous wreck. He'd had to go pee for the last hour and a half but had been terrified that someone would recognize him. He was afraid now that the doorman of Caesar's Palace would identify him and then tackle him for being a terrorist. If David didn't get recognized by the doorman then he would certainly be noticed by some of the hundreds of gamblers. He fidgeted with his seat belt. "So what's the plan?" David asked. "Are we going in here or are we gonna walk outside? Who's going to do most of the talking? Should I walk behind you, or in front with my head down?"

Jerry leaned back and stretched. "Listen, I want to hit the strip and drink and gamble as much as you do, but first thing's first. We gotta get you a disguise. If people realize that you're responsible for killing everyone in the Pacific Northwest then we're going to have a problem on our hands."

"I was thinking the same thing."

"Now I happen to know a guy who works at a very reputable establishment just down the street from here. I did him a favor a while back and he owes me one. Really great guy, actually. He has this dog that he trained to hump anything he points at, seriously. I hope the dog's there when we show up."

"So what do we do after we get the disguise?"

"According to the guy that I talked to on the FBI agent's phone, I'm supposed to take you to that medical convention here at Caesar's Palace and meet with a Dr. Ronald Macaw who is attending."

"Did he say why?" David asked.

Jerry shook his head. "All he said was that Macaw would get you settled into the vaccination procedure."

"Maybe they're going to make me immune!" David said with relief. "That would be great! I've been so worried about my head exploding that I can't stop thinking about it. Maybe they found out I'm important and that I can't catch this exploding-head cold or whatever it is." His phone beeped. David read a message. "Oh no!" he said.

Jerry looked over. "What is it?"

"I just got a message from Maria Valdersmart on Heart Match. She says, 'I don't want to date you because I don't date terrorists. My dad's head is gone! You're a duck!' "

"A *duck?*" Jerry asked.

"I think she means dick." He tossed his phone on the dashboard and slumped into his chair. "I feel like crap," he said.

"OK. So you're giving me a pretty heavy bummer," Jerry said. "Now I know you're sad because you got fired from your job and just got dumped by a girl you weren't actually dating, but just repeat after me." He paused. "*Vegas, baby. Vegas.*"

"Vegas, baby?"

"Close enough. Now let's go get you a disguise and some answers from this Dr. Macaw before people find out who you are. Come on!" he said and got out of the car. "And don't forget that folder."

Knowing that David had never been to Vegas before, Jerry felt obligated to play tour guide and he immediately jumped into the role and led David through the Caesar's Palace parking garage, pointing out dark corners where he had once bought drugs and other places where he had used the corners of the garage as a urinal. "Good spot right there," he said with a look of experience. David relieved himself.

At last they emerged onto the Vegas strip and David lost his breath. Never before had he seen so many flashing lights, so many neon signs, so much going on at once. His phone rang and for the first time in his life he didn't even notice.

"J-Jerry," he stammered. "I – I never knew. It's...*beautiful.* Look at all the twinkly! We should go over there!" he pointed at Treasure Island. "Oh! But first we should ride that roller coaster. Ooo! All you can eat buffet? That's a *great* deal! I can't believe I've never been here before. *Tigers?* They have *tigers* in Vegas? That makes sense, I guess. I think we need to go over there," he said sporadically as Jerry walked in the opposite direction. David hurried to catch up with Jerry.

"OK," Jerry said after they had walked for several blocks. "You wait here."

David looked up at the sign on the building they had stopped in front of. "Elvira's Pawn Shop," he read. "This doesn't look interesting. What are we doing here?"

"I'm going in to buy some things that will help us. Try not to stand out while I'm inside. I'll only take a sec."

David leaned against the brick building and pulled out his phone. To his surprise, he had a voicemail.

There was a strange kind of humming as if the caller did not know the phone had gone to voicemail. This continued for a little over a minute. In the background he could her the musical score of *The Hobbit.* Then the high pitched nasally voice of his mother broke through. "David? Is that you? Are you there?" Silence. "Well, if you're listening, this is your mother - Donna," she reminded

78

him. "I was surprised to see that you made the New Zealand news. Imagine! My little Frodo on every TV station. Everyone's talking about you! It's so exciting! Here all along I thought that you were too timid for adventure, but just look at you! Destined to slay the American dragon, you are. Very neat! I hope you remembered to change your underwear, dear. It would be a real shame if they caught you with dirty underwear. Find yourself a ring of protection. And a cloak of invisibility can go a long way. I'd love to come join the fun but I've got a Wizard's gathering tomorrow afternoon and I'm bringing Oreo Orcs. I've really been working on getting my casting spells memorized so I can-" The message ended.

David looked out across the strip. His mom was right. David was going to have to be as inconspicuous as possible. He had to be a sleuth. A spy. A shadow.

Jerry came out of the pawn shop with a small pistol in his hand. "Check it out!" he yelled, unable to contain his excitement. "Colt .45, motherfucker!"

An elderly couple walking past them screamed and took off running.

"What are you *doing*??" David yelled. "Are you crazy?"

"I know, I know," Jerry said, reading David's expression of horror. "This isn't the most practical gun for the job, but it's small and easily concealed, which I might add, is part of the reason I got it — that and *A*, it was the cheapest gun they had, and *B*, the guy offered to throw in a fifth of Wild Turkey if I bought it right away. You want a shot?" he asked and unscrewed the lid.

"No, I don't want a shot! Jerry, put that gun away. You're going to get us arrested."

"Only because I don't have a license to carry," he quipped. "Relax. It's not like I'm going to shoot anyone who doesn't deserve it."

"How did you buy it without a license?"

"I gave the owner a tube of pills. Mostly unmarked tylenol capsules, I think. Couple hits of Ecstasy. Ready to go to the Palace?" he asked, slipping the gun under his waistband, and setting off down the sidewalk.

David pulled out his phone as they walked.

"What are you doing?" Jerry asked.

"Looking at the news," David said. "I feel lost not knowing what's going on in the world. I think it's important to stay up on what's happening since we left Seattle."

"So, what's it say?" Jerry asked.

"Well, it looks like Kanye West just got a new dog named Kwanye. There's also this article that says corn syrup is really good for your liver. I had no idea," he mused.

"Yep. It's good to take some every day," Jerry said.

David studied his screen. "Wow, those corn corporations really do a lot of studies to ensure the safety of their products. One sec, OK there, posted to social media," David said. "People should know..." he added with a serious look.

"David, you *can't* be using social media. You might as well stand on the corner with a sign that says I'm David Dingle!" he yelled out loud and took another slug of Wild Turkey.

"Oh, crap — you're right. Sorry, it's just habit. I'm better with social media than I am in person. I have time to think," he said thinking about it. "I can be anyone I want to be online. I can be confident, or interesting, or ethnic. Offline I'm just boring old me." He looked up at the twinkly. "I should know by now that my phone keeps me safe. Had I been smart enough to use it in Pioneer Square I would have just sent a text to the police department, told them I was innocent, and then calmly waited until someone official showed up to clear my name."

"You gotta stop trusting everyone and everything," Jerry said. "The only one who can take care of you is *me*. Got it?" he said and took another slug.

David pushed send. "I just sent you an affirmative answer."

Jerry looked up at the casino. "Great. Here we are. Now this whole thing is going to have to be handled very delicately, which is why I'm going to be the one to handle it. You wait outside while I go in."

"Wait. What are you going to say?"

"I'm gonna tell them I lost my room key so we can go upstairs."

"But they'll know you're not staying here."

"I'll just tell them my name is Carlos Santana and if that doesn't work I'll use another name. *Truuust me*, Santana stays here all the time. I've seen him play here live on two occasions. Great performer!"

"Jerry, you don't look *anything* like Carlos Santana."

"Oh no?" He reached into his plastic shopping bag and pulled out a curly black wig and some dark sunglasses. "Got these at the pawn shop, too. What do you think?" he said, trying them both on.

"I think they're going to laugh at you."

"Good. Laughter will loosen them up. Maybe I'll tell them I'm a comedian here for a big show."

"Jerry, this isn't going to work. Why don't we-"

"Yeah, that'll be plan B. OK. You stay here. I'll be right back."

David sighed and propped himself up against the marble wall and waited while Jerry talked to the concierge. He opened his phone and did a search for Dr. Macaw. It didn't take long to find him. A white intelligent-looking man in his fifties stared back at him. Under his name were about a million different degrees and qualifications. Apparently, he was an infectious disease specialist. David quickly typed in Caesar's Palace and Medical Convention. His eyes widened in surprise. What were the chances that a convention on infectious diseases had been planned just one day after the outbreak in Seattle? He tried not to think about it.

"Hey!" Jerry said. "You ready?"

"Did it work?"

"Kind of. You were right in that they didn't think I was Carlos Santana, but I *did* get them laughing. I told them I wanted to stay here, but I had to see the sauna first."

"The sauna?"

"Told them it was a deal breaker for me so they gave me a temporary key. Come on."

Jerry led the way to the elevators at Forum Tower. "Keep your face covered," Jerry whispered. "They've got cameras in the elevator so security can prevent drunk people from having sex in them."

"Really?"

"Oh yeah. I've been busted a few times."

They got out at the second floor and Jerry inserted his key into the slot and pulled the door open to the sauna changing room.

"Sorry," David said. "But what are we doing here?"

Jerry turned around and faced David. "I'm not going to lie. We've been really lucky that no one has recognized you yet. Personally, I thought we were gonna get brought down by the gift shop attendants. Bottom line is we gotta get you in a disguise. Now take off your pants."

"What?"

Jerry grabbed a full length towel off the rack. "Wrap that around your waist."

David stared at him. "Jerry, I didn't come here to relax."

"Would you hurry up already? You gotta look like you belong here. People don't want to look at half-naked roman soldiers unless they absolutely have to. This is Caesar's Palace we're talking about here. There are Roman Soldiers everywhere." He was moving quickly. "Now take this other towel and wrap it around one shoulder. Good."

"I thought Roman soldiers wore sheets, not towels."

"Where are we gonna find sheets in a hotel? There we go," he said, adjusting David's towel. "You're starting to look like a skinny version of John Belushi in *Animal House*." He took a step back and studied him. "Hmm. Something's missing. Oh! I know what it is," he said and looked around. "Awesome! They've got plastic sandals you can use."

"I am *not* wearing those!" David said. "They look moldy."

"Roman soldiers don't wear Nikes when they're in their towels," he said.

"Now hurry up and put them on."

"I don't have a pocket for my phone."

"Give it to me."

David pulled it back possessively. "Are you kidding?"

"David, Roman Soldiers don't walk around carrying their phones, either. You have to look *authentic*."

David looked at his phone like it was his only son who he was sending off to war. "I don't know, Jerry."

"We have no time to argue. You're not the only one that needs a disguise. Now give it."

Reluctantly, David handed him his phone and Jerry put it in his pocket. As David got himself arranged, Jerry began rummaging through the stacks of clothes that people in the sauna had left behind. "Oh my God," he whispered in excitement.

"What?"

Jerry reached into a stack and pulled out a full length doctor's coat.

"What are you doing? You can't take that!" he whispered.

"Shhh," he hissed. "If we want to save the world I have to steal this stranger's coat."

David couldn't quite figure out what the two had in common, but Jerry sounded confident and that was enough for David.

"I found out where the convention is," David said as they walked down the hallway. Jerry was practicing his doctor's walk.

"Good. So the way I figure it, when we find that Doctor Macaw he'll probably want to do crazy experiments on you right away, and we'll convince him that we'll comply, but just before he gives you the chloroform we'll trick him into giving us the information we need."

"Which is what?"

"Jesus, David, you gotta stick with me here. We need to find out why everyone's heads are blowing up and why ours aren't. Personally, I think we both got jabbed in the middle of the night with some secret formula by some twisted underground Nazi organization, but I need to hear it from their mouths first before we release their testimony on Facebook."

"But what if the plan doesn't work?" David asked.

"Well, that's why we brought *this*," he said, and pulled the manilla envelope out of his bag. "If things go wrong, we'll just get the doctor to read this document. Then his head will explode and, well, we'll probably go to Mexico. Tijuana's only a few hours from here, I think."

They stepped into the vacant elevator. Across from them were their reflections in the elevator mirror.

"Dude," Jerry said, "you have *got* to put your hair up. You look like Jesus."

"I do?"

"Spitting image."

"How am I supposed to put my hair up?" David asked.

"What do you mean 'how?' It's *your* hair. Put it in a bun or something."

"Can't you help me?"

"Yuck, no way. I'm not touching another dude's hair. Put it up yourself."

"Fine," David said and bunched his hair into a bun and tied it up.

Jerry looked at him. "That is *not* going to work," he said.

"What? Why?"

"Because now you look like Princess Leia, that's why." The elevator door opened. "Oops. Too late. Run with it. Helllooooo Vegas!" Jerry hollered and stepped out dramatically. "Come on," he waved. "Let's go get some drinks."

It was difficult for David to follow Jerry. Not because his sandals were somewhat slimy, or the fact that he was wearing a towel and nothing underneath, but the sheer volume of flashing lights, ringing bells, and shouting people turned his straight path into a swaying swagger.

Jerry stopped at a sports bar and ordered a beer and watched the baseball game while he waited.

When David sat down Jerry turned to look at him and burst out laughing. "Sorry," he said and covered his mouth. "It's just that you look fucking hilarious. What was I thinking giving you a towel? You look like you took a wrong turn coming out of the pool. I think the buns probably throw people off, though. They'll think you're part of some show."

"Here's your beer," the bartender told Jerry. "You want anything, pal?" he asked David.

David smiled. "No thank-you."

"You better stop doing that," Jerry told David after the bartender left.

"What? What'd I do?"

"You can't make eye contact with people. They'll recognize you."

"Oh. Right," he said and shook his head. This was getting complicated. He lifted his shoulder towel and buried his face in it so he didn't look suspicious. "So what's the plan?"

"Glad you asked," Jerry said after he had slugged back three quarters of his beer. "We're gonna go to this infectious disease conference and find this doctor Macaw. They shouldn't recognize us because we're in disguise."

"But I don't look like a doctor at all."

"That's why we're gonna say *you're* a patient."

"Oh. OK." That seemed to make sense. "So what do I have?"

Jerry rubbed his chin. "Retardation."

"*What?* No, I can't be retarded."

"Are you kidding me? You *definitely* look retarded."

"Jerry, retardation is *not* contagious."

"Not *yet*," Jerry said with a wink. "We'll tell them you're a special case. Which you are," he said and winked again.

"I don't know. I don't think this will work. Besides, as soon as Dr. Macaw sees me he's going to recognize me."

"That's OK. As long as he's the only one that does. Remember, he's *expecting* you, but he has no idea who I am. I'll just tell him I'm undercover. Hey, barkeep!" Jerry practically shouted. "What time does that medical convention start?"

"It started this afternoon. People have been coming and going all day."

"Alrighty," Jerry said. "Here. Take your phone and look up the convention. Let's do this. You nervous?" he asked David.

"A little," David admitted.

"Me too. We should calm down. Can I get two shots?" Jerry asked the bartender. "Tequila."

The bartender poured a couple shots and set them on the counter. Jerry slugged them down back to back. "Phew! Much better," he said. "Let's go!"

David looked at his phone. "This says the convention is in the Octavius Ballroom. That's a neat name!" David looked up and searched for a direction sign. It was hard to tell the difference between information and entertainment. There were television monitors and flashing lights, signs pointing to buffets and strip clubs, and Roman lounge rooms and huge screens blared out music videos and international current events. He squinted. Was he...on TV?

Yes. Yes he was.

David turned 180 degrees and prepared to take off at a sprint towards the Mexican border. Behind him on the screen was a long-haired hippy-looking guy looking stupidly at a plaza of headless bodies. His expression resembled something crossed between puzzlement and constipation. Even *he* thought he looked guilty.

There were two security guards in the direction he was facing. David quickly sat on an empty black stool and hoped to disappear into the slot machine before him. The slot machine tinkled with hopeful glee. Out of his peripheral vision he could see Jerry sit down next to him.

"Everything's cool," he heard Jerry say.

"Did you see it?" David asked.

"I *felt* it, just like you did. These two machines are gonna pay out big time. You got enough quarters or should we put a card in?"

"Not *that,*" he said through gritted teeth. "I'm on TV."

Jerry looked up. "*Really?*" He scanned the room until he saw the monitor. "Oh *shit!*" he yelled. "We gotta get the fuck out of here!!"

David grabbed him by the sleeve. "No one's seen me," he said. In fact, David realized, no one seemed to be paying attention to the news at all. The screen was filled with blood and brains and all sorts of terrible pictures which would inevitably become iconic images for this part of the century – David Dingle: Biological Genocidal Terrorist Assfuck of Forever. Instead, most people were looking for their cocktail waitress.

"OK, well you gotta keep it that way," Jerry said. He passed a trembling wrist over to David and dumped a handful of quarters into his lap, spilling them everywhere.

"Dude!" David exclaimed.

"It's cool. Just play. Pretend like you're really drunk and have been here for a while. Act like you've totally forgotten that you're wearing a towel. We'll hang out for a moment until they shut the news off."

David put a quarter in and reached for the handle but Jerry stopped him.

"No one's gonna believe you're a gambler if you only put in a single coin. You gotta put in three."

David tempered his breathing. Whatever. Whatever. Just. Act. Normal. He watched as the spinning symbols and numbers whirred in front of him like little lunatics.

Seven.

Seven.

Seven.

His machine erupted into a chaotic madness of lights and bells and whistles and voices and a female robotic voice said, "Congratulations, congratulations, congratulations..." over and over. Now people *everywhere* were looking at him.

"Yeah!!!" Jerry yelled. "Fucking Yeah!! This is sooo amazing. You've *got* to be kidding me. Who is this guy?" he said and grabbed a septuagenarian by the shoulder and pointed at David. "It's my boy, that's who! I *told* you I had a feeling about these babies. What's it say, what's it say? How much did you win?"

David couldn't even look. His head was buried in his hands. He wanted to disappear but the sound of a new voice brought him out of his shock. It could only be the police. Goodbye society. Hello Guantanamo.

"Hello, Sir."

When he looked up he was surprised to see a young thin blonde woman standing beside him. It was difficult, however, for David to read her expression. She looked simultaneously polite and entirely unimpressed. She was pretty, though, so that was nice.

"Hello," he said.

"On behalf of Caesar's Palace I would like to congratulate you."

"Oh. Thank you," he said, straightening a little.

"Yeah, thanks a *lot*!" Jerry hollered up at the ceiling. He looked at the young lady with wild and passionate eyes, a look that in some states could very well have gotten him arrested. He was rolling hard on a lucky blue streak that wasn't even his own. He took three large steps toward the cocktail waitress, pulled his trousers up by his belt, and attempted to sling an arm around her neck for a wholly unromantic kiss. Courtney Spears wisely backed away.

"Sir," she said and turned to David again. "I would like to escort you to the winnings locker to finalize your winnings. As long as you're over twenty-one, which you appear to be, everything should be fine. Do you have your ID on you?"

David's face went blank. He looked to Jerry for support who for the first time in his life was stone silent.

"Sir?"

"Um, yeah, actually, well, no. I guess I don't. You know, I was just kind of practicing, really..." he said looking at his hands like a hidden script might be written on them. If he wasn't a Roman soldier he'd pull out his phone and get her to sign something or do something with a fingerprint maybe. She had nice thumbs, he saw.

"He's just joking," Jerry blurted out. "Of course he's got his ID, don't you buddy?"

David smiled through clenched teeth. "*Actually*, I left it in my room."

"Oh no you didn't. I'm pretty sure it's around here somewhere," he said and began to paw at David's towels.

"Jerry, what about that thing that we were talking about not doing?"

"Ahhh, yes, well now that we have all this money we *can* donate to that orphanage, even though we just talked about not doing that," Jerry said and smiled at Courtney.

Courtney gave a look. "Should I get someone else?" she asked.

"NO!" they both shouted.

"Maybe you could get us a celebratory drink?" Jerry suggested. "Right? Like that's probably in the procedures, I'm sure."

"Umm..."

"Yeah, beers are *great*. Thank you *so* much."

Courtney turned to get their drinks. It seemed to be a lot easier than dealing with these two.

"Jerry, you *know* I can't give them my ID. My flipping face was just on the 7 o'clock news. You win some, you lose some. Let's just stick to the plan and get going."

"This isn't some. This is..." he leaned over David's shoulder and looked at the little blue numbers on the machine. His eyelids flickered slightly. "This is more than some, David. Listen, more than likely no one will have any clue who you are. People around here don't care. All they're concerned about are the cheap buffets and titties."

"What about the medical convention?" David asked.

"*Screw* the medical convention. You just won $50,000 dollars! I say take your money and we drive to Tijuana and live like kings for the rest of our lives."

"*No one* lives like kings in Tijuana, Jerry. Besides, there's no way they'll let me across the border. I'm stuck! If you really care about me more than money you'll help me talk to that doctor."

Jerry thought about it.

"Jerry!" David yelled in frustration.

"OK, OK. Why don't we head on over to the convention, make a brief speech on retardation, bop that doctor on the head, call the President, and as soon as he clears your name we pick up your fucking money."

"Please tell me that's not your plan."

"Let's call it a draft. Hey, our beers are here!"

Courtney was back with two tall malty beers which she handed to David and Jerry.

"Thanks, Sweetheart," Jerry said coolly.

She gave him a tight smile. Her eyes softened though when she looked at David. "Is this your first jackpot?" she asked.

David shrugged his shoulders.

"Well, that's pretty exciting. For you, at least. Not so much for me. These things go off all the time. This is like the ninth one today. I could use a bit more excitement. You OK?" she asked. "You look kind of pale?"

David was looking wide-eyed over her shoulder at the television monitor of which he was the subject again.

"Uh, yeah, I'm, I am good."

"He's retarded," Jerry said, putting his arm over David's shoulders.

"Oh!" Courtney said. "Well, that's OK."

"Sure is. Retards got souls too, ya know?"

"I'm not retarded," David said.

"Of course you're not buddy. He prefers the term 'Goober'."

"Jerry!" David said, jutting his chin out, hoping that Jerry would see the screen and take the hint to move on.

Jerry continued. "That's neat, Goober. Quite a trick you've learned. He's been watching Star Wars a lot recently. I think he's trying to impersonate a wookie. So tell me, baby. Ever made it with the friend of a jackpot winner?"

David spun around in exasperation, half expecting a barrage of security agents to be coming through the casino right now. Instead, he saw himself on *another* monitor directly behind him. Without thinking, David grabbed Courtney's hand and yanked her away.

"Whoa!" she yelled. "Where we going?"

"I'm ready to collect my winnings now," he said.

"OK, well then we're headed the wrong way."

"That's OK. I need to walk, been sitting down pulling on the one-armed bandit for so long that it's good for me to stretch my legs. I get clots." He grimaced, realizing how that all must have sounded.

He got her to a less crowded corridor and stopped in a state of mild panic as he tried to figure out what to do next.

"What's your name?" she asked.

"David," he said right away and then cursed himself, quickly deciding to top it off with, "alyiah."

"Excuse me?" she asked.

"Davidalyiah. It's Greek."

"Oh. Well, pleased to meet you, Davidalyiah. My name is Courtney," she said, pulling on her name tag.

"It's nice to meet you, too," he smiled, wondering if the only reason she was being so nice to him was because she still thought he was mentally handicapped. "Do you...come here often?" he asked moronically.

"Yes," she said slowly. "I...work...here." He couldn't believe how big her smile was. She must think he was a real nut case.

"Yeah, of course," he said.

"How about you? Is this your first time in Vegas?"

"Vegas..." his voice trailed off as he looked around. Behind him was another monitor. "Don't you people *ever* get tired of watching TV?" he asked suddenly.

His outburst surprised her and she held up her hands. She looked at the wide screen behind them. "Oh, those," she said with distaste. "Those stupid things run twenty-four seven. No one really looks at them, though, which is crazy, considerin' all that's happenin' right now. Isn't it terrible?" she asked.

"I hate things, too," he said.

"Hardly *anyone* gives a crap. People are so locked into their world they can't see the wood from the forest. If it doesn't affect them directly they tune out."

"We should *definitely* tune out," he said nervously. "I like to put my head inside my towel. Want to try?"

"You know, Davidalyiah, we all live on this planet together. Everything's connected. It doesn't take a genius to figure that out. What happens in Vegas does *not* stay in Vegas. Like, there's the internet and stuff. If we don't start payin' attention to the world around us then we're just as bad as the terrorists." David could see her hands had become balled into fists.

"Hey look! A buffet," he pointed. "That's something around us."

"Listen, I know you're mentally handicapped, Goober, but this outbreak is a big deal. It's already in California! Why for all we know it could have already come into Las Vegas!" She shook her head and her expression hardened. "How could anyone *do* something like that? I hope they find the criminal that did this. And when they *do* find him I hope they get wild animals to tear his nuts off. You like animals, Goober?"

"There you are!" Jerry said in relief. "I thought you two had ditched me to go make out under a stairwell. Or an elevator," he winked at David.

"Where have you been?" David asked.

Jerry smiled sheepishly. "Had to put in a few more quarters while the machine was hot. Just lost fifty bucks. Got another drink, though! You ready to pick up your cash?"

"I – yes," David said, stepping away from Courtney. "Thanks a whole bunch for your help. See ya later."

"You know, you look kinda familiar," Courtney said, as she studied David's face. "Are you sure you haven't been here before?"

"Guilty as charged," Jerry said and stepped forward. "I've been to Vegas more times than I've been to jail, thankfully. I *love* this place. But what am I telling *you* that for? You've got, like, the best job in the fucking world. I mean, you're walkin' through the action on a daily basis. Wish we had these kind of casinos where *we're* from. All we've got is Redman's Blackjack House just outside of Seattle and the odds are tilted in their favor on account of the chickenpox when Columbus came for Thanksgiving."

"You're from...Seattle?" she asked.

"Born and raised," Jerry said and sipped his long-island ice tea. "Best part's the ocean, worst part's the water." His expression changed when he saw David's eyes boring a hole into him.

"Oh my God," Courtney said. She was looking over David's shoulder at the monitor. "It's...you!"

"Alrighty," Jerry said calmly and stood directly in front of Courtney, blocking her view of the monitor. "Everything is *juuust* fine. David and I aren't actually *from* Seattle, we're, well...first off, this guy's name isn't David at all. In fact, it's Lucius the Roman" he nodded. "And *what* a gambler," he clapped his hands. "So why don't we go collect our winnings and we'll be on our way. Phew! Do you know where the bathroom is?" he asked, shaking the ice in his empty drink.

Courtney looked around like a frightened deer. "I know who you are and

I...need to go."

"I'm sorry, Courtney. I can't let you do that. You're going to have to stay with us now." Jerry pulled the gun out of his waistband and flashed it inconspicuously at the hip. It felt *really* good to do that.

"Jerry!" David whispered. "What are you doing?"

"Dude, we can't let her go now. She's only going to take off and tell the cops."

"I won't, I promise."

"That's really nice of you," David said with genuine appreciation.

Jerry glared. "No no. You're too pretty and pretty girls *always* get their way. Sorry sweetheart, but you're coming with us." He turned to David. "This puts our situation in a bit of a time crunch. We gotta get to that convention fast before anyone else recognizes you."

"I'll take you there!" she said.

"Really?" David asked.

"But you have to promise you'll let me go."

"*Absolutely*," David assured her. "Again, we're really sorry for the inconvenience. It's just a precaution kind of thing like a seatbelt or...an exit sign," he said looking around.

She held out a shaky finger and pointed. "It's down that way."

"K," Jerry said. "Let's go." David led the way while Jerry held the barrel of the gun into Courtney's back. "I don't like this any more than you do," Jerry said to her as they walked past the poker tables. "You're real sweet, have a great accent, and you got us those beers like *right* away. This whole thing is just one big misunderstanding. We're not actually terrorists like everyone thinks, which by the way, is why we're here in Vegas - to clear up this whole mess, meet a few girls, jump in a hot tub, you know how it is. The way I see it, this fiasco should be taken care of by breakfast time. Are there breakfast buffets or just the twenty-four hour steak and potatoes kind of thing?"

They rounded the corner. "Holy shit!" Jerry said as they arrived at the ballroom entrance. "There are doctors everywhere. What kind of convention *is* this? It's like they all called each other to look doctor-y for this thing. We're *never* going to find Dr. Macaw," Jerry complained.

"He's over there," David said, pointing as he looked up from Dr. Macaw's photo on his phone. "Standing near the back of the room."

"Dang, Goob. That's some good spotting. OK. So we need a plan and luckily I've thought of one. I'm going to go in there and talk to him. Once I'm in, I'll bring him over. All you guys gotta do is play it cool. Talk to him like everything's totally normal, casually take off the towel around your shoulders, throw it over his head and punch him in the face."

"What? Why?"

"Come on, David, you're a terrorist, remember? Start acting like it."

"Hey, wait!" David called. "What about Courtney?"

"Just keep her here. If she tries to go anywhere, *shoot* her." He slapped the pistol into David's hand who nearly dropped it in pacifistic shock.

"I don't even know how to use this thing," he whispered.

Jerry pushed his fat finger into various parts of the weapon. "Trigger, nozzle, bullet comes out of nozzle. There's a safety on there somewhere, too. Hold it for a moment. Feels good doesn't it?" Before David could respond Jerry turned and said, "Be right back!" David watched hopelessly as Jerry disappeared into the sea of white coats.

Courtney was staring at him when he turned to look at her. "You don't have to do this," she said.

David attempted a smile. "Trust me. This isn't exactly what I had in mind. Our other plan was a bit more logical."

"You mean the one where you beat a man with a towel wrapped around his head at the back of a medical convention?"

"No, not that one. There was another one. I forget what it was though. There are a *lot* of doctors here," he said and looked around.

"So you're plan-less?"

"Yes, but we're trying not to make it look that way. That's why we have disguises."

She gave him a look. "You mean you're wearing that on purpose?"

He rolled his eyes and clenched his jaw as he looked for Jerry. "I hope he still has my clothes," he murmured. David scanned the room. "Oh my God," he whispered. "Jerry is talking to Dr. Macaw. Holy crap. Dr. Macaw is even nodding his head."

"Hey!" Courtney yelled.

David thought she had made a run for it. Or that she had announced her captivity. But when he swirled around he instead saw a short, balding man in a medical coat being shoved away by Courtney with both hands. The man's face reminded David of what Jerry looked like after four beers and a couple of bong hits.

"Whoa," the doctor said playfully. "Sorry about that. I stumbled and must have fallen right into you. You're very attractive," he winked.

"This guy just grabbed my *ass*," she whirled on David.

"Again, so sorry. My name is Doctor Whyzer. I'm from New Hampshire," he said with more than a touch of arrogance. Whyzer took Courtney's hand and shook it. David watched the internal conflict play out over Courtney's face. This sleazeball was the closest thing she had to an escape.

"I'm Courtney," she said carefully.

"You bet you are." He rubbed her forearm with his finger. "Your skin is very soft."

"Ugh," she said and dry heaved. She looked at David. "Do something," she mouthed silently.

This was without a doubt the first time in David's life that an attractive woman had asked him to help with an obnoxious guy. Usually it was the other way around. David jumped into action. "OK," he said quickly and took Dr. Whyzer's hand off Courtney's arm. "Thank you very much for the skin check. I'll be sure to tell her real doctor how soft her skin is. Good lotion will do that it. Get's everything lubricated." Courtney gave him a look. "That is," he stammered, "if that's what needs to happen. Sometimes it's better to remain hard — *callous!* Lotion should do the trick either way, though. Lavender is nice, I think."

The doctor's eyes fell on David's shoulder. "That towel also looks soft." A pause. "May I touch it?"

David held out his arms. "Um. No, I guess, yes," was the last word he got out before the doctor had begun to pet the towel with both hands.

"Wonderful idea to wear a towel at a group event like this," Dr. Whyzer said.

"Are you making fun of me?" David asked.

"Heavens no! I almost came in costume myself. I wish they'd play better music, though. Don't you want to just *dance?*" he said and snapped his fingers like maracas.

Courtney eyed David.

"This is elevator music they got going here, like something you'd listen to in Albertsons," he complained, though despite his negative sentiments Dr. Whyzer was bobbing his head to the soft beat of Michael Bolton. Whyzer looked at David and raised his eyebrows like he was about to share a secret. "You know what? I've been coming to this convention for the last three years and after my *second* year I swore that this stupid convention was so boring that I wouldn't come back unless I did some hard drugs." His eyes widened and he raised a hand to shield his comment from the massive group. "I think my Ecstasy is starting to kick in."

Courtney shouldered hard into David who in turned stumbled backwards a bit. "Well..." he said, "I'm sure that will be exciting." He glanced at Courtney who was clutching David's elbow as if she had begun to embrace Stockholm Syndrome. David took the hint. "I hope you have a nice trip," he said politely. "Best of luck with the music."

"David," a man's voice said behind his ear.

David's heart leapt into his throat. The police had finally found him.

They knew his name. It was over. He turned to face the music, but actually, it was not over. It was Dr. Macaw, a middle-aged man with thin, wire glasses and a face that wore signs of an incredibly uncomfortable puberty. David struggled to identify the Dr.'s expression. It almost looked like awe.

"It's nice to finally meet you, David," Dr. Macaw said with that same strange look.

"Do I know you?" David asked.

"Not really. But I know you. I've been working with you for years now, indirectly that is." Dr. Macaw glanced at Jerry. "You've done very well, Agent Santana," he said. "I know the Organizer was expecting a different order of operations, but I'm glad the contingency plan was smoothly executed." He looked at Courtney. "And this must be the female agent you spoke of?" he said to Jerry/Dr. Santana.

"This is," Jerry said and widened his eyes at Courtney with a look that said, "Don't make me bash your face in." She smiled thinly.

"And I'm Dr. Whyzer," Dr. Whyzer said and stepped forward and promptly embraced Dr. Macaw in a bear hug.

"Oh, hello. Tha-nks," Dr. Macaw said uncomfortably.

"Mmm," Dr. Whyzer said and rubbed Macaw's back with his hands. "It's *sooo* good to meet you."

Dr. Macaw pulled away. "I did not expect another doctor," he said glancing at Jerry.

Jerry hadn't either but he knew he had no choice but to go along with it. "I sent you an emoji," he said quickly. "Two doctors and a heart."

"I must not have gotten it," Dr. Macaw said, doing his best to avoid Whyzer's piercing stare. "Regardless, it does not matter. I trust you have all taken the antidote." He laughed suddenly. "But of course you have!"

"Taken more than one, Dr.," Dr. Whyzer said before his eyes rolled into the back of his skull.

Dr. Macaw rubbed his chin as he studied David. "A fascinating strain of virus, wouldn't you say, Agent Santana? At times virulent, at other times it can remain dormant for hours. My guess is that it has begun another round of mutation, otherwise, everyone here would already be dead."

"Mutation?" Jerry asked.

Dr. Macaw adjusted his glasses. "You're not a doctor so I wouldn't expect you to understand the intricacies of viral evolution. I, on the other hand, have been studying this deadly virus since its inception. Helped design it, actually. You can imagine the work involved on a project like this — a tour de force," he boasted and rubbed his chest as if he were applying menthol. "It is truly remarkable that I have been able to develop a virus that not only attacks a specific intelligence, but also targets distinct personality traits. No one thought it was possible. I've been working alongside The Organization for over ten years to get this thing off the ground," he whispered. "A lot is at stake," he said and looked at David again. "We're lucky to have you with us, David. You're more important than you can possibly imagine."

"I am?" David asked.

"Oh, certainly. The blood in your veins is worth *trillions* of dollars. When all this comes to a close you'll be remembered for hundreds of years. Maybe more. You're going to be a hero, David."

"I *am*?" David asked again.

"Of course you are! Your blood is going to be responsible for saving thousands of lives. After you inadvertently kill millions, that is. You see, the virus inside of you is intelligent and is quickly adapting to its surroundings."

"Wait a minute. You mean I'm *infected* with something?"

Dr. Macaw elbowed Jerry playfully. "I *told* you he was the perfect candidate."

Jerry chuckled, without the faintest trace of understanding. "Would you say this virus is more infectious than herpes?" Jerry asked.

Macaw gave him a strange look and returned his attention to David. "Consider yourself the focal point of America's greatest moment in history. The world is changing, David."

"So when will the virus become active again?" Jerry asked, and rubbed a cold sore on his lower lip.

Dr. Macaw reflected. "How long have you all been in Vegas?"

"A couple hours now."

"Then I imagine it already has. The convention is the perfect place for our secondary phase. Once another outbreak occurs people will be clamoring for the vaccine, which, I'd say, we're on target to develop within the hour." He turned to Jerry and took him aside. "I'd like to get started as soon as possible. There's no need for me to stay here any longer. Once the virus hits the streets there's going to be pandemonium. Follow me to my room and we'll get Mr. Dingle situated." He leaned in and whispered to Jerry, "Once we've created the antidote you will take him behind the casino and kill him."

Jerry, clueless to Dr. Macaw's directions, had no choice but to play along. "I'm afraid I can't do that," he said.

Dr. Macaw looked at him gravely. "Why not?"

"Because I don't have a permanent room key. They won't let me back in."

"You're not *coming* back in," Macaw said impatiently. "I'd prefer to never see you again. Your money will be right where we arranged. In the-"

"Dr., I really need you to look at something," David interrupted.

"What's this?" he asked and turned to David.

David held out the envelope. "It's a document that I think explains how I'm not a domestic terrorist. I'd really like you to read it and maybe sign it somewhere so I can go home and forget all about this."

The Doctor looked into David's eyes and registered an understanding. "Yes, I'm really sorry that it's gone down the way it has. The original plan was that no one would know about you until all of this was over. Unfortunately things happen. I'd be happy to take a look at this and explain anything you need me to. After all, it's kind of a like a last meal, wouldn't you agree?" he asked and held out his hand to take the manilla envelope.

"Ladies and Gentlemen!" a loud voice broke through the auditorium. "Can I please get your attention. I understand that everyone is very eager to discuss the recent outbreak that is taking place in the Pacific Northwest. As you all know we will be speaking about it more at length over the course of the weekend, but I wanted to get a quick jumpstart. I know this is impromptu, so forgive me, but I felt that there is someone here with the credentials and background to, at the very least, give us a quick rundown of what we can expect in the coming weeks. I would like to present to you, Dr. Macaw."

"Fuck," Dr. Macaw said under his breath. He looked at his small group and said, "Wait here, this will only take a moment."

"Wait, wait," Jerry hissed. "Remind me where we arranged the money!"

"Dr.! The documents. You've got to explain them to me!" David called.

But Dr. Macaw ignored them both and walked through the throngs of applause as he made his way to the microphone on stage.

"I hope they'll put on some electronic music while he speaks," Dr. Whyzer whispered to David.

Dr. Macaw smiled dimly behind the podium. "Thank you very much," he said without emotion. Hundreds of pale faces stared back at him expectantly.

"I don't really have a speech prepared," he began. "I am certain, however, that you are very eager to hear my perspective. I have worked in this field for over thirty years and never have I seen a strain as terrifying as what our poor world is currently infected with. The virus appears to be highly contagious, although the rate of infection, along with the incubation period seems to vary." His voice was coming out uneven. "Right now we cannot say for certain why it is targeting who it is targeting."

"Dr., can you tell us what the strain is being called?" someone asked.

"It is known as strain HR-IQ84. It seems that those affected have had their neurons attacked by neuron capacitors that fluctuate between the receptor cells which makes it drastically dynamic in those tertiary terms."

"What did he just say?" Jerry asked Dr. Whyzer.

"I have *no* idea. To be honest," he said casually, "I just use an app on my phone to diagnose my patients. I couldn't imagine having to actually *remember* all that crap. Medical stuff is *hard*," he confessed.

Dr. Macaw was still speaking. "We are at a crossroads in history," he began. "Our planet has not seen an outbreak as deadly as this since the Spanish Influenza. Sadly, the age of bio-terrorism is here. I cannot pretend that I understand the sadistic mind of a person who would willingly infect millions of people. Perhaps there is a religious cause or a political ideology at stake, but we as a people must stand behind those who are currently in power and obey their wishes. President Alan has already come out in condemnation of these people. I feel that it is our duty as citizens and medical professionals to educate the masses just as we have been educated. It is within our right to spread what we know far and wide. We cannot allow the few to affect the many. Whoever is the cause of all this must be taken to the highest court to bear the full weight of justice."

"OK, this is just too much," Jerry said under his breath. "That hypocrite is taking you down Crap Avenue without a motor." He took the gun from David. "We're out of options, Dave. Time to go into Plan L."

"What? Jerry! Don't! What are you doing?"

"Plan L?" Courtney said. "That doesn't sound good."

Jerry left their side and sprinted through the crowd like a linebacker, pushing and knocking doctors over as he ran.

"Oh my God," David said, now holding his hands to his head. "I can't watch."

"Hey, stop!" someone yelled, but Jerry had already reached the stage. He raised his pistol over his head and fired a shot into the ceiling. The entire crowd fell to the floor and cried out in fear. No one knew whether to wait or run.

"Agent Santana, what on earth are you doing?" Dr. Macaw demanded.

Jerry grabbed the curly wig off his head and threw his glasses into the crowd like the actual Santana might do with a sweaty scarf. "This man is *lying* to you!" he shouted and leveled the gun at Macaw's temple. "His story is nothing but lies."

Dr. Macaw looked surprisingly calm. "I don't know who the hell you are," he whispered, "but it doesn't look like you've got long to explain yourself," he said, indicating the red dots that had suddenly appeared on Jerry's chest like fire ants.

Jerry looked down at his shirt. "*What* the?"

"Stand down!" two or three people from the crowd yelled. "This is Dr. Draze from Arizona."

"Dr. Mendez from Florida," another man yelled. "Open carry, bitch!"

"Shit!" Jerry shouted. Who would have figured doctors would have handguns? He had to get this under control. "OK, calm down, calm down, people. I'm not going to shoot him or anyone. I'm just here to inform you all that he's selling us lies. This virus isn't what you think it is. It's a conspiracy, man!"

Now the crowd had quieted down, though Jerry knew he had to act fast before they turned on him. "Behold!" he shouted and held up his recording device. "I was *just* speaking to this so-called Dr. Macaw who announced only moments ago that *he* was the one who developed the virus. Listen for yourselves."

David noticed that Dr. Macaw's face had gone pale. Never in a million years would David have guessed that Jerry was actually smart enough to thwart a conspiracy like this.

Jerry shoved Macaw out of the way and thrust the device in front of the microphone and pressed play. A bit of garble and then Jerry's voice, "Captain's log, I've tried fixing the carburetor of the bong but to no avail. I suspect that it has been tampered with by a friend of a friend at some party I no longer remember. I'll need to find a mechanic."

"Ah, dammit," he said. "Hang on!" he commanded into the microphone and then banged the device with the palm of his hand. "OK. There we go." The voice that came out was soft and of poor quality, but anyone could clearly recognize that it belonged to Dr. Macaw. "I, on the other hand, have been studying this deadly virus since its inception. Helped design it, actually. You can imagine the work involved on a project like this — a tour de force."

The crowd had become absolutely silent. All eyes stared at Dr. Macaw. There in front of them, the poster child for a healthier, safer world, was nothing but a fraud — a Benedict Arnold.

Jerry, on the other hand, had never lived a prouder moment in his life. Very casually he stepped up to the microphone and said, "Sooo, would anyone like to get a selfie with this asshole before we haul him away?"

He paused. Everyone in the crowd was still with shocked silence. In fact, not a single person was moving. "I understand that this can be hard for you to believe," Jerry said. "If I had put my trust in a dick fart without knowing that he was a dick fart, and then I found out that he *was* a dick fart, well, I'd be pretty astounded, too!" He paused, letting that sink in. "I also understand that it may be hard for you medical types to trust someone without any credentials. Rest assured, however, that I have recovered from alcoholism three times and have the paperwork to back that up, so in a way, I'm more qualified than some of you are. This man, on the other hand, is a deceiver, and the first thing we must do if we are to pass through all 12 stages of recovery is to get past that first one involving denial. So, in the spirit of Vegas, let us acknowledge that we have a problem acknowledging when a dick fart is in fact a dick fart, can we do that?"

KABOOM!!!

The auditorium erupted in a wave of exploding heads. The blast shattered most of the ceiling lights and blood and brains splattered against the floor and walls like poorly mixed red paint. Jerry, who had never seen a large-scale infection first-hand stared at the auditorium in shocked horror.

Dr. Macaw, knowing all along that the deadly result of the infection was inevitable, took the opportunity to grab the gun out of Jerry's hand and was now pointing the gun at *Jerry's* head.

"Never encourage an infected population to think for themselves," he grinned. He gave Jerry a hard shove. "Go on, get moving," he ordered.

"You *knew* all those people were going to die?" Jerry asked in disbelief.

"It was only a matter of time."

Jerry scanned the room. There were hundreds of headless bodies slumped over one another, sprawled over tables and chairs laying criss-crossed on the floor; pieces of brains were floating in punch bowls.

"Oh my God!" he moaned at the verge of hysteria. "David! David, where are you??? Oh, God, everyone's dead! What a tragedy!"

"Jerry! Over here!" Near the door Jerry saw a small group of survivors. Among them was David. Jerry ran over like a lost child and hugged his friend tightly. David felt like a doll in the arms of a bear. "Oh man, I thought I lost you. I'm so glad you're OK," Jerry said, tearing up.

David was touched. He wanted to say something but couldn't.

"I think you're suffocating him," Courtney said.

"Oh, shit," he said and released his friend.

"That was a brave thing you did up there," Dr. Whyzer commended.

"I just knew I had to do something," Jerry admitted.

"Well, you really didn't do anything useful at all," Dr. Macaw said. "In fact, if you had just kept up the ruse, you probably would have ended up alive and rich by the end of all this. Unfortunately, you and your friends will likely be buried somewhere in the Nevada desert by dinner time."

Jerry looked at Dr. Macaw with steel angry eyes. He had never been so mad in his entire life. He had been so close to becoming a hero.

"Why would you do something like this?" Courtney demanded. "This is just terrible!"

Dr. Macaw laughed. "Money, Sweetie Pie. Why else?"

"*Whose* money?" Courtney asked.

His expression changed instantly and David noticed the presence of fear in his eyes. "I'd be a dead man if I told a soul."

"They *own* you," Jerry said.

"No one owns me."

"They totally own you. You're like...a pawn, or something. You do all the hard work but you're gonna end up six feet under like the rest of us."

"I don't think so," Dr. Macaw said smugly. "They're not going to kill the only person that can get them a vaccine."

"You mean David?" Jerry said.

"I mean *me*, you idiot! I'm the one who *designed* the virus," he said. "The host — that's you, Mr. Dingle, will self-destruct if the blood is drawn incorrectly. So if you don't mind," he said, leveling the gun at the group, "please follow me to my room where I have a lab already in place."

A loud bang erupted at the back of the room. The emergency exit had been kicked in by two men in black suits who ran into the room like navy seals on a sting operation. One of them in particular looked extremely pumped up.

"Freeze!" the man yelled, and then fired a shot. The bullet sailed through the air and right through Dr. Macaw's chest.

"Fuck!" Jerry yelled. "It's the Men in Black. Go! Go!" He grabbed the hands of Courtney and David and bounded out the room. Dr. Whyzer struggled to keep up behind them.

"Goddammit, Boring!" Fleckle yelled. "I told you not to shoot anyone."

"And I told you not to tell me what not to do!" Boring growled. "The perps have left the convention center – I repeat, the perps have left the convention center." Boring yelled, fantasizing that he had hundreds of agents under his command.

"We're the only ones who know they're here!" Fleckle shouted as they chased after them.

"Then we better fucking catch them. Cool, I shot someone," he said, as he stepped over the dying Dr. Macaw. "Man down!" he yelled as he entered the casino full of people. Not one of them, however, seemed to give two shits that the entire world was about to change forever.

Chapter 12: Vice President Harold Palmdonger

"I do not for one minute believe that President Alan understands the severity of the situation," Senator Guiles said with a concerned and practiced tone. He squared off to the camera, dipped his chin, and continued. "There is nothing simple about the situation. It is dynamic with many moving parts. It will require a team of well-informed people to solve this disaster effectively."

Senator Guiles was being interviewed on live television because the press needed a statement from someone in Washington. The White House had become strangely silent on the issue despite the media's best efforts to get ahold of the President. This, however, was nothing new for SmartNews, a station well-accustomed to finding people to speak in front of a camera. Being an election year, it was only natural to have someone with no authority express their opinions.

"Alan has yet to come up with a plan," Mitchell Guiles continued. "How can the leader of the free world refuse to comment on something so important? What we need is a leader with clear, concise, and *confident* communication. I think the American voters deserve only the best." His teeth glimmered like freshly polished oyster pearls.

"Graahh!!" President Alan shouted and inadvertently turned off the television by throwing a bust of George Washington at it. "I *hate* that man! He thinks he's so charming. Well, my *butt's* more charming than he is!" He yelled something animalistic and strode over to his phone. "Mary!" he demanded.

"Yes, Sir?"

"Send in the Vice President."

"Yes, Sir."

"And Mary," he added. "Have him bring in some sodas."

"Of course, Sir."

He set the phone down and exhaled an angry puff of air. "That damn virus is going to be the end of me," he said to the broken bust of George Washington. "It's like I can feel it watching me. It's planning its attack. Pray to God it doesn't breach the capitol. If it does...well, it will only be a matter of time until I become infected and lose the election." He looked off into the distance. "America would be without a leader..."

Vice President Harold Palmdonger walked through the door. He was carrying a tray with two opened bottles of ice cold Dr. Pepper. His back was stiff and erect, his chin raised, and his eyes were straight and precise. He looked confident. Unafraid. Ready to do whatever the President ordered him to do.

Palmdonger set the tray on the desk and handed the President a drink.

"Thank you," President Alan said and took a long and steady drink. "Drink up, Palmdonger," he offered. "It's important to have rewards in times of crisis." The Vice President nodded cordially and took a sip from his soda pop.

"Harold, I want to talk about the pandemic," Alan said.

"Of course, Sir."

"I have to know everything about it if I am to speak to it at tomorrow's assembly. As you can imagine, I've developed several amazing theories about its origin and how we can fix it. Still, I'd like to explore other options, even if they come from you, believe it or not. I want to know not only what *it* thinks, but what *you* think. I think our thinking can solve this."

"I think the virus is bad," Palmdonger said without hesitation.

"Good," the President said. "I think so too."

"But I think it thinks that *we* are bad."

"Go on..."

"It thinks it wants to find us and kill us because it thinks we are bad. But we are no more bad than a turtle is."

Benjamin Alan narrowed his eyes. "A turtle?"

"Yes, Mr. President. An innocent turtle. Their only burden is their shell, but their shell is also their home." President Alan stared at him as he finished off his soda. "We cannot hide from this virus, Mr. President. We might think we can, but even in our hiding we are still visible. Much like a turtle that has gone into its shell. A hiding turtle can still be seen, even though it thinks it is safe."

The President grimaced. He had hoped this conversation wouldn't get too intellectual. "I'm not sure I follow."

"The turtle is not safe just because it is inside of its shell."

"But its shell is...really hard," the President said.

"Not for an eagle's talons, or the jaws of a polar bear, or a volcano." His eyes revealed that he could continue endlessly with good examples.

The President widened one eye. "Good point." He stared at him and Palmdonger could see two, maybe even three thoughts, swirling around in the President's eyes. "I'm going to be honest with you, Harold. I need help. I have lots of aids and lots of advisors, but no one has as much vested interest in all of this as you do. I mean, you're not going to be Vice President for much longer if I don't get re-elected. Besides, I think you're really smart."

"You do, Sir?" he asked, surprised.

The President moved uncomfortably in his seat. "That's right, I do. You look at things differently than most politicians I know."

"I think about things like this a lot," Palmdonger admitted.

"That much is evident. It's possible that with this turtle metaphor of yours we might just be able to talk our way out of this."

"I'd never really thought of it as a metaphor before..." he said and scratched his head.

"All the better. Why don't you sit down, Harold. This conversation has given me new hope. I think I'm finally ready to speak with my cabinet now." The President pushed a button on his desk. "Mary. I'm ready. Send everyone in."

The door opened almost immediately. A large group of people shuffled into the Oval Office like cattle vying for the best spot at the trough. The air was tense while everyone sat down. No one said a word.

"I'd like to say thank-you to everyone for their patience," Alan said. "I have spent a lot of time going over this issue in my head, racking my brain for the correct road to take. I believe we can all agree that this is a trying time for us all. Only three days ago we were living the King's life and sharing in the abundance of this great nation. Today is no longer that day. It has become Saturday. I'm sure you understand." He paused for effect.

"I have been meeting with Vice President Palmdonger and the two of us have been formulating a plan. We believe that people in this country need to feel safe. They depend on us to tell them that the government has everything under control. Shoot, it's our job to tell them we have *Neptune* under control if need be. Now I've never been to Neptune, don't know if it's got nice weather or beaches or any of that," he shrugged, "but dammit, if the voters need to know if Neptune is nice in order to feel safe, by God, I'm going to tell them it's better than Myrtle Beach in September.

"Now a lot of Americans are confused right now and rightfully so. All they know is that people's heads are blowing up and no one knows why. Do *we* know why?" he asked quickly. Everyone shook their head no. "Wrong answer!" he shouted. "It is wrong because they are *expecting* us to know something that we obviously don't. Now I brought you all in here today to light a fire under your butts. I want you to understand clear as day that it is our responsibility to tell the American public that we have the answers."

"Will you be passing those answers out?" the Secretary of Education asked.

"No, Cathy, because we *don't* have the answers. But that's OK."

"How can we tell the public we have the answers if we don't have the answers?" she asked. There was panic in her eyes.

He smiled like an old friend. "Think back to when you were a teacher."

She frowned. "You mean when I was a substitute teacher?" the Secretary of Education said.

"No, when you were a real teacher."

"I've only ever been a sub," she admitted.

"Well, then think about the assignments you gave to your substitute students. You had never seen those assignments before, yet you had to pretend that you knew what you were talking about."

"I usually just had the kids watch Disney movies."

"Mr. President?" the Secretary of Transportation asked.

"Yes, Phil?"

"All the roads to Disneyland have been shut down."

"Well, that's OK for now because-" the President began.

"It's a disaster for the economy is what it is," the Secretary of Labor interrupted. "Mickey Mouse accounts for fifteen percent of our nation's GDP."

"What about cattle?" the Secretary of Agriculture asked. "Are they still free to roam?"

"Nothing's free!" the Secretary of Defense said.

"You can still buy a car with no money down and zero percent APR," the Secretary of Commerce pointed out.

"I've never understood that," the Secretary of State said. "I think I just don't bargain enough. My wife doesn't like it. Bargaining I mean."

"If we could *please* stay on topic," President Alan said. "There's no point in going off about car shopping when we're clearly talking about elections here. Now I've been thinking a lot about what Senator Guiles has been saying about needing clear, concise, and confident communication. I mean, just saying it like he does feels good."

"It's all the c words together," the Secretary of Education said.

"My point is," the President continued, "we *have* to come across as smooth and non-threatening, otherwise Mr. Butt-munching Fart Head Senator Guiles is going to run away with the American public while we're still talking about Mickey Mouse!" he shouted and shot an angry look at the Secretary of Agriculture who in fact had not made the reference. "We are dealing with a very frightened populace," he said gravely. "The bottom line is they have to have faith in us. Without faith everything will fall apart. Now Palmdonger is going to go a bit more in-depth about safety protocols so I'm going to give him the podium. Palmdonger..."

The Vice President stood. "Thank you, Mr. President." He turned and looked at the group. "I think about a lot of things," he said. "I think about what this great nation would have looked like if we had been alive when the Nino, the Pinto, and the Santo Marino landed at Plymouth Rock. So much has changed since then and I think the Intdians would have been really afraid by our lighters and cell phones, but," he paused for effect just like President Alan might, "I also think we would have brought Democracy a lot sooner because of the internet." Someone coughed. "We can't go back in time and change things, but we can move forward and think ab out new things. I think a lot about how the movie industry has shaped our perceptions of Indians from India..."

"The turtle, Vice President," Benjamin Alan said. "Talk about the turtle."

"Oh! Of course. Turtles have homes..." he began. "Not all homes are safe, however."

"Shouldn't *I* be talking about this?" the Secretary of Housing and Urban Development interrupted.

"I agree. This talk about turtles is irrelevant. What we need is an energy plan!" The Secretary of Energy said. "I've been working this job for eight years and I'll be damned if this virus affects our carbon emissions! Your goddamn turtle better be driving a goddamn coal fired car, is all I can say! Otherwise we just as well open the goddamn doors to Russia and China," he said and looked at the Department of Defense, "because if these dying workers decide to strike, we're gonna have a real goddamn mess on our hands!"

"Folks, if everyone can just pay attention," the President pleaded.

"Russia's bigger than China," the Secretary of Defense said. "But China has Chinese food."

"Mr. President," the Vice President said, "can I use the restroom real quick?"

"Get out!!!" the President yelled. "Everyone – Get. Out!"

The cabinet members begrudgingly stood up and shuffled out of the Oval Office. President Alan threw his empty Dr. Pepper bottle across the room at the door as it closed. "Idiots!" he yelled. "Why am I surrounded by idiots? I'm the President of America, for God's Sake! You'd think whoever fills my cabinet would have a little more competence."

Benjamin Alan walked over to the wide window and crossed his hands behind his back as he looked out over D.C. "Those poor voters have no idea what's headed their way. If only I could help them. But what can I do here in Washington?" He was silent for a moment. "We *have* to find that terrorist."

He reached in his pocket and pulled out his phone. "Boring, is that you?"

"Mr. President?" Boring's voice answered.

"Give me some good news, Boring. What's the status on David Dingle?"

"He's blown up some more heads, Sir." The President clenched his teeth. "He just took some hostages and is currently in a getaway vehicle driving east."

"*East!*" the President ejaculated. "What the hell is he doing coming *this* way?"

"No one can stay in Vegas forever, Sir. One has to tap out eventually."

"Listen, Boring. You do whatever you have to do to find this guy. Shoot him in the spine and paralyze the sonofabitch if you have to. Just don't let him get away. He's the one with the answers. We find him and we end this thing, you got it? Personally, I'd like to get this bastard in front of the media so he can publicly apologize for ruining everyone's week."

"I'll do everything I can, Sir. We just finished our thirds at Triple Sevens All You Can Eat Buffet so we should be out of here any minute."

The President clicked off the phone. "We're coming for you, David Dingle," he said like steam coming off a hot coil. "And when we find you, we're gonna turn your head into a piñata."

Chapter 13: Heading East

"I think we lost 'em!" Courtney yelled as she leaned out the window of the 40 ft. long jet black party bus with larger than life-sized pictures of barely dressed women airbrushed onto the side. At the time it had seemed like the best option for a getaway vehicle.

A sign that read LEAVING ST. GEORGE, UT rushed past them at nearly a hundred miles an hour. David, who was sitting in the driver's seat, leaned back to relax for the first time since they had boarded the bus. With a sigh of relief he took his phone off the dashboard.

"I can't believe you know how to drive like this," Courtney said in disbelief.

"I have a Commercial Driver's License," he shrugged and casually flipped through his phone.

"Really?" she asked.

"Kind of," he said and pressed his thumb on a green "start" button on his phone screen and set the phone back on the dashboard. He swiveled his legs around and looked up at Courtney. He noticed a concern in her eyes. "What's up?" he asked.

Her eyes flickered between him and the road. "Um... shouldn't you be driving?"

He tilted his head. "I *am* driving."

"Then why aren't you looking at the road?"

"Oh! That," he said and waved his hand. "What I mean is that my *phone* is driving. It's a new app," he said proudly. "I just set the bus on cruise control. Don't worry," he reassured her. "This app has mostly four star reviews. It looks like the majority of the one star reviews came from drunk people."

"You mean you haven't used this thing before?"

"Only my second time on a bus, actually." He smiled and looked past her down the aisle. "You've got a really nice bus!" he shouted awkwardly. "Thanks for letting us borrow it." Trish held up a hand. She was sprawled out beside Jerry on a long velvety pillow-thing. The inside of the bus looked more like a strip club than a mode of transportation. A disco ball with a mechanical hum revolved to the soundtrack of *Boogie Nights* and dimly illuminated the interior: half a dozen love seats resembling various forms of genitalia, three poorly built aluminum stripper poles, and a hodgepodge of complementary liquor bottles from the Circus Circus Hotel and RV Park.

"I'm just glad no one got hurt," Trish said, her eyes glazed and gleaming under the disco light.

"Trish," Courtney said impatiently, "a whole convention of doctors' heads exploded! *Lots* of people got hurt. Remember?"

"Oh, right," she said quietly. "That sounds uncomfortable," she said, grinning for some reason, the reason being cocaine.

"We're only alive because we've outsmarted the bad guys every step of the way," Jerry bragged and dragged his fingers over her forearm like a meditation rake. "You're probably risking your life helping us. We're wanted men."

"Is that right?" she said, smacking the words along with the rhythm of her chewing gum.

"You bet your sweet face that's right," Jerry said, his eyes focused and excited. "David here is wanted by the FBI. I'm an accomplice. We're practically gangsters, you know."

Dr. Whyzer dismounted from the dance pole. "*God* that was fun," he said smiling. "Where are we again?"

"Utah," Jerry said. "Ain't that right, babe?"

Trish shrugged. "Long as I don't gotta work tonight I don't care *where* we are."

"We're still on a bus though, right?" Dr. Whyzer asked.

"Damn, Doc. How many of those pills did you take?" Jerry asked and Dr. Whyzer held up a hand and wiggled three or four fingers.

"You all surprised me when you came in," Trish admitted. "When I first saw Courtney I figured she had to use the bathroom. But when I saw everyone else I thought, 'Oh boy, this is gonna be a looong night.'"

"Oh it's gonna be a long night, all right," Jerry said as he playfully grabbed a hold of Trish's waist.

She pushed him off with a laugh. "Gangster! You're no gangster. The only thing you're on the run from is some girl's heart."

"It's *true*!" he said. "Runnin' from love and Johnny Law. Hey, does this thing have satellite TV? I want to see if we made the news."

"TV, on!" Trish demanded.

A screen lowered from the roof.

"Impressive," Jerry said.

On the screen a well-dressed black man stood facing the camera on the upper floor of the Stratosphere. "...I'm at the only safe place in the casino," he said over the wind. "We have recently learned that the virus has reached Las Vegas and infected people in the lobby of the casino. There are multiple people's heads that are confirmed exploded, although at least one of the incidents may have been due to a case of overexcitement from hitting a jackpot. Las Vegas experiences well over 200 head-exploding-fatalities a year due to 'Jackpot Surprise' as it's known locally. But considering the circumstances, Martino Culiano, the mayor of Las Vegas, has put the city on lockdown."

A grainy photo of David and his party of three appeared on the screen.

"We made it!" Jerry screamed. Trish smiled and clutched his arm. "Turn it up!"

"These four individuals are wanted for questioning about their involvement in the incident. The man in the lead, Mr. David Dingle, quickly fled the scene after winning a jackpot. He was last seen at a medical convention where the virus first appeared in Vegas. This is now the second time that David Dingle has been at the scene of the virus's appearance in a new city. He is believed to have two hostages in his possession, a medical professional and some blonde bimbo."

"*Bimbo?!*" Courtney yelled. "My hair is *naturally* bleached, thank you very much."

"See, I *told* you!" Jerry said to Trish. His hand was on her leg now.

"Oh my God," Trish said and stared at David in disbelief. "Did you *really* win the jackpot?" she asked. "I've *always* wanted to win a jackpot. Only been livin' here for fifteen years," she said bitterly. "Sure, I've had *clients* I've escorted who have won..."

Courtney looked at David. "I still can't believe this is happenin'," she said softly.

"Tell me about it," David said.

"I shouldn't even be here. I should be at work."

"*Tell* me about it," he said again.

"I don't want to be a fugitive."

"Technically you're a hostage," he said, trying to be helpful. "When all this is over you'll probably get a book deal out of this. Maybe even a made-for-TV movie."

"What's going to happen to you?" she asked. "Do you think they'll catch you?"

"I try not to think about it," he said with an air of depression.

"So you really didn't kill all those people?" she asked.

"Not on purpose," he said. "It just seems to happen that way. Everywhere I go people's heads blow up."

"That Doctor Macaw said that you're infected."

David looked through the windshield and down the long highway. "I know," he said. "Infected with the worst virus since the bubonic plague, apparently. It's just not fair. I get my flu shots every year."

"From the sound of it, Doctor Macaw has been working under the radar for a while. He seemed to know everythin' about you." She studied him. "If you *are* tellin' the truth and have no idea what's goin' on, then why would they go to all this trouble without your knowledge?"

David involuntarily glanced at the manila envelope on the dashboard.

"What's that?" she asked.

"Oh nothing. Just the answers to all of our questions."

Courtney picked it up. "Well, open it, for cryin' out loud."

"No!" he practically yelled and swiped it out of her hand and shoved it under his butt. "You can't look at it."

"If it has all the answers then why aren't you readin' it?" she asked. "Aren't you even remotely curious what it says?"

"I'm *beyond* curious," David confessed. "But I'm also terrified about what it could say. All I know for certain is that what it says inside is about me and that anyone who reads it their head explodes. I was hoping Dr. Macaw was smart enough to understand it, but now he's dead and I can't think of anyone else who has the brains to decipher what's inside."

"*I'll* do it!" Jerry hollered from the back. "Pass it over here."

David grimaced like he had just taken a bite out of a rotten lemon. "Thanks, Jerry, but I really want to be careful with this. I mean, a lot of people have died because of this folder," he said.

"Are there any patterns?" Dr. Whyzer asked.

David thought back to the first incident in Seattle. "Well, some of the people were kind of...stupid."

"Stupid?" Courtney asked.

"Yeah. Like those nerds in Pioneer Square," David said. "Who in their right mind would still be using Apple products when Nuerolink is by far the superior technology? *Everyone* knows that. I mean, that's not just stupid, that's *idiotic!*"

"But what about all the doctors?" Courtney asked. "Doctors aren't stupid."

"Can I offer a medical perspective?" Dr. Whyzer asked, hanging onto the stripper pole like a tripped-out orangutan. "I'm probably the only doctor in that entire convention that isn't dead. There were a lot of good men in that hall. Boring men, *maybe, b*ut still, very smart and dedicated individuals. Most of those guys were at the top of their game. They were society changers, people ready to solve all types of problems for poor people in Africa. You know the type. That's what I thought about Dr. Macaw, at least," he said, shaking his head. "I had a lot of respect for that guy. But if what your friend recorded is true, which I believe it is, then Macaw pretty much deceived us all from the very beginning. It makes you wonder, doesn't it?"

"That Doctor Macaw is linked in with some very sinister people?" David asked.

"No, that Ecstasy is keeping me immune." Everyone stared at Dr. Whyzer who was chewing on his tongue. "Being immune feels *sooo* good."

"I gotta agree," Jerry said anxiously. "If all those other doctors are dead then it's only logical that we should all take some drugs. Hey Doc, give me some pills before my brain starts leaking out of my ears. She'll take some too, right babe?" he asked Trish who gave a grin.

Dr. Whyzer furrowed his brow with practiced reverence and tapped several pills onto Jerry's palm. Jerry handed one to Trish. "Guys?" he asked Courtney and David.

Courtney shriveled her nose and David politely declined.

"There is a negligible chance that I am wrong," Dr. Whyzer said, "so we should still take precautionary measures."

"What do you suggest, Doctor?" Jerry asked.

"Well, I think that if you get the urge to cough that you should do so into your shirt. Also, let's keep the fluid exchange between people to a minimum."

Jerry scowled. "Well, I can definitely get behind the coughing part."

Courtney stared at David for a moment. "I'm confused. If people's heads explode everywhere you go then why aren't *we* all dead?" she asked.

Jerry perked up. "Yeah, good point! I've been with this guy the whole time. If this shit were so contagious then my head would've blown off my shoulders back in Seattle. I catch colds like a *mother*fucker. It's like I'm *always* sick," he said and downed the rest of his seventh beer.

"Hmm," David said, thinking to himself. "I'll bet my phone has some answers but it's driving the bus right now. Dr. Whyzer, do you think it's possible that the virus is attacking stupid people?" he asked.

"Maybe yes, maybe no," he replied thoughtfully. "I can personally attest that all of those men in that convention hall were brilliant, myself included. So maybe it's targeting the super smart, who, ironically, weren't smart enough to take Ecstasy. Now if *I* were the President, I would round up all the super-geniuses in the country to keep them safe long enough to solve this problem."

"The President..." David said. "Now *he's* smart. If only I could get *him* to read what's in this folder," he said and stared at the envelope. "He'd be able to explain it to me in seconds."

"You sure yer talkin' about the right President?" Courtney asked. "President Alan is about as sharp as a broken thumbtack."

David waved his hand in front of him as if he wouldn't even consider it. "No way. Our President is the culmination of the greatest voting process on earth. You don't just get elected by an ignorant population. *We* elected him, remember?"

"Well, *I* sure didn't," she said. "I voted for the fat guy. Can't say I wasn't surprised that he didn't get elected, though. It's hard for the public to accept a man who speaks his mind."

"He wanted to build a bridge to Vietnam so he could order authentic Vietnamese food. That's just crazy!"

"You're just jealous cause you didn't think of it. Didn't he die of a heart attack last year?"

David shrugged and sat down in the driver's seat again and stared out the window, his thoughts elsewhere.

"So where are you taking us?" Courtney asked David.

"I've set the destination as South Africa," David said.

"South *Africa*?" she exclaimed.

"It's the farthest place I could think of. Right now it's got us routed through Florida. Who knows? Maybe there's a bridge to South Africa from Orlando. That would be nice..."

"So you're just gonna run away?" she asked. "I thought terrorists usually blow themselves up."

"I'm not a terrorist, remember?"

"So who are you?"

He picked up his phone and showed her his Facebook Profile. "This is a pretty good overview," he said, scrolling through his "About Me" section. "Strong work history, lots of great selfies of me in traffic, family and relationships..." his voice trailed off.

"The relationship part's blank," she said.

"Yeah, I was gonna mention something about Jerry," he muttered.

"What about your parents?" she asked.

David sighed. "I never really lived up to their expectations. My Dad wanted me to be a Green Beret and my mom wanted me to become a hobbit. I dunno. I hate doing push-ups and I look ridiculous in anything from Middle-Earth. I still don't know who or what I'm supposed to be."

"That must be hard," she said quietly. "I've been lucky. I knew since I was four years old that I was going to be a famous singer-songwriter. It ain't been easy, though. It's hard followin' your dreams when no one believes in you. I love my family to death but it's been difficult for them to accept my raw talent. One day I just realized I had to pack up and move along if I was ever gonna show the world who I truly am."

David chuckled nervously. "I seem to have the exact opposite problem. Everyone seems to know who I am except me."

"Hey!" Courtney said. "If this bus is headed to Florida then we'll be driving right through my hometown in Arkansas. We could stay with my folks in

Mackanack. We can bunker down for a while which will give you time to think. My family is the greatest! They're super loving, and smart, and politically active. My brother has a whole place prepared for crazy stuff like this. He's even got this website and Twitter name and everything."

"Oh yeah, what's his Twitter name?" Jerry hollered from the back of the bus.

"Um, @Sirtatum," Courtney said.

"No way!" Jerry yelled. "I'm *following* that dude!"

"Really?"

"Yeah, well, I'm following like forty-thousand dudes, but *that* dude I actually know what he does. He's like a prepper. He's got this whole Youtube channel going on about the abolishment of the New World Order and the rebirth of the constitution. Your brother's got like *mad* militia connections."

"That's Tatum," Courtney said, rolling her eyes. "He's real good at gathering resources."

"We should *totally* go there, bro," Jerry called out to David.

"You think so?"

Jerry paused. "Whoa, did you just feel that?" he asked.

"Yeah," Trish said. "My pills just kicked in, too."

A metallic feminine voice came over the loudspeaker. "Obstacle in the road. Vehicle stopping."

"What's going on?" Courtney asked.

"I don't know," David said, turning around in his chair. "The autopilot just detected something. Holy crap," he said looking up. "There are *people* standing in the road."

"People?" she asked. "How many?"

"About twenty."

"What on earth are they doing in the middle of the road way out here?" Jerry asked. "Don't they know it's Armageddon? Who the hell do they think they are?"

"It looks like half a dozen women in their thirties," David said.

"Pick 'em up!!" Jerry yelled.

The bus slowed to a stop and David opened the large door. Standing outside were nearly two dozen individuals that looked like they had been plucked out of the nineteenth century. The women were wearing strange, drab dresses with bonnets over their heads. The men, well, the lone man, was dressed like a preacher in a black vest and white cuffed shirt. Here, there, and everywhere around them were a playground's worth of children.

The lone man looked at David. It was as if the man had suddenly become engaged in a moment that had been predestined by the creator of the

IQ84

cosmos Himself – at least that is what the man's expression conveyed. He flashed a glance at the women around him. They felt it, too. In fact, one of them swooned and another fainted.

"Um, have your heads been blowing up?" David asked them.

They stared at him.

David was concerned about the unconscious woman in the hot sun. He walked down the steps and examined the woman who had fainted. "She's hot, she needs shade. Please, come inside," he smiled.

The Timpson family followed David up the stairs and onto the jet black bus with the large breasted, scantily dressed women painted on the outside. The lone man nodded an overwhelmed hello to the rest of the individuals in the bus who stared back. Jacob Timpson hardly noticed their shocked expression — his attention was locked on David alone. David's sparkly beautiful blue eyes seemed to Jacob Timpson to have all the world's answers within them. There seemed to be a golden aura spread around this coachman — even David's sandals gave the bishop a feeling of hope.

"Are you all headed east?" David asked.

"If that is where the Son is rising, then yes," Jacob said. "Thank you, Jesus!" he said and the rest of his family began a quick rendition of "Oh Lord, My Redeemer."

David, oblivious as usual, did his best to hum along.

"Man," Jerry said, looking at Trish and Dr. Whyzer. "This party just got *good.*"

Chapter 14: The Hubcap

Melech looked up from his device. "That's strange. I just lost reception."

Mason leaned into the train aisle. "I think we're stopping," he said.

"This train is not supposed to stop," Melech said impatiently. "I've taken it hundreds of times. Go find out what's happening."

"I'll look into it, Sir," Mason responded and walked to the front of the train. Ten minutes later he returned with an attractive blonde woman in a yellow halter top by his side.

"Tell Mr. Rothschild what you told me," Mason said to the woman.

The young lady attempted a smile. She looked like she had just pooped her pants and was about to come clean. "I'm sorry, but we are being forced to stop," Beth said.

"That much is obvious," Melech said without bothering to smile. "I assume it's not for gas."

She laughed uncomfortably. "There appears to have been an earthquake."

"An *earthquake*? Where?"

"About ninety miles from here. The epicenter was near the rail line, Mr. Rothschild. The tunnel has been structurally damaged. It is impossible to proceed."

Melech stared at her. He could feel his small heart pick up tempo. "We really cannot proceed?"

"I'm afraid not."

"Very well. What is your contingency plan?" he asked and looked at his watch.

"Well, we're currently stopped at station fifty-seven, awaiting transfer." She hesitated. The last person who had told Melech Rothschild he would have to wait (the woman who had been cleaning the bathroom when Melech had to pee) had been tossed into the incinerator. "From there you'll have to travel to our next pick-up." She gulped. "In Tennessee."

"*Tennessee!*" he screamed.

"Memphis, Sir."

"I assume a helicopter is waiting for me?"

She shook her head, wondering why she had been told to get such an expensive yellow halter-top if it was just going to get burned to a crisp.

"Then how in Satan's name am I supposed to get to Tennessee?"

Beth shifted. "A bus, Sir?"

His fingernails punctured the leather chair. "I must admit," he said evenly, "I do not like the sound of this one little bit."

She shrugged, wondering if her cat Wiggly would also be incinerated. "In Memphis another train will be awaiting you."

"Where the hell are we?" he demanded. "Tell me that we're close."

"Northern Wyoming, Mr. Rothschild."

"Wyoming!" he yelled. "You're telling me that the closest pick-up station between D.C. and Wyoming is in *Tennessee?"*

She nodded, wondering if she should still be shrugging. "I'm afraid so. The earthquake has affected roads and electricity throughout half of the country. It's the biggest earthquake we've seen in...well, it's big, Sir."

Melech pinched his coarse black eyebrows. "This stupid fucking planet. Of all the times to shake things up it decides that today is a good day." He looked up at the woman who was visibly shaking now. "Get everyone you know on the phone. Inform them of the situation. I want a plane ready to leave Cheyenne in two hours."

"That's going to be very difficult, Sir. What with the earthquake and the virus..."

"Just do it!!" he screamed. He slicked his hair down and composed himself. "This is just a little hiccup," he said, pretending that his reassurance was for Beth and Mason and not himself. "I will simply have to take matters into my own hands. Be sure to inform the President of the situation. Tell him I shall be a few hours behind."

"We've lost communications as well. That's what I was trying to say."

He stared at her. "I know a surgeon who could give you another mouth since the one you have has become such a retched blunder-hole. Would you like that?" he asked.

Not knowing if this was a choice between that or the incinerator she nodded yes.

"Sir, she's hardly responsible for this," Mason said.

"Don't get me started on who is responsible," Melech retorted. "*All* you idiots are responsible. Mason, get your things together. You're coming with me."

"Of course, Sir."

"Mr. Rothschild?" Beth asked timidly. "A whole team is prepared to accompany you."

Melech shook his head. "That, Ms. Blunder-hole, is an impossibility. There isn't a person on this train who has the appropriate DNA to accompany me. The virus is attacking individuals within a specific spectrum of intelligence. Everyone is too smart," he said while he gathered together his belongings. "I had planned for everything," he fumed quietly to himself. "Stolen vaccinations, corporate media, economic scandals. Everything. But fucking geological probabilities?!? What next, a meteorite?" He reached down and pulled out his metallic briefcase, set it on the table, and opened it. Inside were two small silver syringes set into a rubber mold. He pulled one out and showed it to Mason.

"This is currently the only antidote in existence. I keep it on hand for emergencies such as this. It will only keep you alive for two or three days, however. The virus is still in a state of active mutation while it reaches equilibrium. Once Dr. Macaw gets the final blood sample from our host you will have access to a permanent solution." He handed the needle to Mason. "You'll need to inject this into your arm before you come up to the surface."

Mason calmly and competently injected his arm with the needle and then handed the empty syringe back to Melech, who took it and closed the briefcase. "What about yourself, Sir?" Mason asked.

Melech smiled thinly. "I've been immune long before first exposure. This one is merely a back-up. An *actual* contingency plan," he sneered at Beth.

"What is the other needle?" Mason asked.

"Cyanide," Melech said and shrugged. "It's good practice to have some cyanide with you wherever you go. You never know whose suicide will need to be faked. Come on. Let's get going before my *own* head explodes with anger."

Beth led Melech and Mason down the aisle to an automated sliding door that released with a *poosh* sound and a hiss of air. "Remember," she said. "The entrance to the station is located in Memphis, Tennessee just behind the courthouse."

"How could I forget?" he huffed. He looked at Beth. "I will use the satellite phone to update my coordinates. And I will need a detailed description of my updated logistics as soon as you have them. I will be on communication the moment I hit the surface. I want a flight ASAP."

"Satellite communication is not currently active," she said, thinking of poor Wiggly. "Someone in Washington must have taken them offline for some reason."

"So you're telling me I won't be able to reach *anyone*? How am I supposed to communicate with Logistics? Or with the President, for that matter?"

"You'll still have your cellphone," she said as cheerfully as she could. "Just call as soon as you get a signal. It shouldn't be a problem."

"Indeed," he muttered. He and Mason departed from the train into the dimly lit cold underground tunnel. There wasn't much to look at besides an elevator and an endless staircase that looked like the exact opposite of 'a good time.' On the wall was a painted black and yellow sign which read: "Station 57. Depth 2,000 feet below ground."

"Ugh," Melech said. "Let's get out of here quickly."

Mason stepped over and pushed the green button on the lift.

"There's no response," he said after a long moment. "It's likely the power is out due to the earthquake."

"I really hope you're not saying what I think you're saying," Melech said.

"We're going to have to climb out."

Melech looked up. "It's been a long time since I've climbed that many stairs," he said apprehensively.

"I could carry you, if you'd like."

Melech thought about it. "Good idea."

Mason bent down and Melech threw his arms over his shoulders and before long he was piggy-backing up the staircase. After seven flights, however, he told Mason to stop. "This is really uncomfortable. My testicles are rubbing against your belt. Whoever designed it should be incinerated."

Off came the belt, but every fourth step Mason's pants fell down.

"This is hopeless!" Melech complained. "I'm afraid I'm going to have to climb the rest on my own."

And so they continued their upward journey. Mason was in his prime and a fine specimen of health. He stood at 6'4 and weighed 190 pounds of pure lean muscle. Melech, on the other hand, was a bit...softer. It was rare that he spent any time exercising anything other than his mind. It was rare that he ever stepped outside, for that matter. At the risk of an understatement, Melech was not a fan of the natural world or any of its inhabitants.

It took the two of them well over an hour to get to the top and by the time they reached the steel hatch, Melech was doubled over in exhaustion. Mason quickly unlocked the hatch and lifted it open. A flood of piercing white light enveloped them. Melech recoiled.

"Aaauughh!" he yelled. "It's so bright. Turn it off — turn it off!"

"It's OK, Sir. You'll get used to it. Give me your hand."

Melech took Mason's hand and felt himself being pulled out of the hollow tube of blackness and into the sunlight. After several moments of excruciating blindness he regained his vision. In the distance, he saw smooth yellow and green hills nestled below a vast and eternal blue sky. The air was warm and the scent of sagebrush hung on the air like a gentle perfume. The buzzy songs of songbirds could be heard rising up from the low bushes.

"Yuck! What a miserable place," Melech muttered as a gust of wind blew dirt into his eyes. "Aaaghh!" He screamed and shielded his face. "Where in Satan's name are we, Mason? Mordor?"

"Recluse, Wyoming," Mason said and pointed at a white and green sign behind them.

Melech looked. "Population 229."

"We are at the edge of town, Mr. Rothschild." He pointed at a handful of buildings in the near distance. "We should head over and see if we can catch some transport out of here."

"I'm going to need some water fast, Mason. I was not anticipating such a workout."

"I'll see that you get some right away, Mr. Rothschild."

The two men walked slowly down the dusty road toward town. Melech's shirt was soaked with sweat and his breathing sputtered like a dying tractor. Mason was growing concerned.

"I appreciate you carrying me back there," Melech said to Mason as they walked. "Why, you didn't even hesitate."

"I apologize for the belt," Mason said.

"Yes, terrible thing," Melech agreed. "I'll be sure to get you an Indonesian brand that I've quite enjoyed. It's made from the underbelly of immature orangutans. They're *incredibly* soft!" Melech was beginning to feel better. "We make them the same time we harvest our palm oil to keep costs low."

They were walking into town now. The buildings, of which there were seven, were rustic to say the least.

"It looks like there's a market up ahead," Mason said. "We'll try to get you some water there."

A bell jingled as they walked through the market door and an obese cross-eyed man looked up at them from a comic book. "H-hello?" he said. "You folks...need somethin'?"

"So this town isn't abandoned after-all," Melech said.

"We'd like to buy some water," Mason replied.

"Buy some water? Heck, we ain't got no water for sale. You just help yourself to whatever comes out of the faucet, over there." He pointed at a rusted sink next to a broken Slurpee machine. "Just grab a styrofoam cup."

Mason grabbed a cup, rinsed out the spider's nest, and filled it with cold water. Melech grabbed it and slugged it down like a thirsty pit-bull. Instantly he began coughing and gagging. This was a far cry from the Chilean glacier water he was accustomed to.

"What's that *taste*?!" he shrieked.

"Hmm," the clerk hummed. "Arsenic, maybe? Only trace amounts, they say, but some of us is skeptical. We also get a bunch of crackerjack minerals in our water due to the mines. We're told they're pretty good for us, though. Ain't no one here had much problems with it." He eyeballed them for a moment with one of his eyes. "You folks from Cheyenne or something?"

Melech scoffed. "Not on your life. Listen, we're trying to get out of this god-forsaken Gomorrah as fast as humanly possible. When does the next bus come by?"

"Bus?" the man scoffed as if he had just been asked when the leprechauns come out to pollinate the flowers. "No buses come through these parts, Mister. Closest city is Gillette and that's 'bout thirty miles from here."

"Are you insinuating that we have to *walk?*" Melech asked, as if he had just been told that his champagne would be served at room temperature.

The clerk shrugged.

Mason broke in, "It's possible there won't be any buses in Gillette either due to the outbreak." Mason turned to the clerk. "Has the outbreak hit Recluse yet?"

The man's eyes glazed over like donuts.

"I take it that it hasn't," Melech said. "Good. In that case we should be able to get out of Wyoming. Mason, take a look at the bus schedule on your phone. Check the trains while you're at it."

"Ain't gonna find no signal," the clerk said.

"Please tell me you're joking," Melech said.

"I ain't the laughin' type, Mister. Dang ol' earthquake has taken out all of the cell phone towers. It shore was scary when it happened. I thought the sky was a-comin' down," the man said reliving the moment.

"And yet your beautiful establishment managed to stay standing," Melech said. "What's it built out of? Popsicle sticks?"

They stepped outside before the clerk could answer and were hit by another blast of dusty wind.

"Look," Mason pointed. "There is someone over there. Let's go find out what he knows."

"Right, perhaps he'll be able to count to three," Melech murmured, but followed along.

A tall exceedingly thin man in his late thirties leaned against a crumbling brick building on the corner of the block. In one hand he held a cigarette. In the other he held a string leash attached to a pig. The man looked up when he saw the men approaching. As they neared, Melech noticed that this man was cross-eyed too. Somehow he was not surprised.

"You guys headed to the big town?" the man asked.

"Yes!" Melech said with a wave of relief. "Are you waiting for a ride?"

"Sure am!" the man said. "Should be here any minute, too."

"Thank Satan!" Melech said.

The man squinted. (Melech assumed that this man spent his entire life squinting.) "Say, where you folks comin' from?"

"Cambodia," Melech said, trying to get a signal on his phone.

"No kiddin'. So yer Chinese?"

"Mmm hmm," Melech said and stared down the endless road hoping for the slightest indication of transit. "We've heard so much about this place that we had to see it for ourselves. And now that we've been here for five minutes we feel satisfied that we've seen it all."

The man nodded. "We had a black guy pass through here about a year and a half ago. That was neat. Don't see too many outsiders, to be honest. We kinda set back from..."

"The rest of the civilized world?" Melech interrupted.

The man spit. "Ya'll shoulda come during the Post Office Festival. It's quite an event. Whole town comes out and mails their letters."

"Sounds enthralling," Melech said, shielding his eyes against the miserable sun. "Say, when is that ride supposed to come in?"

"Any minute now, but I ain't goin'," he said and waved his hand. "I'ma just passin' along my prize pig to the driver. This here's Wilbur," the man said. "Swear to God, Wilbur is the *smartest* pig I have *ever* seen," he said, widening his eyes with excitement. "An' I seen a *lot* a pigs, Mister. Go ahead Wilbur, stand on two feet."

Wilbur grunted with annoyance. "I said two feet, boy," the man ordered. Wilbur grunted again but leaned back and stood up. "Ain't that somethin'?!" the man said and slapped his thigh. "Good boy, Wilbur! Now do your Donald Trump act." But Wilbur only pestered the man for a treat. "He ain't gonna do it unless I give him a snack."

"Smart pig," Melech admitted.

"That's why I'ma sendin' ol' Wilbur here to the pig competition in Gillette. Say, would you fellas mind doin' me a favor and holdin' onto Wilbur for a moment while I grab some beef jerky? I feel bad not given him a snack for his Kirstie Alley impersonation he's been doin' for me." He handed the string to Melech and took off. Melech immediately dropped the string like a hot pin.

Wilbur snorted.

"This is why I stay underground," Melech said to Mason.

"Look!" Mason pointed.

Melech followed his gaze and saw a growing plume of dust coming from the road. "That must be our ride," Melech said in relief. "Looks like it's headed our way...*fast.*"

"*Real* fast," Mason agreed.

Within moments they could see the sun reflecting against the shiny metal grate of the black and white pickup truck.

"That's a big pickup," Mason said. "And is that a...*horse* in the back?"

At fifty feet from where Melech was standing the driver slammed on the brakes and the truck skidded to a stop in front of them like something out of

Dukes of Hazards.

"Oh," Mason said. "It's a donkey."

That wasn't all. Crammed into the back of the pickup were four sheep, three goats, a calf, and an ill-tempered llama. Up front, a clearly intoxicated man nearly twice the size of the grocery clerk peered out of the truck window. He had a massive wad of bubble gum in his mouth which he pushed to the side with his tongue as he leaned out the window. "That Chester's pig?" he asked, his tone familial as if he knew Melech and Mason from the Post Office Festival.

"It is," Mason said.

"Well, toss him in back. You boys lookin' fer a ride into Gillette?"

"Um..." Melech said. "When's the *next* truck coming by?"

The driver laughed. "Most folks are either asleep or in church. Ain't gonna be another ride 'til tomorrow afternoon. I'd offer ya both a seat up front but there's only room for one due to all the chickens, an' they get priority."

"I am *not* sitting next to that man," Melech whispered to Mason.

"Will you be OK in the back?" Mason asked.

Melech looked. The pickup bed looked like a traveling barn. He had never spent much time with animals before, aside from his pair of Persian cats and occasionally as a spectator at an illegal silverback gorilla fight. Still, it looked like there might be an open spot beside the ass. "I'll be fine."

"Well, git yer butts in," the driver ordered. "I gotta git back to the tavern in Gillette before the ball game kicks off."

Melech hesitated. "Is your truck capable of handling the extra weight? Those have to be the smallest tires I have ever seen on a truck this size."

"Got 'em at discount!" the man said proudly. "Pulled 'em off a Honda in a junk yard. But the hubcaps look brand new. (They ain't.)"

Mason lowered the animal bridge at the back of the pickup and waited. To Melech's surprise, Wilbur walked confidently up the wooden ladder and looked back at Melech and gave an impatient oink. Melech sighed and looked at Mason. "Well, I can do it if Wilbur can. You better get up front before our driver eats himself."

Melech and Mason got settled. The driver banged his fist twice on the roof and yelled, "Hang on!" The truck peeled out and Melech was launched backwards and careened into one of the goats behind him. The goat grunted and then sniffed Melech and began chewing on his shirt.

Melech slammed sideways into another goat. "Hey!" he screamed at the driver. "Be careful." The truck was moving considerably faster now and Melech was forced to steady himself on all fours. Carefully, he stood up by holding onto a rope attached to the back of the cab. He clutched the metal frame with both hands. This guy was *hauling.* Melech could already see the dim outline of Gillette in the distance. He opened his mouth to command the driver to slow down but the rushing wind stole his breath. Melech's eyes were bleeding tears and strips of saliva were being ripped out the corners of his mouth like water off an airplane window. An oncoming car swerved to get out of the way.

"This maniac is going to get us killed!" he yelled and fell backwards into another goat. In all his years he had never felt so close to death. Melech Amschel Rothschild owned billions of dollars in military stock. He had helped fund both sides of multiple wars. On two occasions he had nearly led the entire country into nuclear war. He had always been in control. He owned armies of puppets and legions of servants who responded to his every bidding. But none of that had scared him like this car ride. In this moment, every person he had ever manipulated, everything he had ever worked for, everything he had ever *stood* for, was in the hands of a man whose breathe smelled like bubblegum and whiskey.

Melech noticed something up ahead. Whatever it was looked like matchsticks or Lincoln Logs scattered over the road. As the truck rocketed forward, Melech made out the image — a string of downed power lines and a colossal fissure in the earth's surface that ran right across the road like a holy fucking omen of death.

"Oh my Satan! Stop! Stop!" he screamed. He was banging on the roof and then the truck started swerving side to side like a speed-crazed mudskipper. Inside, Mason was trying to arrest the truck's speed by subduing a man that only listened to reason if it was made out of Twinkie filling. If anything, Melech thought, the car felt like it was accelerating. They traveled 1,000 ft. in the blink of an eye. Melech swiveled around and looked for an escape of some kind, *any* kind. There had to be someone or something that could save him. It was then that he made eye contact with the pig. Wilbur's eyes were wide and wild and locked onto Melech's. The pig's expression was one of blind panic and it was in that moment that Melech knew that if Wilbur could speak it would have clearly and intelligently said the word, "Fuck."

The entire accident happened like something in a movie. Melech watched it happen as though he were sitting down in a comfy movie seat chair and digging out a fistful of popcorn. He watched with raw amazement as the truck took to the air like a 1987 rusted tin barn with wings. Bits of hay and crumbs of dried manure filled the air like confetti. He could somehow see every person involved. He saw their driver mid-chew and wide-eyed as they sailed over the cavernous chasm of doom. He saw Mason with both hands on the steering wheel in a last vain attempt to correct the vehicle. And he saw himself standing in back with the kind of monstrous expression that would frighten the senses out of any child who had seen it. That man — himself, Melech – was clearly the villain, and movie-goer Melech saw that plainly as he continued to stuff his movie-mouth with popcorn and soda. He wondered when that awful man would finally get his comeuppance until he realized with terrible understanding (so powerful that it's a wonder *his* head did not explode) that *he* was that awful villain. Now he knew that he did *not* want his comeuppance because he had been one *evil* sonofabitch.

And then, just like that, the movie lights went out.

Melech opened his eyes to a blinding white light. The ground felt soft, as if he were resting on a cloud drifting up towards the Pearly Gates. Had he died? Hell certainly seemed more comfortable than he had anticipated. He knew he had to wiggle his fingers if he was ever going to be able to touch his new wings.

Fingers and toes intact, Melech sat up and looked around. To his surprise, instead of a puffy cloud he was lying on the carcasses of four soft but very dead sheep. The calf and the ass were also dead as were most of the goats. The llama had survived somehow, although its back hoof was broken and its snout was covered in blood. Still, it was standing, although it was very pissed off.

Wilbur was nowhere to be seen.

Melech rolled over and tested the weight on his feet. Amazingly, he could walk. With the exception of a light headache and a few cuts and bruises, Melech had somehow come out of the accident mostly unscathed.

"Mason," he whispered to himself.

The truck was resting on its side more than fifty feet away and the hood of the truck was compacted against a rock wall like an artfully crushed tin can. Both Mason and the driver were dead.

"Aaughh!" Melech yelled. "That idiot must have thought he could jump the cavern! If *only* it hadn't been such a quick death for him," Melech said and kicked dirt at the truck. "Poor Mason. *Now* who's going to take me to Gillette?"

"Oink."

Melech looked down and saw that Wilbur was standing there beside him with an expectant look. Accident over, Wilbur was ready for the trough.

"Yeah, you and me both, you ugly swine," Melech said and pushed Wilbur away with his foot.

"Oink oink."

"I said, 'take a hike,' Wilbur. You're on your own now." He stepped away and began a slow walk towards Gillette on the horizon. "Oh great," he said when he saw the llama walking up to him. "This isn't a caravan, you ugly beast. This is a solo show." The llama lowered its ears, pulled back its teeth, and spit into Melech's face.

"Hey! What the hell is wrong with you!" he yelled and flailed his arms.

Wilbur, who for some inexplicable reason felt a sort of kinship to Melech, turned on the llama and began a cute, albeit persistent attack, onto the llama's bum leg. The llama took off at a trot. Wilbur returned to Melech's side. "Oink oink."

"I don't care even if you *are* a guard pig," Melech said. "I don't need your company or help. Ugh!" he complained. "My head is killing me. We must have been in the air longer than the Wright Brothers. I do hope that idiot suffered some internal bleeding before he smashed our vehicle into that small planet."

He took out his phone and tapped it a few times. "Still works!" he said triumphantly. Unfortunately he could not get a signal. Looking around he saw a sign down the road which read: Gillette – 11 miles.

"I will just have to walk into town myself," he said and began to brush the dust off his Armani suit. "I better check to make sure I don't look absolutely dreadful before I find myself in front of a crowd of proletariats explaining my situation."

Melech leaned down and picked up one of the side mirrors that had come loose from the vehicle. "Still have all my teeth," he said happily. "Just a thin line of blood coming off my forehead is all and..." Melech paused as he stared at the mirror. "Is that a...*hubcap!*...stuck in my head?"

He stared at the strange metal disk for a moment. It wobbled slightly in the breeze.

He quickly squashed a tsunami of rising panic. "It must have penetrated so quickly that it cauterized the bleeding and by the luck of Minerva did not damage anything life-threatening. It must come out at once. It looks like I will be stopping at the hospital on my way out of town."

Melech heard Wilbur pressing something abrasive against the ground.

"Hey! You stay away from that!" he demanded and rushed over and picked up his metal briefcase and then stood and began to walk slowly down the road to Gillette. Wilbur trotted closely behind him.

Melech raised his hand to shield away the harsh sun. "This place looks like it's been nuked," he muttered. Giant terrible columns of black smoke drifted into the sky. The earth itself had been torn apart and a wide gaping hole stretched across the landscape like a horrible tear upon a prized painting. He wondered if part of this was the direct result of the virus, the quick effects of the negligence of stupid men without a leader. It resembled the aftermath of an unnecessary war.

"Oh!" he said in surprise as he read a sign at the edge of the road. "Coal Creek Mine. Hmm. Come to think of it, I believe I helped fund this project. Well, it's good to see that it's still working properly. I think those automation programs I invested in really paid off."

"Oink Oink."

Melech looked around. Sadly, no humans could be seen.

"Maybe it's just because it's Sunday," he thought and walked on. Soon he passed the airport which to his disappointment was likewise deserted, but in the near distance he saw a small suburb of Gillette, and he could see activity. Gillette was a conglomeration of construction companies and mining related industry and this little outpost may have become a refuge for a band of survivors.

Melech was beginning to get an uneasy feeling. It was not because of the apparent collapse of human civilization, but rather because of the untreated drinking water he had guzzled down in Recluse. He realized that he would soon be shitting his pants if he didn't find a men's room somewhere. And fast.

His hubcap flapped in the wind as he ran.

Melech clutched his stomach as he bee-lined toward the closest building. Hopefully it was open. If not, he was prepared to break in. Melech had never taken a shit in the open air before in his life and he wasn't about to start now.

The building he ran toward had a sign on the facade that read, "Mike's Plumbing and Liquid Cleaner." Melech grimaced at the irony, although it did not stop him from assaulting the heavy door with both hands while screaming, "Someone open this goddamn door this instant!" at the top of his lungs.

Melech had already broken into a cold sweat. He knew that he had only moments before his bowels released the vile waters of this miserable county into his $200 silk boxer briefs. He peered through the dusty window of the building but saw only an empty chair and a desk. A liquid grumble in his large intestine sent him dashing across the parking lot. He looked frantically around him for a hiding spot. It occurred to him that only moments ago he had vowed never to shit without the support of a marble toilet beneath him. Now that sounded like the most foolish thing in the world. In fact, taking an emergency diarrhea dump between two large pick-ups seemed downright sensible.

And so he did. Melech Amschel Rothschild pulled down his $1,000 Cashmere work pants and pressure-painted the dirt parking lot with the foulest liquid waste it had been exposed to in nearly two weeks. When he was finished, Melech pulled off his silk boxers and used them to wipe. He then hung them on the large black tire he had been leaning against.

"Hey!" a man yelled, obviously surprised to see what appeared to be a European banker taking a shit on the tire of his Dodge 4150.

Melech, literally caught with his pants down, recoiled in fright and tumbled over sideways. He rolled quickly onto all fours and pushed himself back up, inadvertently sticking his hand in his own shit, and then scrambled to pull up his soiled pants. He smiled at the man like a dead goat.

The man who stared back at him was as tall as a lamp post and half as wide. A thick handle bar mustache crossed his face like a squirrel tail bent at two right angles. The last of a cigarette hung out of his mouth. He scratched his head and pulled down his Nascar hat and wiped a sweat slick off his forehead. The man stared at Melech Rothschild as he put his hat back on. He spit a wad of chewing tobacco onto the dusty ground and rolled up his sleeve.

"Goddammit," he said and spit again. "Why are you shittin' on my tires?"

"I'm trying to get to Gillette," Melech said. "Can you help me?"

"Mister, there are a lot a different ways of catchin' a lift from a stranger. Don't reckon this one's the best. Say, is that a hubcap stuck in your head?"

Melech frowned. "I need to get to the hospital."

The man combed his mustache with his fingers. "There ain't a chance in hell I'm drivin' my shit-tired truck through town today. Don't ya know it's Sunday? 'Tis an offense to The Lord! Why the Good Lord Almighty would no doubt strike me down like everyone else in town."

Melech stared at him. "Has the pandemic been through the area already?" he asked, terrified by what the response might mean for his chances of finding a good doctor.

The stranger took a long drag from his cigarette. "Pandemic. Is that some sort of crockpot?"

Melech sighed. "The virus. Has it hit Gillette yet?"

"Oh!" the man said, now excited, "That! You bet it has! Whoa Nelly! People are dying left and right." Unbeknownst to Melech, Wilbur started pacing frantically nearby.

"Is the airport still running? What about the hospital?" he asked hopefully.

"Everything's shut down, Mister. Why it's as if the whole world has come to a standstill. Seems to me that everyone capable of taking care of things has died. I mean, there ain't even people to make food no more. We're in a whole mess 'a trouble."

Wilbur stopped pacing. He was staring at the stranger as if he were working out the meaning of the man's words. Wilbur blinked. And then, Wilbur's head exploded.

Chapter 15: Veryonica

"There she is!" Daryl said excitedly to Hashim. "What a marvel of human engineering and design!"

The jihadist's eyes widened in awe as the colossal breast-shaped baseball stadium came into view. Daryl pulled off AT&T Way and followed the signs toward stadium parking. "It's amazing," Hashim said, trying to imagine so many infidels packed together in one place.

"That there is Freedom Dome! *Welll* not officially. It's actually called the Global Hope Dome, whatever the fuck *that's* supposed to mean. Nevertheless, everyone knows it *stands* for freedom, and that's what's important." He turned into the parking lot. "Jesus Christ, look at all these people trying to park at the same time. Why some people don't arrive early is *beyond* me," he shook his head. "Look out for a parking spot, Roberto. Oh! There's the flag boy. Wave him down!"

"I think he's waiving *us* down," Hashim said.

"Good good," Daryl said, rolling down his window. "Get me somewhere close," he told the boy.

The flag boy sneered and waved him on and Daryl followed the orange-vested trail of surely flag boys until they found him a convenient spot 50 rows back from the stadium.

"Beautiful day," Daryl said, sucking in a lungful of air and closing the truck door behind him.

Hashim stepped out and gazed at the stadium. Nothing like this could exist in ExxonMobilastan. This was lavish, extravagant, unnecessary — yet somehow too, it was beautiful. The Americans took their freedoms more seriously than Hashim had thought.

"You got any currency?" Daryl asked.

Hashim reached into his pockets and pulled out twelve dollars.

"Close but no See-gar," Daryl said. He pulled a couple twenties out of his wallet and slapped them into Hashim's hand. "I like to sit in the corner box."

"Oh, I couldn't take all this..." he began.

"Take it 'er leave it. Can't be free without money," he winked. "Let's go. First pitch is comin' up."

Hashim stared at all the money in his hand. He didn't know what was more incredible - the fact that Daryl had given him enough money to survive in ExxonMobilastan for several months, or that it cost that much just to get inside the stadium. He stuffed the cash absently into his pocket and trotted behind Daryl like a little boy approaching the Disneyland ticket counter. He couldn't believe how lucky he was to watch an actual baseball game. Maybe he would get a hotdog with his leftover change! Hashim had never felt more excited to blow himself up.

He gawked at the endless lines of people pouring into the stadium entrances like streams meeting at a great river confluence. Men slapped each other on the backs and laughed. Women seemed to be carrying on about the same topics as the women back home, but these women were liberated and gorgeous. Everyone seemed to be in such a good mood, and if the circumstances had been a bit different, perhaps he could have called them all his friends.

Too bad he was planning on igniting a firestorm.

"Hey Hashim," Daryl said, stopping abruptly. "Didn't you have a briefcase with you?"

Hashim blinked. Next, he looked at his hands to see if they were empty. They were. "Yes, Daryl," he said slowly. "I left it in the back of your truck. I will go get that now."

"Well, I won't be goin' back with ya, game's about to start!" Daryl said. "I got a seat in the corner box. It's on the eastern lower middle-upper-deck by the hot dog stand ten pylons past the walkway division. You'll see me," he said and disappeared into the red, white, and blue colors of the Ranger fans.

Hashim jogged off. He couldn't *believe* he had forgotten to bring the nuclear weapon with him. A *real* terrorist would have brought the weapon of mass destruction to the stadium the first go around.

After five minutes of running Hashim stopped suddenly and surveyed the parking lot. They hadn't parked this far out, had they? He scanned the cars looking for the white pickup. *Every* vehicle was a white pickup. Desperately, he ran from one truck to the next in a frantic attempt to recoup the Mushroom Maker, searching, hoping, *begging* and praying to Allah to help him find it.

Nearly two hours had gone by when Hashim spotted an identical metallic briefcase being carried by a large black man walking towards the stadium. Hashim stalked the man silently from behind. The briefcase was definitely his. The man's face was devoid of emotion, like someone carrying out a job. Perhaps he had been hired…but by whom? The government? Another terrorist organization? A friend of Daryl's?

The questions sent him into a spiral of confusion. He knew he didn't have time to answer them. He had to act. Now! He dashed out from behind a Dodge F-150 and skidded to a stop in front of the *much* larger man. The man towered over him, but Hashim couldn't back down now. He squared off and stuck out his chest, almost like what an *actual* terrorist might have done.

"That's mine!" Hashim declared and pointed at the briefcase. "Give it back!"

The man eyed him suspiciously. "What do you know about it?"

"I know it was in the back of a white pickup," he said evenly, holding out his hand.

The man arched an eyebrow. "If it's yours then what's inside of it?"

Hashim tried to arch one eyebrow and nearly made himself sneeze. "That's none of your business."

"Actually, it is," the man said, and tugged at a name tag pinned to his red,white, and blue shirt.

"Reggie..." Hashim said, his voice trailing off. "Who do you work for?"

"Stadium parking security!" Reggie said. "I saw this sitting on the ground next to a pickup. Whatever's inside must be pretty nice because this is one expensive case. I'm taking it back to lost and found. But if you can tell me what's inside you can have it."

"It's...just a game," Hashim said carefully. "A kid's game. That's right."

"A kid's game?" the man asked doubtfully. "That must be some wealthy kid. Helluva box it comes in."

"It's for N-Nolan Ryan's kid," Hashim stuttered.

"Nolan Ryan? He's *here*?"

"You bet, partner," Hashim said, in his most practiced Mexican accent. "Ain't it great?"

"Wooow," Reggie said. "He's my hero! I can't believe we'll get to see him receive a game in a metal box today. So what kind of game is it?"

"Oh, it's just a little game with a couple of buttons and some valves and these tubey-looking things. And a clock. That runs backwards."

"Well, let's see!" Reggie exclaimed. He had always wanted to meet Nolan Ryan.

Hashim set the box down on the ground and cracked it open.

"*Woooow. Verrry* neat. His boy's gonna *love* it. So are *you* going to give it to Mr. Ryan?" he asked.

"Mmm hmm," he said and clicked the box closed. "At halftime."

Reggie stared. "There is no halftime in baseball."

"Oh. Of course not." Hashim scratched his arm nervously and as he did so the box clanged against the grill of another F-150. "OK then," he said, still backing away. "I must be going."

"Say..." the man said and held out his hand.

Allah have mercy. "Please..." Hashim whispered. "It's something I have to do. I must go. Before the game ends. I don't want to screw this up. It's for the entire nation of Islam. "

"You're not...you wouldn't...*mind* if I gave you a picture of my daughter to have Nolan sign would you?"

Hashim could scarcely breath. "You bet, partner." His accent could have been Chinese at this point it was so bad. He quickly snatched the picture and escaped from the star-struck Reggie.

The ticket line was nonexistent since it was already the bottom of the sixth inning. An older woman with orange hair looked disdainfully up at Hashim without lifting her glasses. Hashim nearly threw his money at her, grabbed his ticket, and dashed through the gates.

He was *inside*! He had made it! He was almost a real terrorist. His vibrating hands shook the briefcase with excitement. This was it. He could do it this very moment if he wanted to. He didn't need to be any place special — it was a nuclear bomb, for Allah's sake! It might destroy half the city! Perhaps first though, he should cultivate a bit more hatred for the blasphemous western ideologies and horrors of capitalism.

Hashim looked around. What a dump. Just concrete covered with the favorite red, white, and blue colors of the infidels. There wasn't even a place to water your camel. Surely, any devout follower of Islam would defecate on this terrible place before blowing themselves up here.

Suddenly, he heard a powerful noise. It was like an ocean wave of voices all crying out together in unison. It was powerful — it was incredible! Was it possible that Mecca was on tour, he wondered?

He walked slowly toward the opening and the blue sky came out like a beautiful curtain of eternal freedom. The voices rose again and the sunlight hit his face like a father's loving gaze. He looked out across the green baseball field and he watched as a wave of hands crawled through the crowd like a living organism. Now everyone around him exploded into a joyous frenzy, undoubtedly in celebration of their bountiful freedoms. They stood up and raised their hands to the sky and screamed and laughed and yelled, and Hashim had no choice but to join them in their bliss. They screamed and he screamed and now they were all laughing together like old friends reunited after lifetimes apart. His bouts of laughter had become as uncontrollable as his eye for the freely dressed infidel women.

"That was fun!" people were saying to one another. A stranger slapped Hashim on his back. "Wow!" he said, and Hashim grabbed the stranger by the shoulder and beamed back like the sun itself.

And then suddenly the wave was upon them again, and he shouted with glee towards the sky. The jubilant crowd towered behind him like a massive wall and Hashim nearly tumbled over looking up at them. Tears of joy were streaming down the sides of his face.

"Whoa!" someone screamed, and their collective shriek changed pitch.

"That's a hit!"

"Holy God!" someone yelled. "It's headed our way!"

"Look out, boys, this one's mine," a fat woman called and bounded down the narrow staircase.

Hashim looked out and saw a white object in the distance floating toward him. The crowd swelled like an ocean wave. Hands reached out to the sky as people clambered over one another, desperate to claim this strange object hurtling toward them at top speed as if it were a home run crack from Muhammed himself.

Hashim thought he was going to catch it when an enthusiastic Rangers fan crashed sideways into him, and together they tumbled down the narrow staircase with a dozen other infidels. Hashim found himself at the bottom of an avalanche of bodies. Everyone squirmed and cursed and laughed and eventually someone reached down and hoisted him up.

"Damn, partner. I think I got pushed into you. I spilt my beer, but I managed to save most of my fries. Like some?" he offered.

Hashim couldn't believe his luck. He *loved* the infidels' french fries. In his time in America he had become a connoisseur of these classic treats, which were far superior to the tasteless deep-fried camel strips found in ExxonMobilastan. McDonald's, Burger King, Wendy's, Carl's Junior, Arby's - Hashim knew them all well. It was a *private* passion, of course, for if anyone back home knew that he relished in sampling snacks from corporate America he would surely be castrated in public. But Hashim didn't care. Pure and simple, the infidels knew how to make some damn good fries.

He gobbled them up and soon thought to himself that a beer would sure hit the spot to wash them down. His religious beliefs did not permit him to drink alcohol, but he figured Allah would forgive him so long as he blew himself up shortly afterwards.

The beer garden was packed with men, and Hashim stepped to the back of the line and waited patiently for his turn. Afterward, he planned on finding Daryl and thanking him for his kindness. Daryl had given Hashim the opportunity of a lifetime — to not only see an American baseball game for the first time, but to also blow one up. Never in his wildest dreams had he imagined he would be standing in the center of Freedom Dome. He thought back to how the leaders of Al Kabob scorned American baseball, claiming that it was in direct contradiction to the values of the Arab world. But looking around, Hashim only saw people enjoying themselves — they didn't seem to be harming anyone.

"Fuck that guy!" a man standing next to Hashim barked up at one of the giant screens overhead. Hashim looked up to see an old pearly toothed white man smiling at the television camera. At the bottom of the screen it read, "Senator Guiles for President."

"Just another crooked politician," another man said.

"Trying to take away our freedoms!"

"Can't be much worse than President Alan," another person said.

"Are you *kidding* me? President Alan's the best we've had!"

"Bah! They're all wolves in sheep's clothing. Our forefathers would be rolling in their graves if they knew! Hopefully that virus makes its way to Washington and wipes them all off the face of the earth."

All this chatter confused Hashim. Back home he had been taught that the American people supported their leaders and their murderous policies. But standing here among them all it was evident that wasn't the case.

"Excuse me," he said politely to one of the men who had scorned the President. "Do you not like the American politicians?"

"I think I'd prefer a quick kick in the nuts than suffer through another four years of President Alan, or anyone else in the White House, for that matter. They don't give a damn about you or me, bud. All they care about is money and more of it. They say whatever we want to hear and then do the exact opposite. I'll tell ya, a revolution is brewing."

"A *revolution*?" Hashim said, his eyes wide with excitement. "Who is revolting?"

Another cheer from the fans erupted outside.

"All of us!" the man declared. "People are sick to death of all the corruption."

"Woohoo!" someone yelled. "Another single!"

"All those politicians do is take away our freedom."

"Yeah, when they ain't havin' sex with interns," another man added.

"Excuse me," Hashim said and stepped up to the bar.

Hashim looked at the TV. The image of the smiling politician had faded and in his place was a scrawny-looking white man standing in Pioneer Square. The caption read: Domestic Terrorist at Large.

"It's him..." Hashim said in awe.

The image was replaced by another photo of the same terrorist, now inside Caesar's Palace. Hundreds of headless bodies could be seen behind him. Hashim could not take his eyes off the man.

"Born and raised in the United States..." the reporter was saying.

"Now *that* is a freedom fighter," he said in wonder. It felt like he was experiencing his first crush all over again. Never before had he seen someone so efficient. Everywhere this man went he created chaos. Even more incredible was that he was not from another land but was making a stand against his own government. Just like Hashim, he was fighting for a cause. This man wasn't an infidel. He was a hero! And he was still on the run — it was incredible. More

132

destruction was surely on the way as long as David Dingle still had breath in his lungs. Perhaps the man would get a chance to convert to Islam before he took his own life — that way Hashim could meet him in heaven, sometime following the distribution of all the virgins.

His daydream was broken by a big man behind the counter. "What'll it be?" he asked Hashim.

"Uh, a beer," Hashim said. "Bud Light."

"You got it," the man said. Hashim looked back at the TV. He couldn't help but wonder how the domestic terrorist had done it. He must have had an incredible amount of support and financial backing. Or perhaps he was a genius, working on his own. Suddenly blowing up 50,000 screaming fans just didn't compare to unleashing a nationwide plague.

"That'll be eleven bucks," the barman said.

Hashim handed him the money and looked around. "So where's my beer?"

"Why I just gave it to you," the barman said. "I set it on the counter not ten-seconds ago."

The bar, however, was clearly empty, but in the distance a very small suspicious-looking individual in a green hoody was running in the opposite direction and carrying what looked to be a piss-colored drink.

"I think that's your beer!" the barman said. "Hey! Get back here!"

Hashim had learned after a lifetime in ExxonMobilastan that telling a thief to "get back here" was about as effective as telling a humping dog to heel. If you wanted what they stole from you, you better get it yourself. Most of his young life had been spent in the marketplace and Hashim was adept at making his way through large groups of people. The fleeing individual, however, was fast. Hashim rounded a corner and scanned the crowd. Across the way he saw the thief swipe a deck of cards off a carousal and pause to examine them.

"Hey!" Hashim yelled.

The thief looked up. He was wearing dark sun glasses and a cap underneath the hoodie of a large green parka. Spotting Hashim, the thief fled up the stairwell. Hashim realized he could have let the whole matter go. He could have let the thief run away and out of sight. He didn't even *want* the beer that badly. But it was the *principle* of the matter. Someone had taken something that had belonged to him. It was like those politicians taking away the infidels' freedoms. *They* weren't going to stand for it, and neither was *he*.

He chased the thief up three flights of stairs until there was nowhere higher to go. He trailed quietly behind. Hashim wanted to watch the person unnoticed, give him a false sense of security before he *pounced* like the competent terrorist that had to be *somewhere* inside of him. Maybe the moment after he confronted the individual he would herald the victory by blowing up the stadium. *That* would sure show the thief.

The thief finally slowed down when he arrived at the upper level of the stadium. He was looking around now, making sure that he hadn't been followed. Hashim hid behind a stadium post and watched as the individual sipped on Hashim's beer. He stared in amazement as the sip became a gulp and the gulp became a chug. Within seconds, the beer was gone. The man opened his parka and a shopping cart's worth of items fell to his feet. He snatched up a 24 oz. Red Bull and sucked it down. Picking up another, he repeated. Next, the criminal pulled out the deck of cards he had stolen and began pulling them out randomly one by one and tossing them to the air. Finally, the man pulled out a card which seemed to please him. He held the card in front of his face and even though the man's face was almost completely covered, the seriousness of the draw was palpable. Slowly, the man approached the edge of the balcony and swung one leg over the rail. He was going to jump!

"Wait!" Hashim yelled and emerged from his hiding spot. "Don't do it!"

The man turned and spotted Hashim walking toward him. Hashim expected the thief to threaten him, or cry out, or beg for help. Instead, unexpectedly, the thief smiled. In his right hand was an empty can of Red Bull, which the thief released and watched its fall.

"What are you *doing*?" Hashim asked. "Are you crazy?"

The thief shook his head and smiled. "Can't go back on a bet," he said, though the man's voice sounded funny to Hashim.

"What *bet*?" he asked.

The man held up a jack of spades between his fingers. "It just wouldn't be as fun if I didn't follow through. Are you here to save me?" The thief reached up and lowered the sunglasses and looked at Hashim. The clearest, most beautiful blue eyes Hashim had ever seen stared back at him with visceral excitement. The thief's hand reached up and pulled back the hood of the parka and swiped the black cap off and a bundle of gorgeous long blonde hair shook loose. This was not a man at all. It was a woman — and *boy* what a woman!

She pulled off the heavy parka and let it drop to her feet. She was short but slender and she had the biggest, most patriotic tits Hashim had ever laid eyes on. He could scarcely breathe. This had to be the most beautiful infidel in all of Texas. His hands were so slick with sweat he nearly dropped his nuclear warhead.

"I...can...save you," he stammered.

"Oh yeah?" she asked, her eyes still brimming with excitement and Red Bull.

"Sure," he said and carefully sidestepped over in her direction. He set the briefcase on the ground and reached out for her hand.

She backed away. "I'll do it," she warned. "I swear, I'll do it."

"But why?" he asked.

She shrugged. "Sometimes I get impulsive. Besides, it might be fun."

"Killing yourself is not supposed to be fun, unless you're doing it for a cause."

"Hmm," she said. "I like the sound of that. I could get behind a cause. You got any in mind?"

He thought about it. "How about saving millions of people from the perils of the western world?"

She looked at him. "That could be interesting, I guess. What kind of perils are you talking about?"

"Well," he flubbed, frantically scrolling through his ideologies — he was never any good on the spot. "Coca-cola, the internet, infidelity, debauchery. American Idol, maybe."

"Infidelity!" her eyes gleamed. "Now *that's* exciting. Imagine getting caught having sex with the wife of a serial killer! Or, ooh, the owner of an underground dog fighting ring, but that's more like debauchery," she said thoughtfully. "So how would you go about fighting for this cause you're talkin' about?" Her eyes penetrated into his. *Allah* she was beautiful.

Hashim shook the temptations out of his head. "Well," he hesitated. "A nuclear bomb could work."

"Yeah, but where's anyone going to get a *nuclear bomb*?" she waved her hand.

His eyes inadvertently flashed to the metal case on the ground and the woman's eyes widened with curiosity. "Are you saying, do you mean to tell me...are you a jihadist?"

Hashim nodded.

Her mouth dropped. "I didn't know Mexicans were jihadists."

"I'm from ExxonMobilastan."

The woman rolled her eyes. "Honey, I don't care *where* you're from!" In one motion she flipped her leg back over the railing and charged at Hashim. His instincts told him that she was going to tackle him and pin him to the ground while dozens of armed men subdued him and took him to prison. That, however, is not at all what happened. Instead of tackling him, this beautiful and clearly insane woman, leapt onto Hashim like a cat, wrapped her legs around his waist, and began kissing every inch of his exposed flesh. Her hands were pawing at his face. Her tongue was down his throat. Her body convulsed against his like a snake in heat.

Hashim had no choice but to take it.

After several moments of primal bliss, the woman lowered herself from

Hashim and stood up. Wiping her mouth with the back of her wrist she smiled. "Sorry, I do that sometimes. Name's Veryonica. It's like a switch-up from Veronica," she shrugged. "And you are?"

"Ha-shim," he struggled to say.

"Can I see it?" she asked.

He stared at her. "Well, we just met. Where I come from, women and men don't even *touch* each other until after many dates. But all things considered," he said, and began to unzip his pants.

Veryonica laughed. "No no. Not that. I want to see the motherfucking nuclear bomb you say you have."

"Oh, that," he said, and fixed his pants. He looked her up and down and then he did it again for good measure. "I will show you," he said carefully, "but you must promise not to tell a soul. Otherwise, I will have to blow you up."

Veryonica's eyelids fluttered with ecstasy.

Hashim knelt down and laid the case flat on the ground. He gave Veryonica one last serious look. He had to be certain that he could trust her. He conferred with his dick which told him that he could *definitely* trust her.

He opened the case.

"Oh my Gawd, I think I just had an orgasm," Veryonica said and squeezed Hashim's shoulder like a vice. "That's real, isn't it?"

"You better believe it," he said proudly.

"Yep, I just totally had an orgasm," she confirmed. "You are like, the *hottest* terrorist I have ever met. Take off your pants."

"What? Why?" he asked with a mixture of excitement and horror.

"Because you and me are going to have sex on-top of this nuclear bomb."

"We are?" His teeth were chattering.

"You heard me," she ordered. "And when we're done, I'm going to show you what a *real* jihad looks like."

Chapter 16: Freedom's Fall

President Alan tossed his empty Dr. Pepper can angrily into the waste bin. He was supposed to speak in front of the entire House in ten minutes and he hadn't prepared a single word. Melech was *supposed* to be here yesterday. Benjamin had tried calling him, emailing him, sending video files of himself begging for help — *everything*. Goddamit, if there were a reliable smoke signal he would have used it by now.

"Good evening, Mr. President," a snake-like voice said from over his shoulder.

Benjamin Alan scrunched his face into an uncomfortable smile when he saw Senator Guiles. "Mitchell," he said as a child might say the word cauliflower.

"I trust you've got a good game plan ready to share with everyone. Lots of worried people out there. Our nation is under attack, after all. You heard about the cases this afternoon on the south end of town, I trust?"

Alan's face scrunched up even tighter. "Yes, yes. Of course. We are in the process of shutting down the city."

"In the process?" Senator Guiles said. "You mean you haven't done so already?"

"No, Mitchell, not me *personally*, no. I did not go to South D.C. and help people string up tape across the roads."

"You told people to use *tape?*" Mitchell asked.

Alan unscrunched his face and grabbed handfuls of Senator Guile's shirt with both of his hands. "Now you listen here, you *twerp*. I don't need your *shit* right now. This is the biggest disaster in the history of disasters, OK? My administration is doing everything it possibly can."

Senator Guiles held up his hands in defense, but a wide smirk was scrawled across his face like a last-minute rider on an appropriation bill. "Easy, Ben, *easy*. No need to get riled up so much," he said and pulled the President's hands from his shirt. The senator brushed himself off. "I fear this whole pandemic is stressing you out and you're taking some missteps. It's understandable, Ben. Like the time you tripped over the flag pole at the Congressional Country Club and ruined your chance for par. It was inevitable."

"That was an *accident*," Alan hissed. "But when I'm in the Oval Office, there *are* no accidents. I have all the control in the world."

Senator Guiles winked. "Of course you do, Ben, of course you do. And even if you don't, you have all the help you need. Why you've hand-picked some of the most brilliant men in America to be your advisors. That reminds me, I just overheard your Secretary of Defense talking about bombing hospitals."

"What? Why?"

"To kill the virus, apparently. Yep, all the brightest minds our country has to offer. Still, it will take an army of men to clean up this mess. But don't worry about it. I'll take care of whatever's left when *I'm* President."

"You're not gonna *be* President, *Mitchell*. You're lucky if you're even gonna be a *Senator* much longer what with the Linoleum Scandal."

Mitchell rolled his eyes. "I'd say there are far bigger things to worry about than some silly intern on her knees sucking someone's cock for crack cocaine."

"That was *your* cock, Senator."

He tilted his head playfully. "Sure, but the crack cocaine was a gift from a friend." Guiles took a step back. "You really need to relax. They'll kill you out there," he pointed with his thumb. "Senators and Congressmen are smarter than you think. Chances are they'll sense your incompetence if you don't cover it up. You need a drink or something?" he said, and pulled out a small glass bottle of Whiskey.

Suddenly all the sounds in all the halls of Washington became silent as President Benjamin Alan eyed the half-full fifth of whiskey in the Senator's hand. It had been years since he had taken a drink. Thirteen, to be exact. Thirteen years and eleven weeks and four days. Of not drinking. A drop. Of anything. Besides Dr. Pepper.

"Give me that!" he said and yanked the bottle out of Mitchell's hand. He pulled off the cap and took a good eight-second pull.

"Wowza!" Mitchell whooped.

President Alan flicked the lid with his thumb and caught it on the head of the bottle.

"Impressive."

"It's a trick my second wife taught me," he grinned modestly. "Oh hey, your shoe's untied," he said to Senator Guiles.

The Senator looked down and scowled. "I'm sure an intern can help me with that. I can never remember which way the rabbit goes round the tree."

"Me either," the President admitted. "Now go sit down. I'll hold onto this bottle for you." Guiles gave a smile and sauntered into the House of Representatives. President Alan pulled out his phone, pushed a button, and waited.

"Hello?"

"Agent Boring?" Benjamin Alan asked. "This is the President of the United States."

A brief pause on the other end. "Oh, hey! Is this Ben Alan? What's up, man? How you doin'? Hang on a sec. Let me turn down this radio. I been

138

listening to 50-Cent since Texas. What's up!?"

The President gritted his teeth. "Agent Boring, don't *ever* call me Ben again. My name is President Alan."

"Yeah, sure thing. You're gonna have to get to the point, bud. I just saw a sign for a tunnel. Is this important or did you just wanna talk?"

Alan turned and cupped his hand over the phone and his mouth. "What's the status on our domestic terrorist?"

"Status is good, Sir. I'm tailing him right now. This guy's not going to get away. You wouldn't *believe* what he's driving. You like tits, Sir?"

"Tits?"

"Yeah, *tits!* I'm only asking because there's about ten of 'em painted on his getaway vehicle."

"Why aren't you pulling him over!" the President hissed into the phone.

"Well, that's what *Fleckle* wanted to do," Boring said. Fleckle, who was sitting in the passenger seat, ignored him and thumbed through his phone. "But I figured it would be a lot more useful if Dingle guided us to his terrorist lair and we caught all of them at once."

"His lair? Where's that?" the President asked. He rather liked the idea of catching a whole group of terrorists at once. It was good PR.

"Arkansas, Sir."

"Arkansas?"

"Yes, Sir. I'm tapped into Mr. Dingle's phone right now. I can hear everything they're saying. I'm actually really surprised he hasn't thrown it away yet. In fact, he's still using it to post to Pinterest and Facebook. He's claiming he's innocent. But I'm thinkin', if he's so innocent then why's he headed to Mackanack, Arkansas to, and I quote, 'bunker down for a while?'"

The President didn't have time to think about it. "Listen, Boring. You bring me this David Dingle alive. He's the key to our re-election. If we don't bring him in, you're not comin' with me for a second term. I'll tell you what. You bring me David Dingle, and I'll make you my running mate in 2022."

"You can *do* that, Sir?"

"I can do anything, Boring. I'm the leader of the free world, for crying out loud. You get me what I want and I'll take care of the rest."

President Alan clicked the phone off. Immediately it rang again. Had the POTUS not been four shots of whiskey deep, he would have dropped it in surprise.

"Mr. President, it's Melech."

"*Melech!*" Benjamin ejaculated. "Thank *God*! Where *are* you? You were supposed to be here years ago."

"I'm standing in a cornfield under a cell phone tower in Elm Creek,

Nebraska. I told my driver that I had to urinate. Sir, the virus is much *much* more virulent than we initially expected. People who should not be susceptible are dying. It has begun attacking people *under* the specific target."

"What kind of target?" Benjamin asked. He pulled out a notepad and began jotting down notes.

"Intelligence, Mr. President. The virus targets individuals within a specific range on the intelligence quotient spectrum. An individual's placement on this spectrum can vary and fluctuate over time, even after a single conversation. At the onset, the virus attacked only the very intelligent, but it has evolved quicker than expected. My guess is that there weren't enough intelligent hosts to keep it alive long enough to pass it on. It's mutated."

There was an unsurprising hesitation on the other end. "So...I don't understand," the President said.

"Exactly, Sir."

Benjamin Alan studied the screen. "What do you mean?"

Melech paused. "I mean that you and most people in our nation's capitol will be just fine."

"Oh," the President said, and stole a sip of whiskey. "Well, that's good news."

"The rest of the nation will need your help, however. This virus has swept through the country like a wildfire, but it is unlikely that it has affected everyone. Many people are still in hiding, but when they come out looking for food and water they could likely still become infected. We have to prevent that."

"But how?" he asked.

"President Alan, for a limited time, we are going to have to take more freedoms away from a lot of good Americans."

"F-freedom?" President Alan stuttered, unaware that he had dropped the bottle of whiskey. "But why?"

"Because unless we get a handle on this situation everything that our nation stands for will come undone. It is *imperative* that Americans unlearn everything they know. It is the only way to keep them safe."

"But, Melech! People aren't going to want to unlearn everything. Do you have any idea how many hours the average American spends every day learning about cats on Youtube? Why they'll never accept it! Whoever you've got lined up to deliver this news is going to get eaten alive."

"*You* will have to do this, President Alan."

President Alan was shaking the hand of some congressman whose name he had forgotten. "I'm sorry, Melech. Did you just say I will have to learn more about cats?"

"We must give the public more credit, Mr. President. They know the price of freedom all too well, and they won't give up easily. They have fought for it since the inception of this great nation. Freedom is a powerful thing, Mr. President," Melech said in a calm and confident tone. "Perhaps, it is the greatest idea known to man. We fight for it and we die for it. Yet its paradoxes confuse us. How can something so wonderful make us so vulnerable? How can we ever be free without sacrifice? These are the questions you must answer if our nation is ever to move forward into the night. Though the path ahead is not easy, I believe it shall be our finest hour. If we are forced to sacrifice a few of our abundant freedoms for the good of the whole, well then dammit, I consider it an honor to serve my nation any way I can."

President Alan had tears in his eyes. "That was the most beautiful speech I've ever heard, Melech. Even better than the one I gave at the AIDS conference in Geneva about needing more clowns in hospitals. Just tell me what to do and I'll do it."

"I'm sending a list of points to you right now through my phone. There are some very important things to consider. Look at them carefully. Some of them will be confusing to you, which is understandable, considering your...situation. Right now we have a lot of priorities, but our top one is to shut down all forms of commerce."

"But won't that kill the economy?" Alan asked.

"You let me worry about that, Ben. The American public must learn how to handle crisis situations without stocking their shelves with pop-tarts. People don't know what's good for them anymore. They've been brainwashed by corporate media. We must convince them that the government has their best interests in mind and will take care of their needs. These new needs and protocols are outlined for you, Mr. President. You'll have to give a detailed explanation of each one during your Presidential announcement."

"But I'm supposed to speak in 90 seconds!" he shouted.

"Well, then get off the phone! Read the headers and learn what you can. Ad-lib the rest. You know the routine. Bottom line, we're headed into Martial Law and you have to make it sound nice."

He brushed his hair and felt the alcohol coursing through his blood. "OK. Thank you, Melech. *Hic* I'll do my best."

"And Sir? You may want to put out a National Manhunt for a short Mexican with a Tijuana hat carrying a nuclear bomb in a metallic briefcase." *Click.*

President Alan stared at his phone.

"Ladies and Gentlemen, I give you, the President of the United States of America, Benjamin Alan!" a strong and fatherly voice boomed over the loudspeaker.

President Alan stumbled backwards over the whiskey bottle that had been dropped on the floor. Two secret service men sandwiched him and escorted the President down the hallway as he frantically thumbed through his phone searching for the document Melech had sent. If Benjamin Alan weren't so drunk he would have been terrified. He was about to give perhaps the most important speech of his career, none of which he had yet read, about a plan to implement Martial Law as a favor to the American public. Not to mention the upcoming struggle with the Mexican Mafia. Maybe a taco day in the White House would help rally support?

The harsh lights hit him square in the face and for a moment he wondered if he could go through with this. For an instant it was so quiet one could hear a pin drop. Was there even an audience to address? Had everyone become infected already? Cold terror was climbing up his spine and he knew it had the power to paralyze him, but suddenly he heard that familiar, absolute applause and every single one of his doubts melted away. Alan raised his hand like an old cowboy and gave his signature nod (one eyebrow halfway up, the other halfway down) and he stepped up to the podium. President Alan set his phone in front of him and looked through his files to pull up the one Melech had sent him. Oh, look! His aunt just posted a nice photo of herself on the beach in the Hamptons.

Someone coughed. President Benjamin Alan looked up. "Holy shit!" he thought to himself. The House of Representatives was *packed*. Melech was right. It was as if all the elected officials were somehow immune to the virus.

Aha! There it was! With a nod of renewed confidence, Benjamin Alan adjusted the microphone. "Gentlemen and Lady," he said, acknowledging the Oregon Senator. "We are officially moving into uncharted territory. Not since the great days of Abraham Lincoln were we at such a crossroads. Our industry, our economy, and *dammit*, our voters are suffering out there." He shook his head sadly for effect. "I think the time has finally come to act in the best interest of the American public." He looked out. "We put it off for as long as we could. It was a good run, boys, a mighty good run." Everyone turned to each other and nodded in agreement.

"Now, I imagine a lot of you are wanting some answers, a plan of some kind for this nation during this great time of distress. Well, let me assure you that I've given it a tremendous amount of thought and consideration." He looked down at the phone and read the first few lines. "Whoa!" he shouted accidentally. Melech wasn't pulling any punches. This was serious stuff. Martial Law, NSA surveillance, the abolishment of both freedom of speech as well as the right to assemble. The list just went on.

"Whoa," he said again, this time more calmly in an effort to recoup his blunder. "Whoa, whoa, whoa...what a pandemic it's been, eh? The West Coast is in shambles, people's heads have been blowing up, most of us haven't even had lunch today, I'm sure. Trying times, indeed." He shook his head an extra couple of times for good measure.

"On a more positive note," he said cheerfully, "I'm really glad you all could make it. It feels *good* getting together like this, doesn't it? It's a pity we only do this when everything we hold dear is at stake. Hey, Marty and Geoff!" he said, pointing at the senators from Georgia and Alabama. "When was the last time we went golfing?"

"A few weeks ago," Senator Snood said.

"It's been too long," President Alan agreed. "I almost think we should just regroup at the clubhouse. What do you all say?"

There was a general murmur of approval among the Senators.

Senator Smackenstock hollered from the back. "I suspect it would be difficult to get a tee-time for all five hundred of us on such short notice,"

"True, that's a good point," Alan said. "Next time, then. Well," he shrugged, "why don't we get on with it since we're all here." He looked at the phone again and hiccuped inadvertently, sending a wave of whiskey particles that could be smelled by the Speaker of the House.

"I'm just gonna give it to you straight because I'm a straight shooter," he said, slurring his S's. "I'm gonna tell ya right away that most of you probably aren't gonna like what I'm about to say. There are some big changes that must be implemented if we're gonna get out of this mess by re-elections. Now some of this may come across as both confusing and frustrating. You might feel it within yourself to rebel, or even worse, ask questions. Before any of that happens though, I'd just like to remind you all that being the President in a time of national emergency is kind of a big deal. Basically, I'm a lot like a drug lord," he said, slurring his s's again. "So whatever I say, *goes*, got it? Now seeing as how I've been working on this with my entire cabinet, I can only take most of the credit and not all of it. OK. So let's get going.

"Number one!" he said, raising his finger into the air. Benjamin kind of felt like Dave from the movie *Dave*. It was like he was trying out a new script for the first time. It reminded him of his first few years as Governor. "Due to all the chaos, I have decided to implement Martial Law. Obviously, kind of a given, considering the situation, I'd say. I know you might find that expression alarming, but don't worry, it's gonna be good." He smiled, feeling good about that explanation, and looked back at his phone.

"OoooK. Number Two. National Surveillance. Now this is something I didn't initially agree with until I understood it a bit better. At first I thought it was all about spying on people, but now I try to think of it more like listening in on conversations without people knowing about it. Why is this necessary? Well, I'm glad you didn't ask. But luckily I have answers of which I'm capable of explaining in detail. Just a moment." He squinted at the text. "Why'd Melech have to use such a small font?" he mumbled.

"All right. So this virus, Virus Eighty-Four, is known by that name because that is the highest survival quotient. Hmm. I wonder what quotient means. Let's see…Eighty-Four attacks particular hosts with a particular intelligence quotient, (dang there's that word again) causing an imbalance in the frontal lobe which leads to death." He looked up. "I think maybe that's a reference to the exploding head thing."

"What does that *mean*?" Senator Goblesfroth yelled.

"Hold on. I'm getting to it. It means," he read, "that the virus is infecting people with an IQ...over 84."

Now there was a chatter in the House! Representatives and cabinet members rabbled and bullied about — not because they understood that the only reason that they were alive was because they were too stupid for the virus to kill them, but because they were trying to come up with ways to keep the population dumb enough to survive.

"Why we'll have to listen in on every conversation in the country just to make sure no one is getting too smart!" Senator Monsanto said.

"We should be allowed to interrupt them mid-sentence so we can warn them," Congressman Bigglesbum hollered. "I'm sure many of them would feel grateful that their congressmen cared so much."

"It's not enough!" Representative Pipdick said. "Monitoring their conversations is only the beginning. We must do everything in our power to keep the public at a safe intelligence level."

"There must be more access to reality television and Fox News!" someone yelled.

"We could spray the people's food with pesticides!"

"How about putting fluoride in the water supply?"

The President shook his head. "Sadly, all of those plans are already in place. What we need is something much more drastic."

"The internet!" the governor of Alabama said. "The internet must be abolished. It is spreading far too much information. The public will not be safe for as long as it remains!"

"What about porn?" the Nevada governor asked.

"Well, we'd keep porn, of course," the governor of Alabama concluded.

"I'll see what I can do," the President announced. "I like porn, too. But the internet and porn are aspects of commerce, which, I am afraid, must be suspended for the time being."

"What!" everyone shouted at once.

"Now hold on," he said carefully. "I know this sounds drastic, but drastic times call for drastic things. Americans have become accustomed to being able to buy whatever it is they want at whatever time they want it. Right now people are buying pop tarts and gun magazines when they should be supporting our campaigns! People don't know what is best for them which is why we have to fire a warning shot in the direction of common sense."

"But commerce is the lifeblood of this nation!" Senator McNibbins said. "Without it we'd be like communist China."

"But it's *boring* without eBay," Senator Macinstock said.

"I understand," President Alan lied, wondering where eBay was. "But this is something that I've given a lot of thought to. We all know just how important the economy is. Without it we probably wouldn't even be alive. Now I'm not saying, 'Let's kill the economy.' I'm just saying that we have to stop commerce until we get this pandemic thing figured out and corrected."

"But why??" they asked.

He stared at them. Frankly, President Alan didn't have a fucking clue. He had no idea why Melech had decided that all commerce should be halted. Maybe it had something to do with Martial Law. Maybe it was to keep people from buying books and accidentally getting their heads blown up. Regardless, he had been given an order to get this message across. It was imperative that he get these men on his side. Without them he wouldn't have the support of Washington. A captain was only as good as his crew and right now his crew needed an explanation.

President Alan looked at the audience carefully. "Because I said so."

Now people were shouting and yelling. It was as if the roof were coming unhinged. Pretty soon people were going to start throwing shoes at him. Ben Alan turned around to the Vice President with a look of panic.

"Help," he whispered.

Vice President Palmdonger stood. "Don't worry, Mr. President. I've got your back." The Vice President stepped up to the podium and carefully took the microphone. "Without a shell, a turtle is just a lizard..."

Chapter 17: The Flood

"Welp, that settles it," Jerry said, stepping back onto the bus. "The virus is definitely following us."

"How can you tell?" David asked and pushed the app on his phone and the bus rolled to a start again.

"Because another gas station attendant's head just blew up."

"That's terrible!" David moaned.

"Tell me about it," Jerry said, wiping a dab of brain-goo off his shoulder. "Luckily most of these red stains are from last month's spaghetti night."

"We must be careful," Dr. Whyzer said. "The whole nation is likely infected. Strange that none of us have contracted the virus. In my case I suspect it's likely thanks to my steady prescription of preventative medication."

"I'd agree, Doc," Jerry said. "I've taken three pills and have never felt better. Best meds I've taken in weeks!"

"Jerry, if everyone's infected, you can't go around hugging people," Courtney said.

"Well, maybe it would be a less violent world if more people were open to hugging," Jerry shrugged and stepped forward, preparing to hug Courtney.

She shifted her weight and crossed her arms. "You put us all in danger when you do that," she said.

"Hey, I thought that construction worker was using that hardhat like a gas mask for his head." He shook his head remorsefully. "Fella sure didn't like the back-rub I tried to give him."

"Maybe David's the reason we're all immune," Courtney said.

"Me? Really?"

"Sure. Maybe you're like, reverse infected or something. Maybe everyone you get in contact with stays healthy. Just look at all of us!"

David thought about this new idea carefully. Maybe she was right. Maybe *he* should be the one hugging people instead of Jerry.

"I still think it's the drugs," Jerry said.

Alma stood up. She hadn't said a word since she had gotten on the bus, but David had observed her spiking anxiety. "Do you really think that you're going to escape the Lord's wrath by taking narcotics?" she accused Jerry.

"Now Alma," Jacob Timpson said and began to gently rub her arm with his fingers. "Be still."

"I will *not* be still," she said and jerked her arm away. "I've *been* still. At first I thought we were on a one-way bus to heaven, but the more I listen to this heathen talk the more I begin to realize that we have been led into the devil's chambers."

"What tipped you off?" Jerry asked. "It was the titties on the side of the bus, wasn't it?"

Alma opened her mouth and gasped.

"Good Sir!" Jacob said. "I will not allow you to say such things to my wife."

"Which one?" Dr. Whyzer asked and buried his chuckles in Jerry's shoulder.

"Alma's right," Neleh said and stepped forward. "We've been in the back of this darn bus for hours now listening to these outsiders cuss and talk about such terrible things like drugs and sex and aliens-"

"I swear I saw one back there!" Jerry said.

"That was a homeless man!" she yelled.

"Women, women," Jacob started.

"Don't you women us," Sarah said snidely. "I agree. A real man would have done something by now. He would have at least said something. A real man would certainly not just sit in the back of the bus on this crude velvet thingamajig shaped like a woman's...waiting for Beelzebub to...smack him in the...*sex* organ!" she exclaimed, looking away from the dildo rack.

"Beelzebub?" Dr. Whyzer asked.

Jerry nudged Dr. Whyzer. "Man, I'm starting to think five wives isn't all that it's cracked up to be."

"Been married three times. Thank God it wasn't all at once," Whyzer whispered.

"Mama, mama," little Noah said. "What's a titty?"

Sariha widened her eyes in embarrassment. "A titty is a little bit," she lied.

"No it's not. *This* is a titty!" Jeremiah said and pulled up his shirt and pinched his nipple.

"Jeremiah!" Sarah screamed. "Just what on earth do you think you are doing?"

"One of the girls was doing it in this doctor's magazine."

"I warned you the kid was lookin' over your shoulder," Jerry said, shaking his head at Whyzer.

"Kid's gotta learn sometime," Whyzer shrugged.

Jacob sighed. Even David could hear it all the way up front. David felt bad for the man with 5 wives and 12 children. No one should have to live such a burdened life. He asked Courtney to watch the driving app while he walked to the back of the bus.

"Is everything all right?" he asked warmly.

Jacob froze. He had been avoiding this conversation for fear the Lord Jesus might strike him down in judgement. He knew he was unworthy.

"Y-yes," he stammered.

"Good," David nodded. "I'm sorry we haven't been exactly cordial since you got on. This virus has really shaken everyone up. I haven't even introduced myself. My name is-"

"I know who you are," Jacob said quietly.

David rolled his eyes. "Oh. Of course you do. Yeah, I guess everyone knows me by now. My face is everywhere."

"It sure is," Jacob smiled shyly. "It's in my home, my church. Why it's even at the diner I go to."

"Wow," David said, amazed. "Word travels fast. Of course I guess every place has a TV these days." He looked out the window at the world passing by and echoed Jacob's sigh. "It wasn't supposed to be like this. I was just showing up to do my job. I'm not anyone special. I'm not who they're looking for."

Jacob's eyes widened in amazement. "You're who *everyone* is looking for. People *need* you more than you realize. But who am I to tell you that, Master?"

David gave him a funny look. "I suppose you're right, Jacob. They won't stop looking for me until they find me."

"And why should they?" Jacob asked. "The world is in such a sorry state of affairs. Man's greed and pride and belief in evolution have taken our planet to the edge of oblivion. There was a time when all this could have changed, when everything could have been saved. But I think it's too late at this point," Jacob said and shook his head sadly.

"You think so?" David asked.

"Why else would you be where you are today?"

David looked up at the ceiling. "Maybe you're right. I took the job because I believed that it would allow me to do something meaningful in the world. There's so much poverty, and war, and destruction of the natural world — it just doesn't seem like anyone cares, otherwise they'd do something about it, wouldn't they?"

"People are too focused on what's in front of them to look at the big picture," Jacob said. "I'm a big picture man, myself. It's why I get in front of my people every week. It's important for me to share my knowledge. Don't worry, Master. I work for the same Man you do."

"Really?" David asked in amazement. "Wow, I didn't realize the Division had offices in Southern Utah. Maybe you could help me then."

"You need *my* help?" Jacob asked, stepping back in shock.

"I'm not going to lie," David said. "What I'm about to ask of you is very

148

dangerous."

Jacob turned and looked at his wives.

"Well Peter, Paul, and Mary! Don't just stand there," Alma said. "You've been waiting for this moment your whole life!"

Jacob sucked in a chestful of air. Beads of sweat had gathered on his forehead. His hands had become clammy. "Working for The Master has been a path of mine for many years now. I've done the work with my voice but never with my hands. Do you want me to slay an army of Mennonites? Are you asking me to swim across the Red Sea? Because if you are I'll do it!" he cried.

"I want you to look at a manilla envelope," David said.

Jacob slouched. "Oh. Well, I could do that too, I'm pretty sure," he said with obvious disappointment.

David grinned and dashed up to the front of the bus and returned with the folder. He stared at Jacob with eyes of steel. "I need you to read what's inside. And then...I need you to explain it to me."

Jacob's slouch deepened. "That's it?" he asked.

"It's like phonics practice, Daddy!" Ishmael shouted with a big smile.

"Think you can handle it?" David asked.

Jacob paused. "I can still battle the armies of Gomorrah when I'm done if you need me to." But David just held out the folder. It looked to Jacob like he was holding a dead rat teeming with the hantavirus.

Jacob took the folder and opened it.

"Be careful!" David warned. "Whatever it says inside could change everything about you. It could change everything about everything." David studied him closely while casually moving a titty flier between himself and Jacob just in case the bishop's head exploded. Jacob's eyes widened as he scanned the document. Invisible words formed on his lips. David winced. It was about to happen. This poor bastard was about to...

Jacob burped unexpectedly. "I have no idea what this says," he said.

David's shoulder slumped and he fell back into a soft velvety bean bag shaped like a vagina.

Jacob was mortified. He had failed his Lord Jesus Christ. Now his entire family would be left with the rest of the sinners to appreciate the true horrors of Satan. "Oh, Master! I have failed you. I am so sorry!" He threw himself onto his knees and bowed his head and raised his arms up and down, over and over. "Judge my soul for I am wicked as are the women. But spare the children, Master, spare the children!"

"Hey!" Sarah and Alma yelled.

"Whoa whoa!" David said in alarm. "What the heck are you doing? Get up, man, get up!"

"But Master, I have been unable to serve you. Now I am doomed to the fiery pits of hell. Please, *please* forgive me!"

"Why do you keep calling him Master?" Dr. Whyzer asked.

"Well, why do you think?" Neleh replied.

Jerry shot a look at everyone. "Oh my God. I think I know what's going on," he said and stood up next to David and Dr. Whyzer.

"What? What is it?" Dr. Whyzer asked.

Jerry leaned into David and whispered into his ear. "They think they're *black*!"

"Ho-Lee-Shit!" Dr. Whyzer proclaimed.

"Of *course*!" Trish said. "That totally explains the weird clothes."

"Are you kidding me?" Jerry asked. "That explains *everything*. It's all so clear now. These poor bastards just escaped from a Neo-Nazi Fraternity rush. They've been brainwashed!"

"What?" David asked. "No way!"

"Totally," Jerry said with absolute certainty.

"How would you know? You've never even *been* in college," David said.

"No, but I've been *to* colleges," he retorted. "I used to walk around the Delta houses on Friday nights in Seattle," he grinned. "Those kids are into some craaazy shit, man. I went to this one party where they all thought they were made of asexual metallic bodies. Lot of LSD, I think. Fun party."

David was dumbfounded. Jerry was much more versed in these things than he was. Who knows, maybe he was right! Maybe these people *did* think they were black. He stared at the prostrated Jacob.

"OK, OK, get up, get up," he told him.

Jacob looked up with one eye. "You have forgiven me, Master?" he asked.

"Careful," Jerry warned. "Try to break the spell too quick and their brains will melt. You'll never get 'em back. Best to play along."

Well, that didn't give David much choice. "I forgive you, Jacob. Now why don't you and the rest of your darky family take a break from the cotton fields. It's been a long ride in this here chariot. Master is going to go back up front and drink some lemonade and think about tobacco."

Jacob leaned back and looked at David. "I'm sorry I could not understand the paper, Lord Master."

"So am I, son, so am I," David said. He looked at Jerry who nodded supportively. The two of them walked to the front of the bus.

"They OK?" Courtney asked.

"I don't know," David said, and sat down in the driver's seat. "Maybe I should have set them free."

"They'll be fine," Jerry said. "I once thought I was a totem pole for nearly a week. We'll stop at the next gas station and grab them some fried chicken to cheer them up. How much longer until we get to your family's place?" he asked Courtney.

She looked out the window. "We're close," she said. "Maybe an hour."

"When's the last time you saw your family?" David asked.

"It's been over two years," she said. "Feels like a lot longer, though. I'm excited to see them. Truth is, they miss me even more than I miss them."

"Why'd you leave?" David asked.

"Mackanack is so constricting," she said. "I always felt like a big fish in a small fish bowl, you know? Ever since I was little I had a knack for singing and poetry." Her eyes got big and dewey-eyed. "In sixth grade I won the underprivileged song award," she blushed.

"What's that?" David asked.

"It's where they pick the school's most talented student from the lowest economic bracket to sing at the high school homecoming halftime show."

"Wow," David said, impressed because he just realized how good she smelled.

"It's not like they picked me because I was young or anything," she said sternly. "It was open to the entire town. It also helped that my family was super poor — like flies-around-an-African-baby's-face kinda poor," she said with conviction. "But bein' poor don't make ya stupid. I wrote my own song and they chose me! When I sang my song the *whooole* town of Mackanack was there. I think my singing can invoke miracles, because right after that our football team scored like five touchdowns or something."

"I like the Packers," Jerry said and pumped his arm quietly.

"What was the song?" David asked.

"You mean you want to hear it?" she said, unable to hold back a smile.

"I do."

She looked back and forth between David and Jerry. "OK then." Courtney cleared her throat. "It's called Hail Mary. I chose that name because the town is super religious. Not me though. My God doesn't live in a church. He lives in a sunset."

"That's retarded," Jerry said.

"Jerry!" David scolded.

He shrugged. "Sorry, it's retarded. God definitely doesn't live in a sunset. If anything he lives on Jupiter, which is huge."

Courtney was already warming up and appeared to be doing some sort of gag-reflex exercise. After a moment she composed herself. "Ready?"

David smiled. "Ready!"

"OK. Ahem. Haaaaiiiillll Maaaaaaaaaaaaaaaaaaaarrryy," she sang like a cracking window.

Everyone winced.

"In the air, rouuunnndddd and rounnnnnnddd. Spinnnning. Spiiiiinnniiiinngggg," she said and held out her arms and began an unbalanced twirl.

"Ugh," Jerry said.

"Take the baaaall to the woooorld and let the wooooorld take the baaaall..."

"That doesn't even make sense," Jerry whispered to David, who shushed him.

"Yoouuuuuu aaaarree the greatest plaaaaayer of aaaallllllll..."

"HO-K," Jerry said. "I think we get the idea. Thanks for that. I feel like I'm there and now it's time to go home. Great game everybody."

Courtney smiled. "Wow. I haven't sung that song in a long time."

"I could tell," Jerry said.

"I liked it," David smiled.

"*Really?*" she blushed. "You ain't just sayin' that, are you?"

"No. It had heart."

"Poor guy hasn't been laid in a *very* long time," Jerry whispered to Dr. Whyzer.

"That's so sweet of you to say, David. It was that kind of encouragement that made me want to go to Hollywood."

David's eyes widened. "Wow. You've been to Hollywood? That's awesome! I've always wanted to do something like that. I'll bet it must have been amazing!"

"It was awful!" she cried. "There I was, thinking it was gonna be the greatest thing since sliced bacon and it was just a giant city full of chaos and fakery."

"*Fakery?*" David asked.

"It's a word I invented after going to Hollywood. Everyone is tryin' to be someone they ain't. And they all want you to be someone you ain't, too. They want you to think that life's all great even when it ain't. It's all just fakery, David. This world needs more than fakery. It needs help, dangit!"

"Well, there are a whole bunch of groups that want to help the world. You just gotta sign up for one of them on Facebook," he said.

She made a face. "I ain't got a Facebook account."

"Well, then make one on your phone," he said.

"I ain't got a phone."

"You don't have a phone!" David yelled. She could just as well have told him that her feet were made out of crackers.

"Nope," she said. "There's more to life than looking at the world through your phone, you know?"

"No, there's really not," Jerry said. "You don't have a phone so you clearly have no idea what you're missing out on. There's this new site called Master Fucked where people upload images and videos of themselves trying to take over the world. It's fucking ha-larious. I'd say half of these people are from Arkansas!" he laughed. "I'll bet you even know some of them." He flipped through his phone. "Here, this one looks good. Watch," he said and thrust the phone out in front of them.

On the screen was a sexy white blonde woman with a Mexican-looking fellow driving down the road at over a hundred miles an hour. The man looked incredibly nervous while the blonde woman shouted gleefully into her phone. "We just stole a fucking nuclear bomb and we're gonna blow you all up to kingdom come! Driving east. Catch us if you can, fuckkeeeeers!" She then waved the phone over to a metallic briefcase which she popped open. "This shit is real," they heard her say, then, "Hashim, take off your pants. I'm horny again!"

"Oh damn, this is getting good," Jerry said and scooted into the phone. "I'm up-voting that fer shure!"

"Shit!" David said. "This is not good."

"Oh, it's good all right. She just took off her shirt," Jerry said.

"Not that, Jerry. There's a checkpoint up ahead!"

Jerry looked through the windshield. The sky was jet black and it appeared to be raining heavily. There were red taillights from a row of about ten stopped cars and flashing lights from a military blockade. Frantically, David fumbled with his phone and got the bus to begin slowing down.

"What are we going to do?" he asked.

"Calm down, calm down," Jerry said and looked down the aisle of the bus. Trish, who was wearing nothing but a lacy black bra and panties, was giving Dr. Whyzer a back-rub while he tapped out a line of cocaine and cordially chatted with one of the wives. Jacob was kneeling in prayer, four of his wives were arguing with Alma who had decided she wanted to try Ecstasy, and a dozen children were in the midst of a rousing game of Pin the Sin on the Sodomite.

"Everything's gonna be OK," Jerry said, turning forward again. "We'll just show them the kids and tell the military that we're coming back from a field trip to Las Vegas."

"That is *not* gonna work," David said.

"Not with that attitude," Jerry scolded. "Why don't you let me handle this?"

"OK," David said out of habit. "Wait a minute," he paused. "You're not going to handle this like the last checkpoint, are you?"

Jerry threw up his arms. "I *told* you I was sorry, all right? Is it my fault that this bus doesn't have a bathroom?"

"Jerry, you *pissed* on that German Shepard."

"I thought he was going to get his ding-a-ling bit off," Noah giggled.

They had reached the rain and large drops splattered on the windshield.

"Sorry, Jerry," David said, using his better judgement for the first time in a 1,000 miles. "But I think Courtney should deal with them."

"*Me?*" Courtney said. "What am *I* going to say?"

He thought about it. "Tell them you are a retired stripper coming home to see your family."

"And if they don't believe you, take off your shirt," Jerry suggested.

"I've got some panties you could throw at them!" Trish said from the back.

Courtney pulled at the curls of her hair. "I don't know. This sounds like a bad-"

"OK. Hurry. Cars are moving through quickly," David said and crouched behind the seat. "They probably just want to make sure that no one has been in contact with the infected so just tell them that you take lots of vitamin C and we should be fine. Hurry, switch spots!"

Reluctantly, Courtney got into the driver's seat and seconds later a tall stern man in a wide-brimmed hat flashed a bright light through the window. "License and Registration," he said.

"Hiiiiiii," she beamed nervously. "How the heck are ya?"

"You comin' from Nevada?" the man asked.

"Boy, I'll tell ya, some days I don't know if I'm a comin' or a goin', you know what I mean?"

He peered up at her suspiciously. "Anybody else in there with you?"

"Shoot!" she said. "Why would anybody be in this great big bus with little old me? I'm just a retired stripper coming back from a school field trip."

"You drive that bus all the way from Vegas by yourself?" he asked.

"Sure!" she laughed. "I mean, sort of. That is, when I get tired I use the apple in my phone. It does the rest. What? My what? Oh! My *app*. Sorry!" she smiled. "I use the app in my phone to drive the bus. What? Oh! I'm sorry," she smiled again. "I'm being told, I mean, I'm telling myself I shouldn't tell you that. How are *you?*" she asked and leaned over the window like she was ordering drive-through. "I'll bet you're tired from standing out in the rain. Gosh. It's coming down in buckets, isn't it? Reminds me of when I used to live here. We'd sometimes get floods, but this is ridiculous. Do you ever...Oh! Well, look at that — *panties!*" she said and awkwardly leaned out the window to hang a pair of black Victoria Secrets on the man's hat.

The man pulled the pair of panties off his hat and studied them. He turned to her. His eyes were the cool steel of a security professional. "Ma'am, I'm going to need you to stay right here," he said monotonously.

"Nice job!" Jerry applauded once the man had left. "Great cover with the panties! They weren't my idea, I promise. I'd say you convinced them. They're gonna let us through any minute."

"Are you kidding me?" Courtney said. "That was awful. I'm just *terrible* at fakery. They're probably calling the prison right now to see if there's one more cell available. Gosh, I hope it has a sink. My poor mama! She's gonna see me on the five o'clock news tomorrow," Courtney moaned.

A solid knock-knock shook the side of the bus. "Oh God!" she gasped.

"OK," Jerry said, turning around and addressing everyone on the bus. "First off, better to finish your drugs than to hide them. They always find 'em in the end," he said with a look of experience.

"Done and done," Dr. Whyzer nodded with reassurance.

David had become oddly quiet. He was staring at the floor as if he were thinking on how he could melt into it.

"What about David?" Courtney asked.

Jerry put both hands in David's hair and gave it a good frazzle. "David," he said sternly, "you're gonna have to be a stripper for a moment. Grab a pole and start dancing."

This broke his trance. "*What!?*"

"Trust me. It'll be way more suspicious if they catch you hiding. Just remember, we're from Vegas. If you don't treat the pole like it's your bitch they'll never believe you. Just keep your hair over your face and you should be fine."

"What about you?" David asked.

Jerry reached under a seat and pulled out his wig. "Everyone knows Carlos Santana loves to party," he said and slipped his sunglasses over his bloodshot eyes. After a quick adjustment he signaled to Courtney to open the door.

Five men in helmets and military fatigues were standing outside the door. Each of them carried an assault rifle and wore a gas mask. No one was smiling. The man in front was obviously in charge and his sharp steel eyes pierced through everything he looked at. "We're coming in," the leader said without invitation.

Courtney couldn't believe this was happening. She delicately stepped out of the driver's seat and stood up. "Well, hey there!" she said as cheerfully as possible. "So you came after all. How about that! So much rain I don't blame you. You need a washcloth or something?" she asked.

The leader eyed her suspiciously and then scanned the rest of the bus and did a quick headcount. "Never seen a bus like this before. This some sorta party bus or somethin'?"

"Maybe it is, maybe it isn't," Trish said from the back.

"These your panties?" the man asked, holding up the black thong.

"Not anymore," Trish winked. The men looked nervously at their squad leader. "I take it this is your first time in a Dancer Bus," Trish said. "Sorry about the condition. Let me fix that for you," she said and flicked a switch on the wall. There was a soft hum as lights on the ceiling descended and blue and purple dots danced around the room. Speakers appeared from the sides of the bus and house music with heavy bass began to thump from every corner of the vehicle.

"Whoa!" one of the guards said with nervous excitement. "The tits on the outside of the bus are inflating!"

"That is *awesome*!" another said.

"Well, hello der, gentlemeen," Jerry said with about the worst Hispanic accent known to man. "Joo guys like'a to partee? Or deed joo jess come in to return'a da pantees?" David thought he sounded like one of the Mario Brothers.

The leader shifted uncomfortably.

"We totally came in to party," the guy behind him beamed. Several others nodded.

"What's with all the kids?" another one asked.

"Ees OK," Jerry said. "Meejits."

"Midgets?" he asked.

"Si. Meejits."

"This is the weirdest party I have ever been to," one of them said. "Nice music, though."

"What's the sobriety rate?" the leader asked, peering at the dirty-blonde disheveled woman who was gyrating against a metal pole like a toweled giraffe with Parkinson's disease.

"Leegal," Jerry said, making a valiant effort not to hug all the men in uniform. He had taken 4 Ecstasy pills in the last hour.

"You sure about that?" he said, pointing at David who looked bound to break a bone at any moment. The stripper pole creaked from the stress.

"Oh, joo no need worry about her," Jerry said, waving his hand. "She's jess trying to remeember how to dance."

"I kind of like it," one of them said. "Say, what's your name?"

"Her name ees Brugelga. She's from Brugelzania. She no talk Eengleesh. Oh look! Now joo maker nervous. Eees OK, Brugelga. She is dancing tomorrow night eef joo steel want to see her try to dance. But joo must go now. Bye bye!" he said and began gently pushing them one by one toward the bus door.

The leader, however, wouldn't budge. "Wait a minute," he said. "What's *this* guy doing on this bus?"

Jerry looked over. Instead of a person, the man was looking at a manilla envelope sitting on one of the velvet seats. The folder was lying wide open and David's goofy expression was there for all to see.

"Oh, joo no need worry about that. Ees jess a piece a paper 'bout a guy who keel a sheet ton of peeple. I suggest joo look on Jahoo for an updated version."

"And you have it because...?" he asked and picked it up.

"Because I jess LOVE the girl at Kinkos. That ees like the tenth copy she make for me. I really think she beginning to like me."

But the leader was already reading the contents. "This says Top Secret," he said. "Why would you have a-" He paused. He squinted. He re-read. "Oh my God," he said. "This is unbelievable. Is this true?"

"Ees true joo gonna mess jor mask eef joo keep reading. How about a song? Joo like Black Magic Woman?"

"This is incredible!" the leader said to himself. "Does the President know about this? Does *anyone* know about this? We've got to tell people. The sanctity of our entire country is at risk. This David Dingle is..." he looked over at the gyrating Brugelga. "It's her! I mean *him*! Arrest-"

KABOOM!

Brain blanketed the inside of his mask as if a liquid piñata had burst and the man's body slumped to the floor and halfway down the exit steps. Children began screaming, the stripper began screaming, Jerry was screaming, and the four other military personnel screamed out of the bus like panicked cats on acid.

David lunged from the pole. "Go go!" he yelled. He knew there were only moments before the military would start firing on the bus. He sprinted to the front and slammed his phone on the dashboard, pressed a button to disengage the safety autopilot, and shoved his foot on the gas. The bus blasted through the military blockade like a war machine. Men dove to get out of the way. Sirens flickered and sang. They were only 50 meters past when the first bullets started to fly.

"They're shooting at us!" Courtney yelled.

"Get down!" David cried over his shoulder as he tried to steady the heavy bus by updating the app on his phone. They were picking up speed.

"We'll never outrun them!" Courtney shouted.

"We gotta try something!" he yelled.

The bus dipped suddenly and swerved to the left. David threw himself onto the wheel to try and steady the wounded vehicle.

"What's happening?" Courtney yelled.

"I think they've shot one of the tires!" he cried. The bus lurched across the road like a dying buffalo. "I can't hold it straight for much longer," he yelled. "Courtney, do you know where we are?"

"Yes!" she screamed. "The checkpoint was the entrance to Mackanack County. My town is just a few miles on the other side of that river. Follow the road over the bridge."

"*What* bridge?" he yelled.

She looked out the window. "Oh my God!" she said. "The river's flooded. The bridge is...gone."

"*Gone?*" he said desperately. ".*Now* what?"

"David, you can't keep going. We'll drown!"

"So what am I supposed to do? If I stop they'll kill us."

"You're gonna have to jump the river!" Jerry yelled.

"Shut up, Jerry!!!" Courtney and David shouted simultaneously.

The bus was now tire deep in water. Bolts of lightning illuminated the incredible swath of watery darkness ahead. This was no river — not the river from Courtney's childhood anyway. This was an angry boiling roiling madness of furious liquid on its way to the ocean. There was no end to it, no definition to its edges. It looked like the sea itself.

"I can't go any farther!" he said as the bus came to an unsteady stop.

Bishop Jacob Timpson was peering out the rear window. "They're right behind us. The military. There's tons of them — cars, trucks, even tanks! Master, help!"

"What are they doing?" David yelled.

Jacob looked. "Nothing," he said. "No one's coming out. It's like they're waiting for something."

"They're afraid," Courtney said. "They think they'll get infected if they come in the bus again."

"Wait! Something's happening," Jacob said. "Someone is approaching the bus."

"Oh God, oh God!" Alma was saying.

"Master, you've got to do something!" Jacob yelled to David. "The sinners will crucify us. Save us, already!!!"

David looked around. All eyes were on him. For the first time in a long time he felt compelled to do something about a situation. He wondered, however, what that something was. There *had* to be a way out of this mess. He looked at his phone. Maybe he had an app of some kind...

"Come out!" a voice outside yelled. "Come out or I'll shoot!"

David picked up his phone and began pushing against the screen.
BATTERY CRITICALLY LOW.

David thought he might pass out. He needed his phone now more than ever — and it was *dead*?

"We've got no choice, David," Courtney said. "I think they'll shoot us if we don't listen. We have to open the door."

With a reluctant sigh David pushed a button and the door opened. Standing outside in the pouring rain was none other than Special Agent Jon Boring. His eyes twinkled with maniacal accomplishment. His gun was leveled at David's forehead. Boring's advancement onto the bus was neither cautious nor charismatic. He marched up the steps like a frat boy coming back from a beer run.

"Well, well, well," he said smiling. "If it isn't the most wanted man in America. In my custody, I might add. Do you have any idea what that means?" The bus was quiet as they stared at him. "It means I'm gonna be Vice Preeeesideeeent," he sang. "Ooooh yeah," he said, turning around. "Quite the entourage you've developed, Mr. Dingle Dangle. Let's see, cocktail waitress," he said, pointing at Courtney, "a random Dr. - Dr. Prostate, I presume," he chuckled. "Random butt-naked stripper," he grinned and slicked back his hair, "and what appears to be the entire Walton Family. Nice," he said, and turned around. "Wow, is that..." he paused. "I'm a big fan of your music, Mr. Santana," he said to Jerry, who had forgotten he was wearing a disguise. "Pity you had to get involved in such a scandal."

Boring looked at David. "You have no idea how long I've been following you. That's some shit-hole you've got back in Seattle. Seriously, you play waaaay too many video games. Tom Clancy's Rainbow Six? *Dude*! Everyone knows that Hard Fire is like a million times better. Only pussies play that Rainbow shit."

"Hey!" Jerry yelled and ripped off his wig. "I like those games."

Boring stared. "Well, not anymore because I gave them all to Agent Fleckle cause *he* likes them. You boys won't be playing any more video games for some time, either. Didn't ya hear? President Benjamin Alan just declared a ban on all commerce. Video game sales are closed indefinitely."

"What!?" Jerry screamed.

"How's that possible!?" David asked.

"Because the President said so, and soon, *I'll* say so. So if you want something in particular, it's gonna have to go through me. Commerce is closed boys, and I'm the prison guard. Got any cigarettes?"

"Got some back here!" called out Dr. Whyzer, who was splayed out on a red fur banana.

"Those might buy your friend a cold shower in prison. Sorry, David. You're coming with me."

"What? Why? Where are we going?" David asked.

"A lot of people have been looking for you. Like *millions* of people. People who still have heads. And now, they want yours."

"But I'm innocent!" David said.

Boring laughed. "You're not innocent. You're a terrorist. You've betrayed your country by being a jerk-off. Now everything's fucked up because of you."

"But I haven't done *anything*. There's been a mistake!"

Boring shook his head. "I've seen your files," he lied. Boring didn't read files. Files were boring. "They give detailed descriptions on everything about you."

"Oh yeah, like what?" Jerry asked.

Boring shifted uncomfortably. "Like where you were born, how old you are now, your last name..."

"You haven't read *all* the files," Jerry smirked.

"I have too!" he protested.

"Not this one."

Boring narrowed his eyes. If this dip-shit had sensitive information then Boring had to know about it. "I want to see it," he said.

Jerry smiled cooly. "It's highly confidential. It would be a real shame if it got into the wrong hands, in this age of national security, I mean. What would the President say?"

Boring's eyes lit up. "What is it? Give it to me!"

"Now now, very special agent. Maybe we can make a deal. We give you the information and you let some of us go."

Boring scratched his arm. He didn't like the idea of letting *anyone* go. The more people he brought back with him the bigger the bounty. But if this knuckle-head had something he needed then he just might have to bargain. "OK. Maybe some of the Waltons," he conceded.

"Uh, uh, uhh," Jerry said. "You've got to let me go, too. That's the deal. Let me and the Waltons go, and I'll give you the goods." Jerry turned and winked to Trish and Dr. Whyzer. Dr. Whyzer winked back multiple times.

Boring tilted his head sideways and thought about it. Truth was, he didn't know what Carlos Santana's motives were. For all Boring knew Santana was using the situation to promote a new record.

"Show me the information first. Then I'll get you what you need."

"Suit yourself," Jerry said, trying hard not to smile too much. He motioned for Dr. Whyzer to hand him the manilla envelope. Delicately, he passed it over to Boring.

Boring took the envelope and looked inside. His eyes widened in amazement. "Holy crap!" Boring thought. "This guy isn't joking. This looks like real official top secret information." (He knew this because there was a giant stamp that read **Top Secret**.) Boring recognized David's photo at once. Whatever this stuff meant must truly be very frightening because everyone in the bus was shielding themselves from Boring's head.

He scanned the contents and flipped it over to read the back. "I see..." he said. "This is all *verrry* interesting. I'm glad you've given this to me. You've done your country a big favor." He gave everyone a quick look and a nod.

"You have no idea what it means, do you?" David asked.

"Of course I do!" he said offended. "I'm a government agent, for crying out loud. I understand *everything*. Listen, this is a highly sensitive document. It's no wonder you've been guarding it so carefully. I would too, what with all those big words and everything. We'll have plenty of time to go over the real meaning once we get to Washington," he said and waved his gun. "Now let's go. Everyone off the bus."

"Hey!" Jerry yelled. "You promised to let us go."

"Well, pal," Boring said. "Promise in one hand and shit in the other and see which one buys you lunch."

"That's not how that goes," Courtney said.

"All right. I'm serious! Get going — off the bus!"

Suddenly the bus lurched forward. Many of Jacob's wives gasped.

"Whoa!" Jerry said. "What was that?"

"The water level's come up!" Courtney yelled. "There's water coming into the bus — fast. We've got to get out of here!"

"There's no way I'm getting out!" Alma shouted. "The water will pull us away — we'll drown!"

Boring looked at everyone. He was about to lose control of the situation. He had to do something fast. He brought his shirt cuff up to his mouth. "Agent Fleckle, this is Agent Boring. Fleckle, are you there?"

"This is Fleckle, go ahead."

"We're gonna need some assistance. I need some large trucks to come and get us. The bus is filling with water."

"Copy that. Sending a truck over now."

Water was pouring into the bus at an alarming rate. It was already around their ankles. "Close the door!" Courtney yelled.

David pushed the button and the door closed. Luckily, the seal was tight and only a small amount of water was seeping through. "This is crazy," David said. "Someone should really do something."

"I've never seen it flood like this," Courtney admitted. "It's like an act of God or something."

"Oh Jesus, save us!" Bishop Jacob wailed from the back.

"Quiet slaves!" Jerry yelled. "God ain't gonna help us now."

"We're moving!" Alma screamed.

"What do you mean we're moving?" Dr. Whyzer asked.

"I mean we're moving," she said again.

David felt it too. The bus was noticeably shifting.

"Relax," Agent Boring said. "They've got the bus on a winch. We're being towed by the military right now."

"Agent Boring, this is Agent Fleckle. Come in Boring."

"Go ahead."

"We cannot get to the bus. I repeat, we cannot get to the bus. There is too much water. Our position is compromised. We are pulling back."

"Pulling *back*?" he yelled. "You can't pull back. I've got the suspect right in front of me."

"You're on your own, Boring," Fleckle said and cut transmission.

"Goddammit, Fleckle!" Boring screamed. "If it was me I'd have swum out and pulled the bus out myself."

"We're being overtaken by the water!" Courtney moaned. "We're gonna drown!"

Jacob walked resolutely to the front of the bus and placed his hand on David's shoulder.

"Master, I have yet to abandon my faith in you. I know in my heart that you will save us, as you did once before. Ask our father in heaven for help. He will listen to you. Better yet, see if you can get ahold of Noah." The bus rocked as it hit another wave.

"Whoa!" Jerry yelled. "This is not good — this is sooo not good."

David had never been a religious man. In fact, he had never been to church before. He had only prayed once in his life and that was for a new phone. If there was ever a time to become a born again believer, this was it.

"OK. Everyone take a knee," he ordered with surprising authority. "Heavenly God Man," he said, looking at the roof of the bus. "We could really use some help. I've got, let's see, about fifteen, no, maybe twenty people in a bus, um, in Arkansas...somewhere. I'm sure you can find it on Google. Please send us a helicopter or a hover boat. We've got plenty of water. Could use some food, maybe. Any requests?" he asked, looking around.

"This isn't an order for Burger King!" Alma yelled.

"We're moving fast now!" Courtney hollered.

"I can't get all the windows up," Dr. Whyzer called from the back. "This thing is going to sink!"

"Daddy, look!" Bartholomew called.

Jacob turned around and saw his son pointing out the windows. "What is it, son?" he asked.

"The titties are carrying us to safety."

Jacob looked. He couldn't believe it! The inflatable breasts on the side of the bus were acting like water-wings. The bus was actually *floating*! They were being carried away from the military and toward the lights of town. It was a miracle.

"Praise Jesus!" Jacob yelled and looked at David in profound admiration.

Before David could respond Jerry took the opportunity to slam his elbow into Agent Boring's back who collapsed to the ground.

"Jerry Burger – Super Sleuth! That's for my video games, bitch!"

Chapter 18: K is for K

The sun was high in the sky and another car zoomed past in the opposite direction. The driver of his last ride had kicked him out after complaining that Melech's hubcap was scratching the passenger window.

"Wait!" Melech shouted. "Come back! Dammit!" he yelled and shook his head. He had been walking on the side of the road all day. In that time fewer than a dozen cars had passed him. He felt miserable. The ache in his head had become dull and persistent, and the high winds of the Midwest plains wobbled the hubcap like a weather vane. Even worse, the bright metal magnified the sun's effects. He felt like he had been walking through a fiery desert for over a month. Mason got out easy, he figured.

He looked at his phone for the thousandth time hoping for a signal. It seemed to be hopeless and he kept on walking. As his dull eyes chased the horizon a faint *beep* shocked him out of his miserable stupor. He had signal! "Oh - thank you, Satan!" Melech yelled at the top of his lungs. Still not convinced it was real, Melech pressed a shaky finger onto the number of the only person who could help him.

Several moments later an uncertain voice said, "Ye-low?"

"Mr. President?" Melech asked. "Is that you?"

President Alan sat upright from his reclining position. "Melech? My God, Melech, is that really you?"

"It is, Sir, it really is."

"Oh! Thank the Good God in Heaven! Where are you, man? Are you in the capital yet? You're gonna have a helluva time getting through security. This place is locked down like a sexually paranoid turtle."

"I'm just outside Boonsville, Missouri," Melech said.

"Boonsville?! Is that a restaurant in Georgetown?"

"No, Mr. President. It's a town. In Missouri. Listen, I need a pick-up. Send me a plane or a helicopter out right away. My coordinates are..."

"Are you testing me, Melech?"

"Am I test — what?"

"Everything's been shut down, Melech. Just like you told me to. Flights are grounded. Roads are closed. We're sealed up and holding out. Put out or get out, that's what I say," he said and laughed. Melech thought he heard some glass shatter against a wall.

"Uh, what? Are you sure?"

"Helicopters!" the President yelled. "There isn't a man left in America who can operate a helicopter. They're all dead!"

Melech's shoulders drooped. He felt like he had been stabbed in the heart. "You have no idea how sorry I am to hear that, Mr. President. I'm not going to lie. I'm in a real bind and could use some attention. I've got a hubcap in my skull that-"

"Boy, you're telling me!" the President interrupted. "I've had this popcorn husk in my gums for almost a day now. I've tried *hic* almost everything but can't seem to get it out."

"But you *have* implemented Martial Law, is that correct?" Melech asked.

"Yep. Taken care of. I just forwarded your message to one of my Facebook groups."

"What about commerce? What did you tell them to do about the commerce?"

The President stopped eating his Doritos so Melech wouldn't hear him munching on them. "I - shut it down, just like you said to. What's wrong? Is everything all right?"

Well, at least that was good news. "Yes. Everything is fine. Just don't reopen it, whatever you do."

It was hard to hear the President's voice over the crinkle of the Doritos bag. "I don't know, Melech. I'm starting to think that shutting down the economy was a bad idea. People are not happy about it. Good thing we shut down media too, otherwise I'd probably be way down in the polls by now. Hey, when you get in do you think you could make a stop at Arby's or Dominos?"

Melech ignored him. "Listen, I'm not far from where I need to get. I'm about eight hours from Memphis. Once I get there I've got a straight shot to D.C. When I arrive there are a few strategies I'd like to get configured before we move into the next stage of actionables. A lot is at stake, Ben, but if we do this right we'll be on Easy Street. How are you? How have you been holding up?"

The President fell into a bean bag chair. "It's been an emotional roller coaster, this pandemic. I've had so many mixed feelings since I found out about it. So much has been lost. It's terrible — just terrible. I can't help but think of all those poor, dying voters," he said and burped suddenly. "It's strange, Melech."

"What's strange?" Melech asked.

"Being the only intelligent person left in the country. I've locked myself in the Oval Office. Don't worry, I have plenty of food and liquor. Also, the Vice President is with me. I know *he's* not contagious and he knows *I'm* not contagious. We're working on a plan to save the rest of America - we've already built a pretty good model out of Legos. We've decided to scratch the turtle idea and are moving away from amphibians in general..." He continued, "I think you're right about the virus. Congress is only alive because they're all too stupid to die. I was lucky enough to barricade myself inside before I came in contact with the disease. I'm telling you, Melech. We are lucky! There's not another capable intelligent person alive, *believe* me! It's only me and the Vice President."

Melech suddenly felt nauseous.

"Hey, you haven't seen any vigilantes on horseback, have you?" the President asked.

"Vigilantes? No. Should I be concerned?" he asked.

"Maybe, maybe not. All I've heard is that there is a large army headed east toward D.C." There was a pause. "Hey I didn't know we had girl scout cookies," Melech heard the President say in a muffled voice.

"Found them under one of the couch cushions," the Vice President could be heard saying.

"Don't go anywhere or do anything," Melech ordered. "Or say anything to anyone," he added. "America's on pause until I get back."

"Be careful, Melech," the President said. "It's a dangerous world out there. Morons have taken over the country."

"Yes," Melech said sadly. "I know."

He clicked the phone off and looked down the empty road. If he didn't get back, America's shutdown could be permanent. The hubcap wobbled in the wind.

Suddenly the phone rang. Melech looked at it. CALLER ID BLOCKED. "That's strange," he thought. He pushed the on button. "Hello?"

A deep, gravely voice answered him and Melech's eyes widened in terror. He broke into a cold sweat at once. "Oh! Hello!" he squeaked out, unaware that his non-phone hand was balled up into a fist and punching a mile marker. "Yes, yes, of course. Certainly, Master! Everything is just fine. I'm a-" he looked around the endless cornfields, "on my way. I ran into a bit of a transportation — what's that?" He pinched his arm nervously. "Yes, I know. It's bad. Indeed. Very, very bad. David Dingle? I, um..." He turned around and looked at the endless cornfield behind him. "I have him with me. It's just like I told you. He has been with me the whole time. No, I'm afraid you can't talk to him. He's, uh, drunk. *Chloroformed*, I mean. That's right. I will, Master. We will be there shortly. Your wish is my command. Goodbye."

Melech Rothschild turned his phone off and threw up all over his shoes. His vomit was chunky and lacked a watery consistency; he was clearly dehydrated. Melech was not accustomed to speaking so timidly to his Master who would almost certainly torture him for his behavior. This time it might even be worse than the time when Melech had been responsible for botching the Bay of Pigs. His pace quickened to a near trot. He was riding on the edge of panic now. He *had* to find David Dingle. His life depended on it.

He noticed a momentary flash far off down the interstate. It was a vehicle! Melech edged to the middle third of the road and waved his arms over his head. "Please, please," he said to himself over and over again. "Stop - just stop."

As it neared Melech could see that the blue and white pick-up truck was slowing down. The engine purred and a friendly looking white man wearing a cowboy hat leaned over and rolled down the passenger side window. "Holy God!" the man said when he saw the hubcap. "What in the hell happened to your head?"

"I've been in an accident. I need help."

The man gave him a look. "You ain't sick, are ya?" There was a calm reserve about him, a subtle confidence, a stoic reverence. His arms looked like bulging pipes.

"Not in the way you might think," Melech muttered under his breath. "Not with the virus, at least."

"All right, well hurry up and get in."

Melech felt a colossal weight lift off his shoulders. With briefcase in hand he stepped into the truck. "Thank you so much!" Melech said, overwhelmed with gratitude.

"Name's Lindin Bradshaw," the man said and took Melech's hand and shook it with a firm grip.

"Pleasure to meet you," Melech said politely. "Where are you headed?" he asked.

"Memphis, Tennessee."

"Oh!" Melech said and thought he might start to cry.

"Everything all right?" Lindin asked.

"You have no idea how glad I am to hear that you're heading to Memphis. I've been on the road for several days now. I'm on my way east but my train broke down. Earthquake."

Lindin nodded. "Heard about that. Is that how you got that thing in your head?" he asked.

"Oh, that," Melech said and shook his head. "I've endured a great deal of hardship since the earthquake. I got in an accident with a friend of mine. He died and I survived, but only barely, as you can see," he said, indicating the metal shrapnel lodged in his skull. He shuddered to think of the germ-laden infection that had inevitably begun to set in.

"Well, I know a few folks in Memphis that might be able to help you out," Lindin said. "Couple of them are doctors."

"*Really*?" Melech asked. "Oh wow, that would be wonderful. I was beginning to believe that all the doctors were, well, dead."

Lindin pursed his lips and bobbed his head as if to say he understood completely. "This virus has been a real challenge for a lot of folks, wouldn't you say?"

"It wasn't supposed to be like this," Melech said.

Lindin shrugged. "Well, I can't say anything about that. The Lord works in mysterious ways and who am I to say who goes and who stays? The way I look at it is maybe some of those folks were meant to go. Maybe it's a cleanse of some kind."

"Oh, it's a cleanse all right," Melech agreed. "Say, what's your background?" Melech asked. "You seem like an intelligent guy."

Lindin looked at him and smiled. "I wouldn't go that far," he said modestly and took off his cowboy hat and pushed back the few remaining thin hairs over his bald scalp. He set his hat on a pile of white clothes in between them and said, "I'm a carpenter by trade, but I dabble in a lot of things. I guess you could say I'm a community organizer. Nothin' makes me happier than gettin' a group of people together around a common cause."

"You're religious?" Melech asked.

Lindin shrugged. "Sure, but not like that," he said and waved his hand. "I go to church every so often — not necessarily every week. I've got my God and my God's got me, but I don't preach or knock on doors or anything like that. I'm more interested in culture, you see. We're a great country and a fascinating people with a rich history. This ain't the first time America has been up against a wall, you know? America has had a lot of problems in the past and, well, I suspect we got more problems to come. Why just look at all this mess," he said as they passed by the giant swaths of agricultural lands. "This once used to be a beautiful prairie with rich forest and diverse species of fowl. But all that's gone now. They've turned it all into mono-cropped madness — poisoned the earth with their pesticides, genetically modified our seeds 'til practically all the seed diversity's been lost, and for what?"

Melech looked out the window trying to imagine what it would all look like with prairie and pockets of forest instead of dirt. Lindin was right. There wasn't much to look at.

"That ain't even the worst part," Lindin continued. "Most of these farms aren't even owned by local people any more. They all been bought up by big industry names like Syngenta and Monsanto. Back in the good old days folks used to go out and till the earth with their bare hands. Well, forget about that! These days they use big old machinery and technology. They say it's good for the economy — *everything's* for the economy!" he growled. "Those idiots don't know a damn thing about local production. Instead of people workin' for 'emselves they got machines and debt. Well, let me tell you, it's better to have people workin' for you than machines. Bring back the niggers, is what I say. Bring back the God. Damn. Niggers."

It was right about this time that Melech noticed the confederate flag draped halfway over the rear window of the pickup. "You want...slaves?" Melech asked.

"Gotta do somethin' with all those niggers!" Lindin said with a wild grin. "My family's been hangin' niggers since they emigrated from England. But too many niggers to hang, that's the problem," he said, shaking his head in amazement. "You let 'em hang around too long and they breed like rabbits, am I right?"

Melech chuckled nervously.

"That's what I mean about this virus. I'm thinkin' it's a cleanse. I been on the road since the outbreak and I ain't come across too many spooks. That's a good thing, if you ask me. They're too dumb to survive somethin' like this. But there's always gonna be a few left over. See, that's why I'm headin' down to Memphis. Big rally goin' on tonight."

Melech shot a glance at the pile of white clothing sitting in the middle of the front seat.

"You ever been to a Loyal White Knights rally?"

"I don't think so," Melech said quietly.

"Oh, you'd know it if you had because they are FUN!" he laughed, and slapped the steering wheel with his hand. "Great group of members. And I'm not just saying that 'cause I'm one of them. We get together and talk about things like community, immigration, burn a cross or two, maybe. I'm serious. You should come!"

"I sure would love to," Melech said. "It's just-"

"Oooh no," Lindin said and shook his head. "All the excuses in the world aren't gonna make up for missin' out on this. *Trust* me. This one's going to be important. What with everything that's happening - I see this as a real chance."

"For what?"

"To cleanse America of Niggers and Jews, goddammit!" he yelled and punched the steering wheel with his fist.

Melech Amschel Rothschild chuckled nervously and a dribble of pee escaped from his small penis.

Chapter 19: A Good Cause

The stolen convertible screamed down the road at 130 miles an hour. Hashim and Veryonica had been traveling for almost a day. They hadn't spoken much. There hadn't been much to say. At this point it was a physical relationship — and *boy* was it physical! He appreciated the dangerous sex but he wanted to know more about this mysterious woman and share his life with her, but every time he tried to speak to her she drove the car into oncoming traffic or down a ravine. Though his fingers ached from gripping the metal door for so long, Hashim was beginning to find her more and more attractive, despite her efforts to kill them both.

Veryonica set her cellphone down for the first time in 40 miles. "I've been texting an ex-boyfriend of mine. He just got out of prison," she said cheerfully. "He said half of Arkansas is under water." She fluttered her eyelids at Hashim and those big beautiful eyes, which could have belonged to a multitude of female Disney princesses, gazed at him wistfully. "Maybe we should turn around. I've always wanted to drive a car into eight feet of raging river."

He feigned a smile. "That sounds nice. I'm not a good swimmer, though. I don't want to drown."

"Well, maybe I do," she said haughtily. She tossed her phone in the backseat. "Pull out that nuclear weapon again, wouldja sweetie?"

"Again?" Hashim asked. He sighed and reached back and showed her the metal box for the eighth time in the past hour. Its metal sheen had become synonymous to Hashim with hard kinky sex.

"You tired or somethin'?" she asked, her lips pouting.

"No - no," he said quickly. "It's just, well, I think I'm getting dehydrated."

She nodded her head. "Makes sense. You've lost a lot of fluid."

He looked at her carefully. He didn't know how to put this. "I'm growing concerned that we are going to set off the nuclear weapon if we have sex on it again. Your butt was inches from the red button the last time."

"Can't say I wasn't trying," she grinned playfully. "But you're right. We need to preserve it. I mean, how often do you have a nuclear *fucking* weapon in your possession for, Christ's sake, or Alibaba's sake, or whatever."

"Allah," Hashim corrected.

"Oh, right, I remember. Allahu Akbar, Allahu Akbar!" she screamed and pressed her foot deeper into the gas pedal. "Hashim, my boy," she said and the vehicle settled into a cool 140 mph coast, "you and me need to start talkin' about how we're going to use this thing. Never in a million years did I think I'd have the

170

opportunity to blow up a whole goddamn city. Not that I *want* to, mind you," she said quickly. "I don't particularly like the idea of killing other people."

"You *don't?*" he asked in shock.

"Nope. Just myself," she grinned. "Wanted to ever since I was old enough to hold a bottle of bleach. Nasty stuff," she said and made a face. "I dunno," she shrugged. "Killing other people has always just seemed wrong to me."

"Even if they're infidels?" Hashim asked in disbelief.

She gave him a perplexed look. "Is that a type of shoe?"

He shook his head.

"Well, I wouldn't know much about that," she admitted. "I just know that people should be free to make their own decisions. If someone doesn't want to die then it shouldn't be right for someone else to kill them. No matter *what* kind of shoes they're wearing."

"But what if there's no other choice?" he asked. "What if people in America, normal people who should care about the violence and injustice perpetrated by their own government, what if they just aren't listening and the only way to make them listen is to blow them up?"

"Listen, I get that you're a terrorist and that you're basically doing what the Palestinians have been doing to Morocco for thousands of years. It's like, history repeating itself, or whatever. I think the reason it keeps happening is, and no offense, but it's because you read that stupid holy book of yours and believe that everything it says is the word of God. I mean give me a break!"

"The Koran *is* the word of God," Hashim said evenly.

"What's the Koran?" she asked, and steered the car back into the right lane.

He furrowed his brow. "Our holy book."

"Oh, *really?* I was talkin' about the Bible."

"Muslims don't read the Bible."

She stared at him. "Really? Well, why the hell not?"

He thought about it some more. "No one really sells them. Just Korans."

"*That* explains it," she nodded. "Anyways, I don't want to judge all you poor Muslim bastards for having been brainwashed into believing that by blowing up a shopping mall you're doing God's will. I mean, me *personally*, I think it's sexy as hell. Heck, my whole life I've been trying to kill myself for no apparent reason other than the fact that it turns me on. A *lot*. But you, *you're* doing it for a cause. That's admirable, Hashim."

"It is?" he asked.

"You bet your brainwashed brain it is. This world *needs* more causes, if you ask me. Just look at our crummy world! Rain forests gone, oceans are drying up! *Trust* me. If we all took a stand for something important there'd be a lot less problems in the world."

Hashim stared at Veryonica. He was unable to take his eyes off of her. She was without a doubt the most beautiful woman he had ever seen before. The way her blonde hair waved in the wind, the way her hands clutched the steering wheel like a throbbing desire, the way her eyes searched the wide world for anything to kill herself with. She was erotic.

"Time to gas up!" she yelled and jerked the emergency break upwards, setting the car into a 200 meter drift. Hashim clutched his seatbelt like a parachute release as the car dropped into a shallow ravine off the interstate and came to a slow stop. "Dang it!" Veryonica said. "We didn't even roll *once*. I guess I probably should have turned the wheel. Oh well!" she said cheerfully and drove the car out of the ravine and into the gas station.

Despite it being one o'clock in the afternoon the gas station looked completely vacant. The gas pumps were not glowing with friendly yellow lights, the neon sign of the shop was turned off, and not a single person could be seen for miles. Both Hashim and Veryonica stepped cautiously out of the convertible.

"It looks like it's been abandoned."

"Just like all the other gas stations," Hashim said.

"Maybe there's some food inside," Veryonica suggested.

The door to the gas station was unlocked and Hashim stepped inside. It was dark and musty smelling. Slow currents of dust drifted through the rays of sunlight. The aisles had mostly been picked clean, but there were still a few bags of chips and car supplies.

"Welcome. How may I help you?" a meek and shallow voice said from the shadows.

Hashim spun around. Behind the counter was a younger man in his late twenties. He was pimply faced with glasses and greasy hair. They had apparently walked in while he was restocking cigarette cartons.

"What are you doing here?" Veryonica asked.

"I work here," the man said in a startled voice.

"Oh. We didn't think the place was open," she said.

"Well, technically we're not," he said. His words revealed a deep depression. "President Alan shut down all commerce the other day," he shook his head sadly. "It's illegal for anyone to be buying or selling *anything* right now."

"What? Why?" she asked.

The man shrugged. "Your guess is as good as mine. Maybe it has to do with how money can have a lot of germs on it."

"Nah, I doubt it," she said. "I once ate eleven dollars in coins and never even went to the hospital. Just pooped 'em out."

The man opened his mouth, but didn't have a response.

"So what are you doing here if the store is closed?" Hashim asked.

The clerk looked at him like a soldier who had never left the battlefield. "I don't know anything else to do," he admitted. "I've never had any other job. I don't have any hobbies or a girlfriend or friends or even a dog. I have a car, I guess. Nowhere to go though, other than here."

"Wow. Now I *really* want to kill myself," Veryonica said. "Seriously, there's a *lot* more to living than working at a gas station."

"Yeah, like what?" he asked.

She thought about it. "Like low altitude skydiving. Scuba diving with a quarter tank of air. Robbing a bank without a gun. Tons!"

He shook his head. "I've never been one for trying new things. I like to do what I know. Hopefully they'll open commerce again soon. Everything is so boring and meaningless without it. Well, commerce and porn."

Veryonica maintained small talk as she stuffed a bag of chips, a quart of oil, a box of tissues and some sunglasses under her shirt. "You guys still have gas?" she asked and swiped a handful of lighters.

"Sure, but I'm not allowed to sell you any."

"I'll steal some, if you don't mind?" she said.

He shrugged. "Where you guys goin'?" he asked.

"Don't know," she said. "D.C. probably."

"What's in D.C.?"

"Freedom."

"Freedom?"

"Yep. Freedom. Gonna blow some up. Wanna come?"

He thought about it. "No. I still have to refill the soda machine and mop the floors. Thanks, though."

They walked out and put gas in the vehicle. When it was full, Veryonica poured some on the trunk of the car then set the flowing nozzle on the ground. She got in the car and took off at a slow start. "Hey Hashim, would you mind holding the wheel for a sec?" she asked.

He was putty in her hands. "Of course, my dear."

"Good. Hold it straight now." She ripped open the box of tissues and flicked the lighter. When the box was almost fully aflame she threw it as hard as she could toward the gas station.

"Whoa, wait! What are you doing?" he asked.

"Move it!" she yelled and grabbed the steering wheel and floored the pedal.

Hashim watched in horror as a line of flame rose up behind the car like a ten foot tall red and yellow snake.

"This baby's *gonna* blow!" she yelled.

"Drive, woman, drive!" he screamed.

The car hit sixty within moments and soon they had left all danger behind.

"Phew! That was close!" she said in exhilaration, oblivious to the mushroom cloud of fire which had engulfed the gas station. "I told you there was a reason it took me so long to pick out a car. Needed a *fast* one."

"You're crazy!" Hashim said, oblivious that his fingernails would need to be pried out of the door again. "I didn't sign up for this."

"You bet your crazy mustache, you did," she said, and yanked him closer by the corners of his handlebar mustache and shoved her tongue down his throat. His arms flailed like the appendages of an upside down camel trapped in the sand, but his heart fluttered like a hummingbird's during the spring mating season.

He collapsed back into his seat and sucked in a chestful of air. "I've never met a woman like you before," he said and smiled as his gaze dissolved into the horizon.

"One of a kind," she agreed.

Hashim mused, "Back home all the women are so conservative. A woman would *never* kiss a man first. It is forbidden. But you, you are as free as the wind," he said and looked at her admiringly.

She avoided his stare. "Now now. None of that."

"What?"

"Don't ruin a good thing, Hashim. I don't belong to anyone."

He studied her. "And that is what I love about you," he said at last. "You do anything you want. You are your own woman. You are more powerful than all the virgins in heaven."

"Well, I've never thought about it like that before," she admitted. "I just don't want you getting the wrong idea. You're a nice guy and all, but you *are* a terrorist. Your mission in life is to kill people and destroy America. That's not really my thing."

"What is your thing?" he asked.

"Well, it changes from moment to moment, but right now it's to *almost die* for a cause."

"I can help you do that!" he exclaimed and inched closer to her like a begging puppy.

"Listen, buddy. I'm helping *you* do that, got it? I don't need your help or anyone else's. Free as a bird, remember? The last thing I need is your help and the second to last thing I need is you falling in love with me. You're gonna die soon, remember? Don't forget that you have a mission, Hashim - blowing yourself up."

Hashim looked off into the distance. "Maybe I should rethink my cause?" he said thoughtfully.

"What? No way!" she said and shook her head. "You've got a *great* cause. Blow yourself up with a nuclear weapon. Great, great cause! As long as you believe in it, that's all that matters."

His eyes traced the horizon. "So much has changed since I began," he said. "I'm not who I used to be. Sure, there is still anger and the hatred inside of me, which is good," he pondered. "The longer I am in this country the more I understand that the infidels are not the ones responsible for killing my family."

"Someone killed your family?" she asked.

Hashim stared at his feet. "It was a drone strike, years ago. My family was in the market, my children were playing in the streets. I was at work. I made little money because of the U.S. embargo so I rarely got a chance to see them because I worked so hard. One day the U.S. Government bombed my village because they thought we were terrorists." Hashim shook his head. "We were not terrorists. We were just normal people."

"That's awful!" Veryonica said.

"It is. Death is a terrible thing. People in America are lucky because they do not have to witness it every day. They are isolated from the wars that their government creates. I believed that if they saw more death in their own country then perhaps they would pressure their leaders to stop killing other people in *other* countries. But now I know that to be wrong. Americans do not even care if their *own* people die. It is not because they are evil. It is because they are stupid. They believe that as long as it is not happening to *them*, then it must not be happening. They only care about money and freedom, neither of which is real. If those symbols were destroyed, then perhaps all of this would change."

The car settled into a calm cruise of 85 miles an hour, but Veryonica felt like they had stopped moving entirely. She could not stop thinking about everything he had just said. Suddenly her eyes lit up. "Hashim, you just gave me an idea."

"I did?"

She nodded and looked at him. "Have you ever been to the White House before?"

Chapter 20: The Family Reunion

"The sun's starting to rise!" Courtney said in excitement. "We're gonna be OK!"

"It feels like we've been drifting for hours," David said and rubbed his eyes.

She looked at her watch. "We have."

The inflatable titties had done a good job of keeping the bus afloat. Agent Boring was sleeping in the fetal position with his hands tied behind his back. Courtney and David both looked quietly out the windshield which was halfway submerged with water. Now outlines of broken buildings began to come into view.

"Oh my God..." Courtney said in horror.

"What is it?" David asked.

"My town. It's been...destroyed."

She was right. Most of the buildings in Mackanack were almost completely under water except a handful of second stories and the golden arches (of which there were six).

"I don't see a single person. Do you think the virus has been through here already?" she asked David.

It was likely that it had. Before his phone had died, David had seen that the virus had swept through the entire nation. There wasn't a single place that hadn't been infected. Still, he wanted to give Courtney at least some hope.

"Maybe everyone died from the flood," he offered.

"Oh, it's just awful," she said and began to cry softly. "This used to be such a nice town. Right over there was the bowling alley and pawn shop. And over there was the Walmart Super Center."

"Does your family live nearby?" he asked.

Her eyes widened. "Come to think of it, they live on a little hill. It's possible the flood didn't destroy the house. Oh, David, maybe they've survived!" She looked out the window full of hope. "It's less than a mile away, but with all this water we'll never make it. We've got to find a way to get the bus where we want it to go. If only we could see better."

"How about the hatch?" he said, pointing at the air vent on the roof.

"Yeah!" she said.

David popped open the vent and he, Courtney, and Trish climbed up onto the roof of the bus. The morning air was cool and humid, and it felt good to be outside for a change. The water was so still it seemed like they were on a lake.

176

The bus drifted slowly down the main drag of town.

"Their house is way over there," she said pointing. "We've got to find a way to propel this thing."

"I've got about a dozen spanking paddles stashed in one of the bus compartments," Trish said. "They're pretty long, too. Every now and then you get a client that you just *don't* wanna get close to. I'll help paddle, but I doubt you'll be able to convince Jerry or Dr. Whyzer to give you a hand."

"Why not?" he asked.

"Did you *see* how many Ecstasy pills those boys took? I'd give them some space if I were you. Jerry about ripped my head off for asking him to move his leg."

"Shoot," Courtney said. "We won't be able to move this thing on our own."

"Unless..." David said. "Hang on." He leaned down and poked his head through the vent. "Hey Jacob!"

"Yes, Master?" Jacob said, sitting up.

"Are you and your sinful family ready to work for your Lord?"

"Day and night, Master."

"Good, then get up here!" he ordered. Pulling his head out of the vent he looked at Courtney and shrugged. "It's kind of nice having slaves, actually."

Five minutes later Jacob and his five wives, along with most of his children, were sitting on top of the bus stroking in unison.

"Stroke!" he yelled.

"For our Lord and Savior!" they responded.

"Stroke!" It was quite effective.

"Geez, we're gonna be there in no time," Trish said, impressed.

After about twenty minutes of paddling Courtney screamed and threw her arms around David. "Land ho! I can see it!" she said, overcome with joy. "It's my family's house!"

David looked toward the horizon. A tiny knoll rose out of the water like a single boob. There wasn't much land, but enough for a multitude of structures. None of them, however, resembled a house.

"Thank God Tatum was able to persuade my folks to move to the butte," Courtney said. "Otherwise they'd be sunk like everyone else."

"How long have they lived there?" David asked, spotting the dilapidated trailer and looking at all the junk that surrounded it.

"Couple years," she shrugged.

"Wow, they really have...a lot of stuff."

"My parents always did have a hard time parting with their possessions. My daddy collects cars, and swing-sets, and burn barrels, and lawn chairs, and, hmm, let's see," she said thinking, "Oh! And chicken wire, and paint cans, and shotgun shells, and pickle jars, and telephone cords..." her voice drifted off. David looked over and saw a tear rolling down her cheek. "I haven't seen anyone in my family in over two years. Oh, David!" she said, and hugged him again. "You're just gonna love my family. They are the nicest, sweetest people you ever did meet." She turned around. "Come on, slaves, hurry the fuck up - Momma's waitin' for us!"

The bus slowly picked up speed and several minutes later it ground to a halt in the sand in front of the hill. "OK, everybody," David said. "Let's all get off the bus and wait outside."

"Yayyy! Salvation!" Jacob's children chimed together in unison.

"Just a bunch of regular little Noahs," Alma beamed.

One by one everyone scooted down the hatch leaving David and Courtney alone on the roof. Courtney looked at David and took his hand. "I never would have been able to make it back here without you," she said. "All this craziness that's happenin', all them heads that are explodin' and burstin' all over ever'thin', well, this kinda makes it all worth it." She leaned over and kissed David on the cheek. "Come on!" she yelled.

David was left alone on the roof. He touched the side of his face where Courtney had kissed him. He began to wonder if maybe things were going to work out after all. Maybe, this whole pandemic was a *good* thing!

Back inside the bus, Jerry was slumped over a barstool in the back and Dr. Whyzer quietly rocked back and forth and muttered words which reminded David of something out of *The Exorcist*. Boring was snoring peacefully. David decided to let them rest.

Still dressed in his toga towel, David stepped out of the bus and into the shallow water. It felt like he was arriving on the movie set of a low budget horror film. In front of him, through a maze of rusted machinery parts and plastic pink flamingos, he saw the brown and blue mobile home that looked as if it had been placed there by an F-4 tornado. The scene was eerily quiet aside from the clucking of a few hens perched on the roof of the trailer. It appeared no one was home.

Courtney sensed it too. "It ain't usually like this. Normally, Daddy's sittin' on the porch with a beer watchin' the world pass by. Momma'd be inside watchin' her shows and the little ones would be out in front playin' 'hit the dog'. Oh Gawd, David. You don't think they've all been infected, do you?"

David hesitated. If anything, they had been eaten by their trash. "Why don't you go knock?" he said.

"I want you to come with me," she said, and squeezed his arm.

David walked slowly with Courtney toward the trailer. The old plastic porch creaked as they walked up the steps.

"Since when have the windows been boarded up?" Courtney asked, more to herself.

"Maybe they thought it would seal out the water?" David suggested.

Courtney reached for the door and turned the handle. "It's locked," she said, with a look of alarm. "This ain't normal, David." She pounded against the door with her fist. "My parents are the most trustin' folks in the whole world. Momma! It's me, Courtney. Momma! You in there? Open the door!"

They waited. Minutes passed but no one came. Courtney looked at David. It appeared she could burst into tears at any moment. "They're dead, David!"

"Now, now," he said carefully. "Let's not jump to conclusions. Maybe they all just got drunk last night. It is...Tuesday, after all."

Courtney shook her head. "No. They're active people. Daddy's usually up at the crack of dawn to check his possum traps. I'm tellin' ya. This ain't good."

"Maybe we should just go back to the bus and wait a minute. Maybe they went for a swim or something," he said.

"OK. Wait here just a second while I go around back and see if anyone's shootin' beer cans with the sling shot."

David agreed and took a seat in the old rocking chair on the deck. Suddenly, he heard a sound coming from inside. It sounded like a heavy piece of furniture being dragged along the floor.

"Hey, Courtney! Courtney!" he yelled. "I hear someone." David stood up. "Hello!" he called through the door. "Anyone in there?" He lifted his hand and pounded on the door. "Hey - open up!"

The door flung open and a 300 pound man wearing a gas mask burst out the door like a linebacker. In his hands was a sawed-off shotgun.

"Whoa!" David cried and took a step backwards and tumbled ass-over-teakettle down the porch steps. The man had something wrong with one leg and so trudged down the stairs like an injured grizzly bear. David had a split second to read the man's neon orange shirt that read, "I sleep, eat, and brush my teeth with my Smith and Wesson."

The man raised the gun and popped off a shot into the air.

"Holy shit!" David cried. "Hang on, man. Don't shoot!"

"What in tarnation you doin' on my doorstep?" came a muffled reply.

"Your daughter brought me, your daughter brought me — she's in back looking for you!"

"Wrong answer!" he yelled and cocked his shotgun and leveled it at David. "Gots about two-seconds to give me the right one before you learn how to chew gum without teeth!"

"Oh fuck, man!" David screamed. "Serious, I'm serious. Courtney's here — your daughter, is HERE! Please, I have a roommate and a phone! For *God's* sake!"

"Daddy!" Courtney screamed.

The injured bear turned his head to see the young unnaturally-bleached-blonde girl behind him. "C-Courtney?" he said in disbelief. "That you?"

"Oh, Daddy!" she yelled and ran like an abandoned puppy into his arms. "Oh! It's so good to see you! I love you - I love you - I've missed you so much!"

"Sweet Jesus!" he cried and dropped his gun and embraced his daughter. "Why you an' yer friend nearly gave yer old man his fourth heart attack! Praise the Lord. It is so good to see you."

She pulled herself away and stared lovingly into his gas mask. "Daddy, I've been through hell gettin' here. I didn't think I would make it. But now it all seems worth it — oh, Daddy! I love you," she said, and embraced him again.

After a touching moment Courtney's father turned around and shouted, "'T's alright! Y'all can come out now. It's Courtney!!"

The front door squeaked open and two identical twelve-year-old girls bounded down the stairs and into Courtney's arms.

"Delilah and Delilah!" Courtney squealed. "Good heavens. You've both gotten so big!"

"I knews you were a-comin'," Delilah said.

"I knews it too," the other Delilah said.

Courtney wrapped both of her arms around them and beamed. Then her eyes suddenly widened as another gas-masked face emerged through the front door. "That you, Sis?" the figure called.

"Tatum!" she squealed. "Oh, Gawd, Tatum! Git over here!" Her brother's shoulders softened some and he set his AK-47 against the porch and trotted down the steps to meet his sister. Her brother was short and about as round as he was tall. When he took off his gas mask David could see that he had on thin-rimmed smart-looking glasses and a healthy colony of pimples in all stages of development.

"Great to see ya, Sis," he said and gave her a gentle hug. "Been wonderin' about you. You normally call every other day. Was startin' to worry. Ya shoulda told us you was comin'. We'da saved you some fried pickles."

"Dat you, Courtney?"

David, who was still lying in a fetal position, looked up. If Courtney's father was a bear, Courtney's mother was that bear's great-aunt's hippopotamus. Her voice sounded like it was trapped inside a 100 foot well. Momma too, was wearing a gas mask.

"Momma?" Courtney said and looked up. She nodded absently to her siblings who released her and Courtney walked slowly toward the trailer and up the stairs. She stopped several feet from her mother, who was apparently wearing a hot pink My Little Kitty king-sized bed sheet, and smiled. "I thought you was sick," Courtney said quietly. "That's what Tatum said, at least."

Momma sighed (which took about 15 seconds). "Turns out I was just havin' soda withdrawals." She spoke slowly. "Luckily...Tatum got me a few crates...b'fore this storm kicked up. Should be fine...fer the next coupla days, I 'spect."

There were lines of tears coming down Courtney's face. "I don't think I've ever been happier in my whole life," she said softly.

"Come here, teddy bear," Momma said, and wrapped her short arms around her daughter.

"Hallelujah!" her father hollered suddenly.

"Hallelujah!" Jacob and his family said in Pavlovian response from beside the bus.

"This here's a miracle!" her father said. "Why I just can't imagine how hard it's been fer you to get here. Why the whole nation's on lockdown!"

"You can take that mask off, Daddy," Courtney said. "All y'all can. It's safe...I think."

"That ain't what the news says."

"Dammit, Pa!" Tatum yelled. "How many times I gotta tell ya? The news is controlled propaganda!" He looked at Courtney. "Y'all made it all the way from California without masks?" he asked.

Courtney said it was.

Tatum hesitated for a moment and then pulled back his mask.

"Tatum!" his mother bellowed.

"Momma, if Courtney says it's OK then it's OK." He gave Courtney a curious look. "You know, I gotta admit, I had my suspicions from the very get-go that this whole pandemic was one big hoax." For the first time he noticed David lying on the ground looking up at him and smiling awkwardly. "Looks like you brought quite a crew," Tatum said. "Who're yer friends?"

"Well, there's Trish, and Jerry, and Dr. Whyzer and this here's David Dingle!" Courtney smiled. She walked over to David and yanked him up off the ground. "He's *real* nice," she said with an extra punch in her Southern Twang.

Delilah and Delilah screamed like two demons from *Children of the Corn* and dashed behind their father. "David Dingle - holy *shit*!" Tatum yelled and scrambled to yank his mask back over his face. Their father stumbled backwards while fumbling with his mask, which he successfully got on sideways. Leaning down to pick up his shotgun the big man fell over backwards like a toppled dresser. Despite his obvious injury and enormous breadth, David was impressed by the man's ability to scoot away faster than a racing crab. Momma on the porch could only clutch her slowly beating heart and wait for her head to explode.

"Are you plumb crazy!" her father yelled at Courtney. "What in hell is wrong with you!?"

"She didn't do this! She's a hostage!" her mother bellowed. "Savage!" she yelled at David and threw one of the plastic porch gnomes at him.

Tatum was a good frisbee toss away by now. He was looking back and forth among the water, the trailer, and David Dingle. He did not have one fucking clue what to do next.

Courtney began waving her arms and tapping her feet in what looked to be the Arkansas version of the Charleston Dance. "It's OK," she cried. "He's innocent! He ain't no terrorist, promise! And he ain't contagious, neither. None of us are. In fact, we're completely immune. Everything's fine, seriously. Look. If he was contagious would I be standin' here talkin' to y'all? No! Know why? Cuz he *ain't* contagious!" Her little dance ended as quickly as it began. "Now take off your darn masks an' say hello. Fer cryin' out loud. It's like I never left."

Tatum began a cautious walk back toward Courtney. Very slowly he took off his mask. David could see that Tatum was holding his breath.

Delilah and Delilah took several shy steps toward David. "You're that guy on the TV, aincha?" one of them asked.

David brushed off his hotel toga towel which was now covered with mud and wet leaves. "I am," he said.

"But he ain't guilty," Courtney said. "It's all one big wet clumsy noodle. Tatum, you were right. All that stuff they're sayin' on TV is one big lie just like you said. Ya know, ever since the beginnin' I had this funny feelin' that - Tatum, you have *got* to take a breath! Yer face is about as blue as a beaver's butt."

"Beaver's butts ain't blue!" Delilah giggled.

"It's a euphamajism," she winked and giggled along.

Tatum walked over to David, and David held out his hand but Tatum wouldn't take it.

"Oh come on, Tatum!" Courtney said. "This just ain't polite. David is our guest."

"He's a wanted terrorist, is what he is!" Tatum said. "An' you done and brought 'im to our front porch. Hollywood musta made you crazy or somethin'. You want our heads to explode just like everyone else?"

"Tatum, there ain't nothin' inside yer head to blow up!" she said angrily.

"You take that back!"

"All right — knock it off, you two!" Momma yelled from the front porch. "It's evidence enough that he ain't got the eBOla virus 'er whatever you kids are callin' it these days. What we *don't* know is why yer hangin' out with him."

Tatum shifted his weight and crossed his arms.

"I think I can clear all this up," David said. "I'm a government worker."

"Wrong answer!" Tatum yelled and did a strange and angry dance similar to Courtney's. "Grab yer gun, Pa. Shoot this Timothy McVeigh sonofabitch where he stands!"

"He's a *peace* worker!" Courtney said.

"Yeah, I'll bet. Piece of this freedom, piece of that freedom — they're all the same. I see how it is. You're a terrorist colludin' with the government, are ya? Who you workin' for? Soldiers without Borders?"

"I work for United Agency of Reform," David said

"Uh, huh," he said, putting his hands on his hips. "Reform the constitution, is more like it."

"Anyway," David continued, "I was just finishing up my route and just happened to be at the epicenter of the attack when it happened."

"Well, what a coinkidink!" Tatum said sarcastically.

"And because everyone thought I did it, I had to flee to Las Vegas. But when I got to Las Vegas it happened again."

"And what are the chances!" Tatum scoffed.

"That's where I met your sister."

"Well, now I know he's lyin'!" Tatum yelled. "Courtney don't *live* in Vegas. She's in Hollywood workin' on a movie with Jodi Foster."

"Heh heh," Courtney chuckled nervously. "Funny thing happened. They ended up cancelin' production on account of money. You know, too many big named actors fighting over paychecks. They wanted to offer me a million dollars but Jodi Foster and that one guy from Saved by the Bell - what's his name, oh yeah - Screech, they wanted their cut too, so they both quit. So I figured I'd try my luck in Vegas and that's where I met David. Ain't that right, David?"

He looked at her blankly.

"What in the *fuck*," someone behind them grumbled. David turned around and saw Jerry ankle deep in mud and water. His eyes were the color of fire ants and about as angry. "If this is a dream I am ready to wake up now." He looked around. "Where the hell are we? The theme park for Texas Chainsaw Massacre? God, my head feels like shit. I can't believe that bar is out of liquor already. What kind of Vegas Party bus only stocks a bar for three nights?" He looked at David and Courtney. "OK. I recognize you and you," he said. "The rest of you better start introducing yourselves quick. I'm pretty sure I'm about to throw up."

"Who in God's name is *that*?" her father said.

"Uh, that's our friend Jerry," David said. "He's a bit under the weather right now."

"That doesn't even begin to describe it," Jerry said, hobbling toward David. "I think I'd rather have the virus than this miserable hangover. Dear God! Ugh, what time is it, noon-thirty? Someone turn off the lights!"

David looked up at the cloudy sky. "It's 7:50 in the morning," he said. "Even worse."

Courtney dashed over and held Jerry back with both arms.

"What are you doing?" he asked crossly.

"I don't want you huggin' my family," she said.

"That's your *family*? Jesus. I thought those were animatronic figurines made out of butter. Speaking of which, I could go for some food right about now. There a Wendy's around nearby?"

"Jerry's been in contact with a lot of infected people," Courtney said. Her family took a collective step backwards.

"I don't think he's contagious, but it's hard to know anything for certain, these days," David said, thinking about his phone which had run out of power.

Courtney's father hiked up his pants. "Better lock him up just to be safe. Say, pardner," he said amiably to Jerry. "Ya like chicken?"

"Do I!" Jerry said, his eyes lighting up for the first time.

"I'll just stuff him in the chicken coop for now," he whispered to Courtney and slipped on his mask.

"Why don't y'all come on inside," her mom said from the porch. "I need to get me a soda before I start shakin' agin."

"It's OK, David. Come on," Courtney said.

David turned around. "Trish, will you keep an eye on Dr. Whyzer and that agent?" he asked.

"Sure thing," she said. "I think he's out of Ecstasy, but I should check just in case."

"Hey, Jacob, why don't you guys stay outside for a moment." David asked.

"Sure thing, Master," Jacob hollered. "Praise God!"

"They think they're black," he said to Tatum matter-of-factly as he followed Courtney up the stairs.

"Oh, Momma, you cleaned!" Courtney said when they stepped inside the double-wide.

If Momma had cleaned David didn't want to see what dirty had been. It looked like someone had dumped a closetful of clothes on the living room floor. There were narrow paths that resembled game trails that guided people from one room to the other — all of which seemed to converge at the vinyl couch in front of the television.

"You're a fan of wrestling?" David asked, admiring the framed portraits of Hulk Hogan and The Undertaker hanging on the wall. The two photos were facing one another in an eternal stare down.

"Momma's got every match ever matched on DVD," Delilah said.

"That ain't true," the other Delilah said. "There's a bunch on VHS she just don't know how to convert."

"Find a seat anywhere, David," Courtney offered.

"Uh..." he said and inched toward an upside down milk crate guarded by a raccoon-sized cat.

"That's our cat, Hokum," Courtney said. "Hi kitty!"

Hokum hissed.

"Never did like that cat," she muttered

A high and shrill squeal cut through the air like a siren.

"What is that *sound*?" David asked, holding his hands over his ears.

"That's Captain Morgan," Momma said.

"Who?"

"Our jungle bird. Don't worry. He does that all the time."

"Doesn't it drive you crazy?"

"Does *what* drive me crazy?" she asked.

"You'll get used to it," Courtney said quietly.

"Whoa!" David yelled and ducked into a chair as an enormous white parrot came out of nowhere and clipped him on the side of the head.

"Captain Morgan!" Momma yelled. "You play nice. He's real territorial," she admitted. "He'll politen up once he gets to know ya."

"Probably sus*pects* somethin'," Tatum muttered.

"And that's our dog Happy," Courtney said. "Hiya, happy!" Courtney leaned over and gave Happy a gentle pet. Happy did not respond. "He doin' OK, Momma? Poor dog must be a hundred years old by now."

Momma shrugged. "He been movin' a lot slower lately."

"Momma, he's cold," she said with a look of concern. "How long's he been lyin' here?"

"'Bout a week."

"That's a long time to be lyin' down," she said.

"Not for a dog's favorite spot. 'Member that time he didn't get off my bed for the whole month of October?"

"No."

"Hmm. Maybe that was me. Y'all want some sweet tea? Girls, go get us some glasses."

"Sugar!" they both squealed and darted off to the kitchen.

Courtney put an arm around her mother's monstrous shoulder and squeezed it affectionately. "I'm so glad y'all are OK. What with the virus and the flood...why, y'all musta had a rough go of it."

"We're not alive by chance," Tatum said and stepped forward. "I've been takin' some mighty calculated moves ever since you left. I knew the shit was gonna hit the fan sooner or later. What I didn't know was how it was gonna play out. Personally I figured it was gonna end up bein' an alien invasion," he shrugged. "Yep. I'm prepared for just about anything. Riots, civil war, Nibiru. It's all gonna happen, eventually. Just in what order is what I haven't figured out yet. I will though. The way I figure it, the Illuminati have begun their Master Plan by high-jackin' the weather. They got those HAARP installations up in Alaska and are now in the process of tryin' to drown us out like rats. Been some real crazy weather lately. All over the country — earthquakes, tornados, this here flooding. There was even a huge hurricane that just took out most of Florida."

"Really?" David asked amazed. "And you think the ... *Illuminati* are doing this?"

" 'Course," he said again as if he had just been asked if humans breathe oxygen.

"But why?"

"Illuminati don't care about you an' me. All they care about is their Master Plan."

"Which is?"

He raised his eyebrows. "Oh, nothin' much, just the enslavement of the human race is all."

"Tatum..." Courtney said, as if she had heard this a million times.

"You think I'm still kiddin'? Look around, Sis! Our town is underwater, the country's on lockdown, and the Vampire Agenda is finally being revealed! Gosh, sometimes you're so stupid, Courtney."

"I guess I just have a hard time believing all of this is being done to us," she said. "Why can't some things just be the way they are? Why does everything have to be one big conspiracy with you?"

"Because it is!" he shouted. "Nothing is as it seems. We're all being lied to. Our media is controlled by a handful of individuals to dumb down the population, our food is being poisoned, our freedoms are being taken away, our government says one thing and does another, and goddammit, vampires are real! If you'd spend a little bit more time on Youtube and start educatin' yourself more, you'd have realized that bringing this time bomb home," he said, thumbing a finger at David, "was a horrendous mistake."

"But I told you, David's innocent."

"Innocent my ass!" he yelled overcome with emotion. He looked at David. "Listen, you look like a nice guy and all, but you've got sleeper agent written all over you."

David blinked. "Sleeper agent?"

Tatum shook his head and looked at Courtney. "Poor bastard doesn't even know who he is." He glanced back at David. "You ever hear of MK Ultra? Project Monarch? Project PaperClip? You've been programmed, man — tricked into thinking you're someone you ain't."

David blinked again. "Really?"

"*Yeah* really! My guess is you were probably born in Russia, trained in Israel, and in your late teens got your eyes taped open and forced to watch Disney movies for three months straight. I'd be surprised if you don't have a bomb strapped to your belly and don't even know it," Tatum said.

David quickly checked. He heaved a sigh of relief after finding his belly button free of explosives. He picked out some lint.

"Oh come on, David, you don't really believe any of this do you?" Courtney asked.

He scratched his head. "I don't know *what* to believe anymore, Courtney," he said. "I mean, to be honest, I don't remember anything before age five."

"But that's normal," Courtney said.

"Oh yeah?" Tatum said. "I remember I got stung by a bee when I was four."

"I choked on a turnip at age two," Momma said.

"We fell down a well when we was three," the Delilahs said holding a tray of sweet tea.

"Come to think of it, I didn't really have loving parents. My dad left when I was a baby and my mom was always casting wizard spells in Discovery Park. All I remember was a sweet Mexican lady tucking me in and singing me lullabies."

"That was probably your nanny," Courtney said.

"Nope. That was your stand-in mother hired by the Illuminati," Tatum nodded. "Her job was to instill in you a deep hatred for the government."

"But I *love* my government!" David said.

"Not subconsciously you don't. Trust me. Deep down you hate it. I gotta admit. They did a real good job programming you. Here you are thinking that you'd do anything for your government until one day you'll be sitting around and a little chip in your brain will go off and you'll decide you have to assassinate the President."

"But why would the Illuminati want him to assassinate the President?" Courtney asked.

"Because the government didn't do this to him — the *shadow* government did this, and as soon as the President is killed they'll be able to roll out their New World Order. Y'all don't believe me but it's true. Look it up on Youtube."

David clutched his head with his hands. Maybe Tatum was right —

maybe he *was* a sleeper agent destined to overthrow the government so the Illuminati could implement their plans for world domination. It made a lot of sense the more he thought about it.

Courtney put her hand on his shoulder. "David, don't go listening to my crazy brother."

"Too late, Courtney," Tatum said. "He's beginning to remember."

"I have to go outside," David said on the verge of tears. "I've got a lot of thinking to do."

David took one of the game trails to the front door and walked down the creaky plastic porch steps and looked up at the sky. The clouds hung heavily in the sky and it looked like it could rain at any moment. David had never felt worse in his entire life. He felt lost and alone. Unlike Courtney he didn't have any family to console him — not his mother, not his father, not even his phone. A tear dripped down his cheek as looked down at the ground. "Help," he said softly.

Jacob and his family were standing at the edge of the water giving each other mock baptismals in preparation for the Rapture. When Jacob saw David he stood up. "Hello there," he said kindly. "You look troubled, Master. Is there anything I can do to help?"

"Oh, I don't know, Jacob. Everything is so confusing right now. I've been trying to find myself for almost thirty years, and just when I think I know who I am, I realize I was never me to begin with."

"We all go through a crisis of identity at some point, my Lord," Jacob said. "You should know this better than anyone."

"What do you mean?"

"Well," Jacob said carefully, "For thousands of years people have said you are someone who you are not. They've taken your message and twisted it and wrangled it to suit their own values and beliefs, never trusting that the world is in fact six thousand years old."

"Wait, what? Six thousand years old? Really? Arrgghh, if I only had Google!"

"What I'm saying is that you are the Lord Jesus Christ back from the dead here to save this planet and all of God's faithful Christians from the bowels of hell."

This certainly came as a surprise. "I *am*?"

Jacob laughed. "Well, of course you are! You're so diligent about testing my faith, good Master. Try as you may, we all believe it and we'll follow you to the ends of the earth."

"Wait a minute. Your whole family...thinks I'm *Jesus*?"

Now all twenty Timpsons were looking at him. The smiles on their faces glowed like the sun itself. The women were hugging each other and the children were happily rocking on the balls of their feet. "We sure do, Master," they said. "We've believed it since the day we were born."

"You mean I'm *not* a sleeper agent?" he asked.

"In a way, perhaps," Jacob said. "You have chosen this path to understand what it means to be fully human."

"I *have?*"

"To understand the trials of being human gives you the gift of compassion. You have seen just how much we suffer here on planet Earth, and now knowing that, you can save us, as is your destiny."

"My destiny..." he said, his voice trailing off.

At that moment the sun broke out of the thick ceiling of clouds and a ray of golden light fell upon David's shoulders. His long hair was bathed in sunshine and his soiled toga robe looked like the garbs worn two thousand years ago.

David looked at his followers who stared back at him with reverence and awe, waiting for their Lord to say something profound, but after a moment's hesitation David said, "I am so friggin' confused."

Chapter 21: The Rally

The roar of Lindin's engine dominated the quiet streets of downtown Memphis. The town was mostly deserted, save for the occasional crack addict or homeless person wandering around aimlessly as if nothing out of the ordinary had happened. The burnt-out shells of automobiles littered the black asphalt like props from some apocalyptic horror film. Dead headless bodies could be seen everywhere — whites, blacks, it seemed the virus favored no race.

For the past six hours Melech had kept quiet during Lindin's continuous racial tirade about the horrors of society and the necessity of a master race. It was evident that Lindin cared deeply about his cause. It was also becoming painfully obvious to Melech that his own curt and quiet demeanor had caused Lindin to grow quietly suspicious. Twice he had accused Melech of being a nigger sympathizer and a Jew lover. Ironically, there wasn't a living creature on planet Earth that Melech either sympathized with or loved. Despite his blaring racism, however, Lindin was obviously educated. His long-winded rants included annotated abbreviations from the Articles of Confederation as well as plenty of well-documented footnotes from *Mein Kampf*. Lindin's intelligence was most certainly floating somewhere near 84.

"Damn shame what's happened to this town," he said. "Goddamn niggers ruin everything."

"I highly doubt they are responsible for this," Melech said, more than eager to reach his destination and get far, far away from this lunatic.

"I don't like that you keep sayin' that," Lindin said and glared into Melech's face.

"Sorry," he replied and fiddled with his hubcap.

"Sorry don't repair the *desecration* of an entire *nation*. You say sorry to George Washington and Thomas Jefferson if you have to. But not to me."

"Sorry," he said again, accidentally.

"Used to be such a nice town with little convenience stores and pharmacies and churches, big plazas and all that. We had big buildings and big cars driving down the street. Too bad that's all gone now 'cause of the niggers." Lindin sighed. "We did all we could. I have given every beat of my heart to our cause. I held gatherings and get-togethers. I organized *dozens* of rallies. It felt *good* getting together and standing behind something important. It felt good doing something meaningful with our lives. Molding society."

Melech straightened in his seat. "Absolutely. Only fools complain about society. One must *create* society."

"Goddam niggers and Jews," Lindin said again and Melech sighed.

"Is there a chance that we're anywhere near the courthouse?" he asked.

"Is there a chance?" Lindin laughed as he turned the corner. "Why that's where the rally is at!"

Melech's eyes lit up. "Great Minerva!" he said and looked out the window. Sure enough, over two hundred people dressed in white clothes with white hoods stood near the steps of the courthouse.

"This is gonna be great," Lindin said. "Looks like most of the audience is still on their way. I have a spare outfit you can wear to help increase our numbers. Quick, put it on."

"I'd rather not," Melech said and turned up his nose. "It smells atrocious."

"It shouldn't. It was years ago when the guy who owned it died in it. He was a big fella, though, so it should fit over that metal plate of yours."

Melech dry heaved.

Lindin glared. "Is there a problem?" he asked. "You aren't sympathizin' again, are you?"

He shook his head. "I regret to repeat myself, but I am in *much* need to see the courthouse."

"The courthouse is closed," Lindin said thinly. "On account of the niggers."

"What if you all broke inside?" Melech suggested.

Lindin thought about it. "Now *that's* a possibility. Why don't you suggest it to my friends?" he said, and shoved the hood into Melech's face. "Get going."

Both dressed, Lindin led Melech across the plaza to greet the protesters. Melech's hood protruded oddly on account of the hubcap. As they approached the crowd Lindin turned and faced Melech. For the first time Melech saw the front of Lindin's costume. He couldn't believe his eyes.

"You're a *dragon*?" His voice came out muffled from under his moldy hood.

"*Grand* Dragon," Lindin said and proudly rubbed the red cross on the front of his chest. "Now I expect you to be real polite with this group," he said. "I wouldn't want them taking whatever you say the wrong way."

A throng of individuals swallowed them. Men hollered and screamed together as they surrounded Lindin like a pack of wolves greeting their alpha and hoisted him into the air. Lindin made no effort to restrain them and embraced the exaltation like a cape around his shoulders. He pointed down at Melech and gestured for him to follow.

At last, the crowd reached the stage and gently sent Lindin onto the steps before the courthouse. Melech inched his way forward as he worked on his escape plan. "Brothers!" Lindin shouted into the microphone. "I welcome you, *Brothers!*" They waved and cheered like maniacs. "Exciting news I bring. Another Klansman has joined our cause!" he exclaimed. "I picked him up along the way. Our kind is everywhere. Hurrah!" he yelled.

"Hooray!" they yelled back.

"Today we are supposed to embrace acceptance," he said and held the microphone closer. "In today's world we must accept each other as we are. Well, I'd say we've been a mighty accepting group of people. We assemble peacefully, we vote, we gather and exercise the rights that our Founding Fathers set into motion — we're doing it all by the books! Today they say that it is time to accept that the white man is at the end of his rope. Is that something we can accept?"

"No!!!"

"Never!!!"

"Our Founding Fathers wanted for us, their *children,* the future stewards *of this great land,* to have all the freedoms that they died fighting for. They died so we could bear arms and so we could vote, and so that we could worship the Lord Jesus Christ freely. Those men, Thomas Jefferson and George Washington, those *white* men had *slaves.* And they are considered some of the greatest leaders of all time. Now you think about that."

There were murmurings of conversation from the crowd.

"So how can it be, *hundreds* of years later, after *aaaaall* this social change, that we cannot even pronounce the constitution as it's written today? Everything about it has changed. *Everything!* Laws have changed, the rules have been changed, society has changed, but not us — *we* will not change!"

The crowd roared with approval.

"I know my freedoms and I know my rights. And I'm pretty sure I *used* to have the right to own a slave or kick a Jew. I'm also pretty sure that I used to be able to talk about anything I damn well pleased. Well, what I got to say ain't pretty, folks!"

"Tell us!"

"Hear! Hear!"

"I'm just tellin' it like it is," Lindin said proudly. "And that's why you all are out here today, isn't that right?"

"You betcha!"

"Let's burn a cross!"

"Now now," he said. "All in good time. What *needs* to happen is a change in direction. Quite frankly, this country should be on another course and I think it's high time that our representatives start representing us. I am more than convinced that the Shelby County Courthouse has quite a list of phone numbers. What do you all think about givin' old Mr. President Benjamin Alan a call right now? Why we'd have to break in, of course, but that wouldn't be so bad, would it?"

The crowd screamed in agreement.

"That won't be necessary," said a clean and crisp Jewish-sounding voice. Lindin looked over his shoulder and saw a Klansman in a misshaped hood holding out a cell phone. "I've got his line on right now. It's dialing his number."

"What?" Lindin said. "Are you crazy or something?"

"Go ahead, see for yourself," he said, and handed him the phone.

Lindin took the phone as if it were a beating heart, but he held it up to his ear all the same. "H-hello?" he said.

"One moment," an automated voice said.

"Ye-llow!" Benjamin Alan asked. "Is that you Melech?"

"M-Mr. President?" Lindin asked.

"That's the name. You called so you're talkin'. Whaddaya want?"

"Um, uh, my name's Lindin Bradshaw," he said, looking around at the silent crowd. "I'm with the, um, the Ku Klux Klan. I'm a Grand Dragon, hope to be a Wizard someday. I...just..."

"The KKK?" the President interrupted. "Yeah, I think I've heard of them. Out of Tennessee, right? Where you goin' with this? You want a check or somethin'?"

"Well, sure that might be nice, but what I'm really callin' to say is..." he paused, "we want the white man back in power."

"Never left it, baby," the President said. "Hoping to make it another four. You voting for Mitchell Guiles this year, son? Because I think that would be a mistake. Why don't you leave your address and email and we'll send someone out there to campaign you. You have a number someone can reach you at?"

"Uh," he looked around. "Is this...I mean...let's see I can probably borrow someone's cell phone here..."

"Ow!!" the President yelled. "Sorry. I just got hit in the head with a bean bag. The VP and I were playing bean bags when you called. How did you *hic* get this number by the way?"

"Uh, Melech, Mr. President."

"*Rothschild?* That old yitze is *always* handing out my number. I got people calling in favors left and right."

"Did you say Rothschild?" Lindin asked wide-eyed. "He wouldn't be Jewish now would he?"

"Only about as Jewish as Kosher pizza. He's got a place in Brussels that makes the Queen of England look like she's living in a *homeless* shelter. Why? Did he schlepp something out you, that miser?"

"He's a Jew!" Lindin screamed and dropped the phone and turned around to strangle Melech. But Melech was no longer beside him. Melech, wisely, had taken the opportunity to escape. As soon as Lindin had taken the phone, Melech had slipped off to the south side of the courthouse. He didn't need to break in. He just needed a distraction, which had worked out rather swimmingly.

At the south end was an inconspicuous dark corner with a subtle Freemason symbol etched into the old brick. Melech pushed the heavy potted plant aside and brushed away the dirt to reveal a tiny handle to an otherwise invisible panel. He gripped the handle and with the last of his strength lifted it up and out of the way. The opening was small, but he knew he could fit. He sat down and swung his feet over the edge until he felt them touch a metal ladder somewhere in the darkness beneath him. With a sigh of relief he began to lower himself down after immediately flipping Memphis, Tennessee a much needed middle finger.

He would have made it, too, had his hubcap not caught against the opening. There was the slightest bit of wiggle room, but Melech was most certainly stuck. Desperately, he tried to free himself. Whatever position he attempted, however, only seemed to make things worse. He looked down, hoping that he could place his feet against the ladder while twisting his torso at the same time. He knew, however, that he had to be extremely careful, otherwise the hubcap could shift and pierce something vital.

But suddenly, he was rising, and within moments he was free. There had been no pain, no prying, only a swift and smooth upward yank from the hand of the Grand Dragon of the Ku Klux Klan, who had pulled Melech out of the escape hatch by the neck.

In one motion Lindin ripped off Melech's white hood and spat in his face. "I should have known!" he yelled. "That kike nose is a mile long, shaped like the Brooklyn Bridge itself. Come on, you! You've got some questions to answer." Lindin dragged Melech by both arms until they were standing at the podium again facing hundreds of angry protesters.

"Why the hell are you here!?" Lindin demanded. "Who the hell are you and why on earth do you have the President of the United State's phone number? What kind of tricky Jewery are you up to?"

"He's a friend of mine," Melech said meekly.

"A friend of yours, is he? Boy, I should have known! Just when I thought our nation couldn't get any worse. Why, I'll bet that hubcap of yours is the result of some sick twisted Jewish ritual, like circumcision or something. Before you know it, people in this very town will get hubcaps installed in their heads because they think it's cool."

"Boo!" the audience yelled.

Lindin grabbed the mic, eager to turn this moment into a talking point.

"This man beside me may look white, but pure he is not. The pureness of the white race has been tainted!" he yelled. "For so long we have marched, and rallied, and lawfully expressed our God-given hatred for blacks and Jews, (Mexicans too, but they mostly live in California), yet where has it gotten us? No matter how hard we try we are still strugglin' to keep our heads above water. While we are busy keepin' the black man in his place, the Jews are cavorting with *our* politicians and perpetuating the enslavement of the white man!"

"It's not the Jews," Melech said without emotion.

"What did you just say?" Lindin asked and turned an icy face towards Melech.

"I said it's not the Jews who are to blame for the fall of America. It's mainly the Zionists."

"The...*Zionists?*" Lindin squinted, unfamiliar with the term.

"Sure, the Zionists."

"What's a...*Zionist?*"

Melech gently pried Lindin's hand off his shirt as he deftly plucked his cellphone out of Lindin's other hand and leaned into the microphone. "Zionism is a nationalist and political movement that supports the re-establishment of a Jewish homeland in the territory defined as the historic Land of Israel (roughly corresponding to Palestine, Canaan or the Holy Land). Its roots lie deep in the Cabalistic tradition, an ancient practice devoted to by gnostics, heretics, and holy men of many cultures. The beliefs of such a system rely on calendrical systems precisely correlated with astral and lunar positions. Though the political movement is shrouded in much secrecy, it is deeply imbibed with traditions born by the Freemason movement, a fraternity of oath keepers that do the bidding of an unnamed architect in charge of the cosmos. So in all reality, no, it is not the Jews, or the blacks, or any culture or person you remotely understand. The one to blame for all this beautiful disaster and mayhem is *me*, motherfuckers!"

KABOOM! Lindin's head exploded into hundreds of pieces and Melech's clothes caught most of the brains.

The crowd gasped!

Melech ducked and dashed away in escape.

"The Jew is escaping!" someone yelled "Get him!"

But Melech was a terrified Jew, and before they knew it, he was gone.

Chapter 22: Taken

A full day had passed since arriving at Courtney's home. The water level had dropped considerably since the bus docked outside the mobile home, and the full extent of the flood's destruction was being revealed. Fenceposts, dead cattle, and overturned cars were just some of the items littering the streets of Mackanack, Arkansas. The sun had finally come out, however, and the twittering songs of curious birds could be heard from the treetops heralding a new day.

Most people had spent the previous day resting. David, thinking he might be Jesus, locked himself in a bedroom and tried to raise his phone from the dead. Courtney talked with her parents and caught up on the happenings during the last two years of her absence. Her mother had informed her that Mackanack had recently acquired its fourth Arby's and a second House of FlapJacks, though she abruptly stopped her dialogue several times to pray for their structural integrity against the flood.

Her father inquired if Courtney was here to stay, and, if so, if she had any interest in finding a job at the logging mill. This led into a long and difficult conversation about Courtney's views regarding the destruction of the environment. Her father was a life-long resource extractor and believed that man's sole purpose in life was to cut down every last tree, otherwise — and he stumped her with this one — why would God have planted 'em? After a long and frustrating argument, one thing did finally become clear to her: her old man just didn't like her living so far away from home.

"Could always use a pretty face down at the mill," he said. "Buncha rednecks ain't all that grand to look at. The boys shore would be happy to get a slice a sunshine during the work day, though. Who knows? Maybe even one of 'em would marry ya? Yer cousin Donny keeps askin' 'boutcha, ya know?"

She stuck out her tongue. "Gross, Dad. I don't want any of them good ol' boys. All they care about are tits and trucks. That just ain't me. My tastes are a bit more cultured," she said and puffed out her chest.

Her father crossed his arms and spit on the carpet. "I can only imagine what those idiots in California think about. Culture," he huffed. "Just 'cause California's filled with Mexicans and sushi-lovers don't mean it's got more culture than we do. I got more culture in my little finger than all of Jodi Foster's movies put together." He stuck his fingernail between his teeth and looked at his daughter. "Boys in this town ain't near as bad as that beanpole terrorist ya brought home with ya. My God, Courtney. He's worse than that one-legged albino fella ya took to prom when you was in high school."

196

"Stop it, he is not. David's a good fellow, honest."

"Good enough to shut down a whole country, eh?"

"It ain't David's fault, Daddy. That dang ol' President of ours just made some rash decisions, that's all. Couple folks get sick and he decides to close all the stores? Now what good does that do?"

"Why don't you ask yer boyfriend?"

"He *ain't* my boyfriend, Daddy. He's just a guy who got caught up in a bad situation. Heck, I *wish* he was my boyfriend. He's practically the only fella who's ever treated me with half an ounce of respect. He even likes my songs," she said and brushed off her lap.

Daddy scooted back involuntarily. "You ain't gonna start singin' now, are ya?"

"Oh just *quit* it, already! God gave me a voice and gosh darnit, I'm gonna use it to inspire the world." She snapped her fingers. "Why what with David's fancy phone I'll bet he could help me whip up a music video."

"Better auto-tune it," her father advised.

A door opened and Tatum emerged from his bedroom holding an empty pot of coffee. His eyes were red and bloodshot.

"You been up all night, boy?" Daddy asked.

Tatum nodded "Couldn't sleep. Had so many ideas in my head I just had to sort them out. Somethin' about that David Dingle has been rubbin' my cornstalk the wrong way. All ya gotta do is look at the guy to tell he's a damn buffoon. I mean, he was wearin' a toga when he showed up on our lawn, for Christ's sake! And that damn expression of his standin' there in that Seattle plaza lookin' like he mighta crapped his pants – Jesus! Media's been painting him as some sort of criminal mastermind, but the more I think about it the more convinced I become that he's a sleeper agent."

"How can ya tell?" his father asked.

"Well, it's a bold conclusion," he admitted, "and to be honest, I felt kinda bad comin' outta the gate and accusin' him of such a thing before I even shook his hand. I mean, if Courtney says he's a good character then we should trust her, since she's family an' all."

Her father squinted. "Don't mean she hasn't made bad decisions, though. Like that time she brought a raccoon home thinkin' it was a stray cat," Daddy said and shook his head. "I had *just* painted the kitchen."

"Or what about when she gave that homeless man with the orange jumpsuit a hacksaw only to find out that he was an escaped convict?" Tatum laughed.

"Or the time-"

Courtney stomped her foot. "OK! So I ain't got the best track record, all

right? But this time it's different. Just 'cause every person in the country thinks
that David Dingle is a terrorist don't make it so. They haven't spent time with him
like I have. They don't know that he's a real person with real feelings."

"Bet he's feelin' real dumb right about now," Momma said.

"Why you say that?"

"Cause he's sleepin' in the other room locked up with Hokem.
Guaranteed that cat's gonna piss all over him." Momma shrugged and looked up
at Hulk Hogan. "Pissed on me *plenty* a times."

"Oh, shit, that reminds me," Daddy said. "I should go out and feed the
chickens. Should probably give that nut job Jerry some water while I'm out
there," he said and lumbered off through the forest of dirty laundry.

"Anyways," Tatum resumed, "I had to know the truth about David so I
took down my flat earth theory collage and started hanging up all the articles I've
been collecting about the pandemic. Turns out David Dingle wasn't born in
Seattle at all. He was born in a town called Tacoma which just so happens to be
home of the Grand Lodge of Free and Accepted Masons."

"So?" Courtney said.

"*So?*" he asked. "Sooo...that lodge is only a couple miles from where he
was born. No doubt that's where he was initiated. He also happens to have been
born on the twenty-first of December which is of course solstice, which means
that the Satanists had preordained his birth and knew that he was coming.
Because they brainwashed him at such an early age, he thinks he's just a normal
guy with a normal job, but that couldn't be *fuuurther* from the truth," Tatum sang.
"The fact of the matter is that he's been programmed like an old Atari. All he has
to hear is a secret word or phrase and he'll turn into a zombie and blow up the
President's head, which would of course cause mass hysteria. Now, I think we can
all agree that President Alan is just a puppet for the Illuminati, but I guarantee
you that as soon as the plan is in motion, our TV's will turn on by themselves and
we'll all witness the leader of the free world get assassinated just like what they did
to Kennedy and Tupac."

"But if he's just a puppet then what's the point of it all?" she asked.

"The point of course is to create a collective synaptic shock-link in our
brains. We become helpless and fearful when we witness trauma which causes us
to beg the government to take away the last of our freedoms in the name of
national security. With President Alan out of the way, Vice President Palmdonger,
who undoubtedly sides with the Vampire Agenda, will begin to unveil his plans
for blood camps and soylent green taco trucks."

"Tatum, this is ridiculous," Courtney said and looked up at The
Undertaker.

"It is *not* ridiculous!" Tatum yelled. "Your boyfriend is a sleeper-agent and

I got the proof spread all over my wall. It's funny how things work out," he said,
composing himself. "It's actually quite fortunate that you've brought him here.
Since we know where he is and what he's capable of we can actually prevent any
of this from ever happening by locking him in the food cellar and feeding him old
potatoes!"

"No! Absolutely not," she said.

Tatum rubbed his chin. "If only I could get an internet connection. What
with all this new information and no way to spread it I feel like I'm letting down a
lot of my Twitter followers."

"You can't just feed me chicken scraps!" Jerry yelled as he emerged
through the back door. There were thin red scratches all over his hands and face.
"I need real food, dammit."

Courtney's father looked flustered and nervous. "Dang kid slipped ma
grasp. Come on, fella. Why don't ya come on back with me? I'm sorry ya got all
tangled up with the two cocks. They're mean this time a day."

"Courtney!" Jerry yelled. "Tell this maniac that I'm not a chicken. Tell
him I need a quart of ice cream and some pizza. *Anything*! You guys have a
shower? I think I slept on a dead animal last night."

"It's OK, Daddy. Jerry's fine. Just hungry it seems."

"What is *wrong* with you people?" he asked, looking around. "You guys
running a refugee camp or have you just gotten accustomed to living in your own
filth?"

"Now you listen here," Momma said and attempted to sit up. It was a
brief attempt and soon she was out of breath and back in the reclining position.

"Good God, what did I just put my hand in?" Jerry asked and looked at
the green slime strung between his hand and the book case.

"I think that used to be a cucumber," Tatum said.

"No," Momma said. "Ain't had no vegetables in our house for years."

"Jesus, Courtney. Your family's about as athletic as a bag of Cheetos.
Your dad nearly tripped over his own feet trying to find them. I sure do
appreciate the southern hospitality and everything but I think I'm about ready to
find a Denny's. Where's David?"

"He's sleepin', Jerry," Courtney said evenly. "You're just gonna have to be
patient."

"My ass he's sleeping. This place is about as peaceful as a concentration
camp."

"You're right. You should go," Tatum said. "We ain't got room fer
shitheads."

"Good one, butter ball," Jerry pointed. "Welp, it sure has been fun
meeting you and the rest of the Adams Family, not to mention the comfortable

room you set me up in. Let me just find my friend and we'll be on our way."

"I'm afraid I can't let you do that," Tatum said. "David has decided to stay."

"*David* cannot decide if he should breathe or not unless you tell him to. Now which room is he in?" he asked and started moving through the house like an anxious golden retriever.

"Hey!" Tatum said. "What do you think you're doing? Stop right there."

But Jerry was already at the last closed door which he flung open with panicked bravado. But instead of finding his friend sleeping on a piss-stained bed, he only found an angry cat staring back at him.

"Tatum?" Courtney asked. "Where's David?" The entire family (minus Momma who had managed to make it to an angle 65 degrees above the horizontal) peered into the empty room. Hokum hissed. "This is where he went to bed isn't it?" Courtney asked.

"It sure is," Tatum said. "Maybe he went for a walk?" he suggested.

"Look!" Courtney said. "His phone is lying on the floor."

"Uh-oh," Jerry said. "David doesn't go anywhere without his phone."

"That's funny," she said. "It's got power all of a sudden. I thought he said it ran out of battery."

"That phone can do some amazing things," Jerry said. "For all we know it could be self-aware."

As if sensing their presence the phone screen suddenly blinked on and the words: "My Master is gone" appeared.

"*Creeepy*," Jerry whispered.

"I don't get it. What does that mean?" she asked.

"Oh shit! Check it out!" Jerry said and held the phone which had begun to play a video for them. In the video they could hear David's voice.

"W-who's there?" he said groggily.

"Wake up, jackass. You're coming with me."

"Agent Boring?"

"The one an only. Put your shoes on. We're going to Washington."

"Seattle?"

"Fuck Seattle. I'm taking you to the capitol. There's a V.P. suit I gotta try on."

Courtney looked at Jerry. "I thought you tied Boring up?" she accused.

"I *did*!" he said. "I even used a slip-knot so it would be easy to untie him later. I hate untying tight knots," he said and rolled his eyes.

"We've got to stop him!" Tatum said. "Or the President's head is going to explode. The Vampire Agenda! The Vampire Agenda!" he kept yelling.

"What'll we take?" Courtney asked.

"The water level's dropped quite a bit. As long as that bus still drives we can take it."

The phone made a beeping noise and Courtney looked at the screen. It read: "I want to drive. I miss my human."

Chapter 23: A Terrible Realization

The 68' Firebird's engine wheezed as Agent Boring pulled away from downtown Mackanack and merged onto the open interstate. The engine sputtered and then wheezed again, angrily and painfully like a lion that's been mortally shot. Boring pressed the gas pedal the rest of the way down until it hit against the sleek black metal floor and the Firebird struggled and coughed and the speedometer topped out at 36 miles an hour. Not bad for a car that had recently been upside down and under water.

"I've got to find a way to make it go faster," Agent Jon Boring said, more to himself than to David who sat buckled in beside him.

"It didn't look mechanically sound when we got in," David said.

"Of course it did!" Boring retorted. "It has a *lightning strike* painted on it, for Christ's sake! Besides, I poured water in the wiper fluid intake. The car should be fine."

"It seems to be shaking," David said with a look of concern.

Boring hung his arm out the car door and patted the side loudly. "She's doin' juuust fine," he said authoritatively. "We'll get there when we get there."

"And where are we going?" David asked.

Boring eyed David Dingle and smiled for the first time since he had marched David out of the house and gotten his first taste of kidnapping. Target-napping is what they should call it, Boring thought. David Dingle was a target, a terrorist, an enemy of the state and only Special Agent Jon Boring could take him down. *That* was why he had smiled.

"We, my unfortunate friend, are going to the White House."

"Really?" David asked. "Oh man! Are we going to meet the President? Because if we are I *really* need you to drive us back to Courtney's house so I can pick up a folder that I need the President to read for me. He's probably the only guy in the world who can make heads or tails of it. I'm serious. Once he reads it this whole situation will get resolved. We might even become friends," he pondered.

"You poor, stupid, sonofabitch," Boring said and smiled sadly at David. "The President doesn't want to be your friend. No way! He's gonna want to punch you in the face because you thought you could get away with it, didn't you? You thought you were above the law, but you failed to account for someone like me who was gonna take you down. You sorry bastard. You *should* be sorry — it didn't have to come down to this. I'm not a violent guy, Mr. Dingle. Don't like violence, really. I'm more of a peace lover and lover maker, you get my drift?" He

shrugged and smiled, thinking about sex. "The God's honest truth of the matter is that there are bad guys out there who don't want neither peace nor love and that's where *I* come in," he said and pointed to himself with his thumb. "I'm the guy people call when the dirty work needs to get done, when the bad guys need to be caught and brought down, and I just brought you down, *big time*!" he said and jeered at David.

Boring paused to catch his breath. There was more he wanted to say about himself. "I think while we're at the White House I'm going to look around for my next master bedroom. Know why? Cuz I'm gonna be the President's running mate!" he clapped his hands and the car swerved and groaned. "I gotta hand it to you, Mr. Dingle. You put up quite a chase. It was neat back there with the inflatable tits on the bus. That was cool — didn't see that coming one bit!" he laughed. "But your friend, oh my God, *what* an idiot! And a loser!" he nearly spat. "Plays video games all day, pretending to be these huge glorified avatars with huge glorified fucktabulous guns and impossible villains that are just *begging* for a hero to bring them down. *Fuck* those made-up games! What *I* do is real. What *I* do is the only way it can be done. No one can do it like Agent Boring does."

David wasn't really listening to Boring's self-congratulatory rant. "I know you don't believe me, but for what it's worth I didn't do it."

"Didn't do what?" Boring asked.

"I - um - am not responsible for the pandemic."

"Wait, what's a pandemic? You're talking about the virus, right?"

David nodded. "Yeah. Just because I was there doesn't mean that I had anything to do with it."

Boring looked off into the distance as he thought about it. "Oooh!" he said suddenly. "I get what's going on. You didn't plan any of this at all did you?"

David shook his head. "No."

"Gotcha," Boring said as if understanding perfectly. "Sounds like you got jabbed, then."

"*Jabbed?*"

"Mmm-hmm. In your sleep. Trust me, it happens all the time. I jabbed a guy myself once, actually," he said, recalling the memory like a lost marble. "Puerto Rican fella, if I remember correct."

David rubbed his arm. "I don't...*think* I've been jabbed."

"You wouldn't remember. They put chemicals in the syringe so that you forget," he nodded with certitude.

"But why would anyone do that?" David asked.

"Well, because you're a patsy, *obviously*," Boring said. "I didn't think so at first. At first I thought you were a criminal mastermind, but then..." he said and gave David a look.

"But what?" he asked.

"*Clearly*, you're not." His tone was both condescending and sympathetic at the same time. "You're just a *regular* guy with a *regular* job, that does idiotic stuff on his phone all day, and plays video games, and never goes anywhere or does anything exciting, or has a girlfriend, or a family who loves him. Come on! You're not a mastermind, Dingle. You're a dumbass! Any intelligent person would have looked at their life years ago and said, 'Holy fuck! I'm a total loser. I should do something meaningful with my life.' Face it. You're just a dumbass guy that was easy to take advantage of. Sorry, but it's true," he said and started humming *Rock me like a Hurricane* as the vehicle crept over 40mph.

David stared out at the horizon and tried to push down the rising swell of pain. The sharp sting of truth had hit him square in the face and it hurt something fierce. He knew the secret agent was right. David was about as smart as a flip phone. All his life he had relied on other people to work out his problems for him. Ever since the outbreak he had allowed Jerry and any other carbon-based life form to tell him what to do. If David had even the slightest shred of confidence he would have told Agent Boring that he was a capable individual with views and opinions of his own that could make rational decisions and think for himself. Instead, he burst into tears.

"Are you serious? Are you fucking *serious?* You're *crying?*" Boring asked. "Geez, I'm sorry. I'm really sorry, all right? Just knock it off, would ya?"

"I can't!" David moaned. "My life is a mess and it's all because of me. I do what everyone tells me to do because I'm afraid of the consequences if I make a wrong decision. There are *so* many decisions, Agent Boring. Like who am I? *That's* an important decision! Why I could be a once-jabbed sleeper-agent suspect of a national pandemic that has destroyed the economy, communications, and everything necessary to civilized life in America. *Or*, I could be Jesus." David brushed his hair and looked out the window. "I *hope* I'm not Jesus. That's a lot of pressure. I would probably have to have read the Bible at least once. I don't know if I've even *seen* a Bible before. Performing miracles might be cool, though. I've always wanted to try red wine."

Boring shook his head. "You need to get out more, man. It's a big world out there. Red wine is like on the bottom of the To-Do List."

"Yeah, but the world's kind of scary, too. Just look at it," he said and pointed to the empty factories that towered over what had once been pristine virgin forest. Garbage littered the sides of the road and dirty sludgy water ran slowly down a rocky ravine. "Everyone seems so certain that they're making the right decisions, but what happens if everyone's decisions turn out to be wrong? I'd like to tell some people that, Agent Boring, but like you said I'm just a regular guy with an awesome phone that can tell me whatever I need to know. I think if more people had better phones there'd be a lot less problems in the world." He shook his head while he pondered this deep thought. "I hope Jerry didn't die of an overdose last night."

Agent Boring waved a hand. "From here on out you don't have to think about a thing. You're along for the ride. Just sit back and relax while I take you to D.C. where you'll likely become the scapegoat for this entire national catastrophe. From there you've got a handful of possible outcomes. They'll either hang you, electrocute you, or jab you again on live television and then bury you next to a bunch of child molesters on the outskirts of Detroit, Michigan. It's where they put Lee Harvey Oswald," he nodded.

"Oh God!" David said and clutched his head. "This is terrible. I didn't do it," he repeated. "This shouldn't be happening."

"Just embrace it," Boring said casually. "Hey, want something to help you relax? You like White Snake?" he asked, and turned up the radio. "Hey look, we're picking up speed."

David's eyes widened. "We're going down a big hill. I think you might need to slow down."

"No chance in hell, kid. This baby's gonna be our slingshot." Suddenly Boring's phone started ringing. Boring reached down and squirmed for his cellphone under his leg. "Hello?" he asked. "*Who?*" He squinted at David. "*Who* is this? His *mother*? Are you kidding me? How'd you get this number? Uh-huh? *Really*? *My* mother gave it to you? Sharon Boring, huh? You do? Well, no kidding. OK, you can talk to him, but only for a second." He passed David the phone. "It's your mother. She probably wants to know if you're still alive. You can say hello but if you tell her where we are or anything important at all you won't be alive for long. Got it?"

David nodded and took the phone. "Mom?"

"David! It's Courtney. Thank God you're alive! Listen, I don't have much time, but we found your phone."

His heart fluttered to life and he sat up in his seat. "Is it OK?" he asked.

"It's fine. When Agent Boring shot the Dr. in Vegas your phone took a picture of him. This morning when I found it, your phone automatically pulled Boring's profile off the internet and hacked his cellphone number. It's a really smart phone," she said.

"It is," he nodded fondly.

"Anyway, it knows where you are and we're coming to find you."

"You *are*?" he asked and a small puddle of hope gleamed in his heart.

"We got the bus up and running again and we're already on the road. Just stay alive, David. Huh? What?" David heard Courtney say to someone. "Oh. David, my brother Tatum wants me to tell you to put newspaper in your ears."

"What?" he asked.

"He says you just need to plug up your ears so you don't hear your trigger word and go offline and kill the President. Plug your ears," she said again.

"Whoa!" he said suddenly to Boring. "You've gotta slow down!" he cried. "We're going really fast. I think the wheels are about to fall off."

"It's fine!" Boring hollered. "Now hold on, we're coming to the second wiggle from that wiggly road sign back there. Only two more to go!"

"David, what's going on?"

"Nothing, Mom!" he hollered. "Got it loud and clear. It was good talking to you — oh my God!"

"David!"

"Boring, slow down!"

"Calm down, calm down!" Boring said, gripped by raw adrenaline. "It looks like we're straightening out."

"What is that??" David yelled.

"I have no idea," Boring said and stared at the objects in the road ahead of them.

"You've gotta stop the vehicle!" he screamed.

"I can't! The brake pedal just fell off!"

"Oh my God! Look how many of them there are!" David yelled. "We're gonna die!"

"David!!" Courtney yelled, but the line had gone dead.

Chapter 24: The Hitchhiker

Veryonica fluttered her eyelids at the cross-eyed soldier guarding the checkpoint out of Arkansas. "We just *have* to get to our nation's capitol," she said with an extra squeeze of honey. "We have an appointment to meet the President."

The guard stared at her tits. "Really?"

She *tsk-tsked* her tongue. "Now would *I* lie to you?" she said for the eighth time today.

The guard apparently didn't think so and waved them on and the stolen convertible cruised through the roadblock. Veryonica shook her head bitterly. "Those idiots believe anything you tell them. He barely asked a single question. I was at *least* hoping he'd frisk us," she said with disappointment.

"I'm glad no one tried speaking to me in Spanish this time," Hashim said with relief. He had nearly blown it at the last checkpoint when one guard had asked him to see his papers and his response had been, "*Yo tengo mechanico nachos. Tres tacos.*" The guard, thankfully, did not speak Spanish either and had waved them through.

The car sped past a road sign of a giant vinyl record jutting out of a lightning bolt which read: Welcome to Memphis. Hashim sat up. "Oh my!" he said excitedly. "This is where rock and roll comes from, isn't it? I remember one afternoon in ExxonMobilastan some blasphemous rock and roll penetrated the open market space and I couldn't help but want to go for a very fast camel ride. I remember the band's name was *Nickleback...*" he said remembering that moment.

"Never heard of 'em," Veryonica said. "Seriously. For a town all about music and rock and roll there sure is a lot of abandoned cars and trash in the roads."

"I think it might be because of the pandemic," Hashim said.

"That makes sense," she nodded. "Outta the way!!" Veryonica yelled and honked at a few desperate survivors who seemed in need of help and were trying to get the convertible to stop. "Still no excuse not to keep your town clean. Just because there's a pandemic doesn't mean people should be walking in the roads." She swerved suddenly to clip the shopping cart of a homeless person and then sped through the wide intersections without stopping. "It used to be so exciting running red lights," she said. "Now without any cross traffic it all seems so pointless. I'll tell ya, Hashim, if we don't get to D.C. soon I'm gonna lose the will to live."

"With all the checkpoints we've passed I wonder how strong security will be at the White House?" Hashim asked as they drove through town.

"Something tells me it's going to be heavily guarded. I mean just look! We're witnessing Martial Law, Hashim. The whole *country's* on lockdown. If they care so much about some stupid checkpoint in Tennessee then I guarantee you they've got the President's ass covered by *multiple* men in black suits," she said and licked her lips.

"I suppose," Hashim said. "He is the most powerful man in the world, after all."

"Whatever you say. My guess is that he's got about as much power and control as a pet chihuahua. Personally, I think he's an idiot. Cute though," she said and checked her reflection in the rearview mirror.

"That's what most Americans think about him, I've learned," Hashim said.

"Yeah, you can't fool the American public," she said and shook her head. "We watch a *lot* of TV. There's like, so many channels, that it's really easy to stay current and like, fact-check. President Alan is always gonna stand there in that nice ol' suit of his and talk with them big fancy words about how much he cares about climate change and football season, but for the most part it's all a show. Point is, he's an idiot and we all know it."

Hashim thought about this. "But didn't you elect him?" he asked.

"Sure!" she said.

"But why?"

"Because democracy is what makes America *great*," she said and looked at him. "I know it's hard for you to understand, Hashim, seeing as how you've come from the Middle West where no one has any rights and women have to cover their face with bandanas, but here in America people are free to vote once every four years. It must be weird for you to witness real democracy in action," she said as they passed an armored tank heading the other way.

"But if you don't like the President then why did you vote for him?"

"Oh my God, you should have *seen* the other guy. He was like, fat and stuff. Nuh-uh," she shook her head. "I don't want no fat President. I'm serious. President Alan is the *only* President I have ever voted for. As stupid as he is, he is still one sexy motherfucker and I would *not* mind getting me a little Monica Lewinsky action before you blow him up — if you think we'll have time, I mean."

Hashim watched the horizon. "I would barely recognize him," he said. "I've only seen him once before on TV. It was when I was living in ExxonMobilastan. I was at my village's only remaining store after all the others had been destroyed. My fellow villagers were flipping through the channels trying to find some news or information on why our village had been bombed to rubble. Finally we found a station with a handsome man standing in front of the American flag who said that he was the leader of the free world. That morning he said that his drone army had dropped bombs on our village because he had received intel that we were harboring freedom-hating terrorists." Hashim looked at his hands. "It was the first time in my life that I learned that Americans thought that ExxonMobilastan pre-schoolers were terrorists. Your President seemed very proud to have killed them all."

Veryonica was silent as they drove down the road. She kept glancing at Hashim out of the corner of her eye. She noticed a tear running down his cheek.

"I lost everything because of that man," he said. "Everything. My wife, my children, my community...my dignity. You may think that I *want* to be a terrorist," he said, "but that couldn't be further from the truth. I want to go back to selling figs in the market where I used to live. But that market is gone now and so is everything else that I had to live for."

"I'm sorry," Veryonica said quietly. "I had no idea. Here I thought that people in ExxonMobilastan loved us."

"Quite the contrary," he said and sat up. "It has become a longtime tradition in our country to hate America with all of our hearts," he assured her. "It is culturally expected of us to vow vengeance against the United States before we hit puberty."

"*Really*?!"

"Sure! We have this really fun song we sing about lighting Micky Mouse's head on fire with a grenade. It gets the whole community involved. Think about it. America has more military bases in other countries than any other country in the world. It kills more innocent people than all terrorist organizations combined. Besides that, the U.S. Government uses its economy to destroy the livelihoods of ordinary people just trying to survive. When they want to build a McDonald's overseas they just bomb a plaza because it's cheaper than hiring a demolition crew."

Veryonica tightened her grip on the steering wheel. "I can't believe I've been *lied* to," she said through clenched teeth. "Here all along I'd believed that the President was making the world a better place with his Affordable Global Shopping Mall Act. But now you're telling me that it's just the opposite? Ugh. I think I'm going to be sick. I can't help but feel responsible in some way." She looked out along the road and Hashim could see that she was thinking. "You know, Hashim," she said, "maybe you're right. Maybe it *is* OK to kill other people, as long as they've been killing other people first."

"What are you saying?" he asked.

She looked at him and smiled. "Maybe we need to kill the President, after all."

Hashim wiped the tear from under his eye and perked up. "I like the sound of that."

"If I don't kill us first, that is," she winked.

Hashim blinked instead of winking. He didn't like that idea. Frankly, her driving scared the holy shit out of him.

"Oh, it's OK," she said, noticing his anxiety. "I'll do my best not to kill myself until we get to D.C., how's that?" She put two fingers on her heart and closed her eyes as they sped down the road.

"Praise Allah," he said.

"Now, if someone *else* wants to kill *me* that might be fun." She opened her eyes again. "Hey look! A hitchhiker! Oooh, he looks dangerous!!" The car skidded from ninety miles an hour to a stop, kicking up a humongous cloud of smoke and dust and rock until it finally settled fifteen feet from a man in a blood-stained white robe.

"Nice hubcap!" Veryonica yelled at the stranger as he approached the vehicle. "Did you do that yourself or were you born that way?" she asked.

Melech tried to catch his breath from running to the car. Only three cars had passed him in the last four hours and none of them had been brave enough to pick him up. "Can I get a ride?" he asked.

"Well, that depends?" Veryonica kidded. "Are you a wanted felon?"

He shook his head. "No."

"An ax murderer?" she asked hopefully.

"I am not," he stated.

She pouted her lips. "Well, what's with all the blood and that disk you got jammed in your head?"

"Car accident. Pandemic. Listen," he said impatiently. "I'm trying to get to Washington D.C. Is there any way you can help me?"

"D.C.?!" she exclaimed. "That's where *we're* going!"

"Oh, thank Satan!" he said without thinking and then slapped a hand over his mouth realizing what he had just said.

"Oh boy! A Satanist!" she squealed. "Get in!"

Melech gave a sigh of relief and maneuvered himself into the back of the convertible. "I really appreciate it," he said and grimaced, still not comfortable with saying polite things to normal people.

"You're not contagious, are you?" Veryonica asked.

"Absolutely not. It is the one thing I can guarantee."

"Rats. Well, maybe we'll pick up someone who is. Name's Veryonica," she said and looked at Melech through the rearview mirror.

"Charmed," he said and cracked a smile like an agitated crocodile.

"And this here's Hashim. We're going to Washington to kill some-"

"Time!" Hashim said quickly. "Yes, lots of time needs to get killed in D.C.," he said.

"That's right!" Veryonica nodded. "Good one, dear. Yep. Nothing like killing lots of time to make you wonder, 'where did all the time go?' Ever thought about killing yourself?" she asked.

"Uh, no, actually," Melech stated. "Why are you asking me that?"

"Oh, just tryin' to get to know ya. Seein' if we have anything in common."

"Nice convertible," Melech said and rubbed the vinyl interior. "It looks expensive."

"Really?" she asked. "I just picked it off the lot. Owner probably paid a lot for it, I imagine." Hashim covered his eyes with his hands. He couldn't believe Veryonica was sharing all of this.

"Are you saying you stole this vehicle?" Melech asked.

"I like to think of it more as fate," she said. "This baby practically jumped in my lap. Which reminds me! I've been so busy driving it I haven't gotten the chance to check and see if there's anything useful. Would you take a look under your seat and see if there's any caustic soda or dynamite or anything?"

Melech looked down and saw the shiny metallic briefcase on the floor of the car. He raised an eyebrow. "There is a very expensive looking briefcase back here. Looks a lot like mine, in fact. Same model even."

"Oh!" she exclaimed. "That's ours! Just got it actually. My, er — grandmother's head just blew up, and that's my inheritance. Yep, old grandmother Rubycash, God rest her soul. Her dream was always for us to go to D.C and buy the Washington monument."

"That's...odd. So, you two must be married?"

She looked at Hashim and laughed. "*God* no! I mean, yes! Of *course* we're married. Been married for years now. Don't we just look like we've been married since the day we were born? I've always had a thing for ExxonMobilastan men, myself. I think it's the way their untrimmed mustaches feel when their face goes into my vagina."

"You're from ExxonMobilastan?" Melech asked.

Hashim squirmed in his seat. "Yes?" he said more like a question.

Veryonica beamed like the sun itself. "Born and raised. Only been in America for a few weeks now."

"But I thought you said you were married?" Melech asked.

"Oh, that's right. Yeah. We decided to do it via email. We just couldn't wait. We're so *impassioned*," she said and leaned over and kissed her pretend husband.

"And now you're going to D.C.," he said. "To kill some time and buy the Washington Monument..."

"Mmm-hmm," she grinned. "What about you?"

Melech leaned back. He hated talking about himself in front of proletarians. "Oh, I live there," he said.

"You *do*? Well, how do you like that! Maybe you could show us around then?"

"That would be nice," he lied, "but I have some business that I must attend to first."

"Oh yeah? Like what?" she prodded. "Does it have anything to do with that hubcap jammed in your head."

He made a face. "Yes and no. I have a meeting that I am terribly late for and so it is of the utmost importance that I get to it at once."

Veryonica involuntarily pressed deeper onto the gas pedal. "Where's your meeting? Where are we dropping you off at?"

"I need to go to the White House," he said quietly.

"The *White* House? Who are you meeting with in the White House?"

He sighed. "Well, if you must know it's with the President."

"The *President*!!" they both exclaimed at once. "You're meeting with the President?"

He eyed them both. "The President is a close friend of mine. I am one of his top advisors and it is imperative that I speak with him in regard to the pandemic."

"Does he know you have that hubcap jammed in your head?" Veryonica asked.

"Would you *please* stop referring to my injury in that manner?" he said angrily. "I am well aware of the dirty metal object implanted in my parietal skull and I don't need every single person I encounter to adopt a medical position, all right?"

"Touchy," she said quietly to Hashim. "Well, Mr. Satanist, I think it's just *great* that you've got that thing jammed in your head," she smiled. "The color clashes a bit with your complexion, but otherwise I think it looks really nice."

"Thanks," he grumbled and held up his cell phone looking for coverage.

"No signal out here, I'm afraid," she said. "That idiot friend of yours, President Alan Dumbass, shut down all lines of communication. Can you imagine that? During probably the biggest catastrophe in American history? Heck, I can't even look at my Facebook to see how many of my friends' heads have blown up!"

"I have a special phone," he said.

Her eyes widened like dinner plates. "Of course you do! That makes sense. I guess when you're the President's top advisor you have to be able to get a hold of him, whether you have a metal plate jammed in your head or not. Whoop! Hang on!" she said and jerked the steering wheel suddenly sending both

Melech and Hashim into the side of the car. Melech dropped his phone which fell to the car floor.

"What's wrong with you!" he yelled. "You almost killed us!"

"Almost," she smiled.

Melech leaned over and searched for his phone.

"So are you *really* a Satanist?" she asked.

His fingers clutched his phone and he sat up. "Mmm-hmm," he muttered as he opened his phone again.

"That sure must be interesting. Not that I believe in any of that garbage. I mean it's cute and all that you believe you're communicating with the Devil, but seriously, that's like, Loony Tunes. That's even crazier than ol' Hashim here thinking that there's a browned-skinned God in heaven waiting for him with a bunch of virgins."

"Hey!" Hashim said.

"No offense."

"So I suppose you believe in a white God sitting on a cloud?" Melech asked sarcastically as he put the phone against his ear.

"Are you kidding me? What do I look like, an *idiot?*" she asked and jerked the car again suddenly, sending Melech's phone back under the driver's seat. "No way! I don't believe in any of that nonsense. Not anymore, at least. I grew up in a very strict religious family," she explained. "My family's Catholic. I've got nine brothers and, um, maybe eleven sisters. *They* all got the brains and all I got was this bangin' body fit for Hustler Magazine. Heck, my father was so strict he barely let me out of the house. Who could blame him, with tits like these?" she winked at Melech in the rearview mirror.

"Anyway, I was just sooo bored bein' locked up in my room all the time that I took a real shine to masturbation." She had their full attention now. "In Catholicism, masturbation is a sin, just like everything else," she rolled her eyes. "Our priest always told us that everyone is a sinner whether they like it or not and that the only one who can save us from our sins is Jesus. I believed all that hogwash until one day when I got ahold of the Karma Sutra and realized that sin is the best part about being alive. I started stealing and having sexually charged adventures every chance I got."

"And then what happened?" Melech asked, wiping the drool from his chin.

"Well, I got caught having sex with a carny in a stolen hot air balloon by a news chopper and I spent a week in jail. It was really depressing. I realized that as long as I was in this body, pleasure was only a temporary thing and if I could just escape from the confines of this sex-sack I'm carrying around then I could live in bliss for the rest of my life. *So*, I attempted to hang myself by my underwear, got caught by the jail guard and had the best sex I'd had all month. I've tried to kill myself nearly a hundred times, but every time someone has stopped me. It's been great!"

"Maybe Allah wants you alive for a reason," Hashim suggested.

"Maybe," she shrugged. "But I don't believe in Allah or Moses or any of that. Ever since I left the church I've been searching for meaning of my own. There just has to be more to life than what's in front of us. I've taken more of a spiritual approach and have become more Native in my beliefs. I believe that we're surrounded by spirits who communicate with us and that everyone has guides that help with our journeys."

"You really believe that?" Hashim asked.

"Of course I do! How else can you explain why I'm still alive? I've tried to kill myself so many times that it's the only thing that makes logical sense. I have no question that I'm being watched over and taken care of by all of the earth's spirits and guardians. What I like most about the Native American belief system is their connection with the plant and animal kingdom. They believe that mother nature speaks to us."

"That's ridiculous," Melech said and finally got a hold of his phone again.

"For someone with a hubcap jammed in their head you're not very open-minded."

"Said the pagan driving the car," he said under his breath.

Veryonica shrugged. "All I know is that I feel a deep connection to this earth and all its animal inhabitants. They speak to me in ways I can't explain. Like the deer," she said thoughtfully. "We have so much in common. We're beautiful, elegant, and we both have a death wish — like this one does!" she yelled and swerved the car toward an eight-point buck who had walked onto the shoulder of the road.

"Ahh!" Melech yelled and dropped his phone for the third time. He couldn't believe he was about to be in another car accident. "You crazy bitch! You're going to get us all killed."

Hashim turned around in his seat. "You'll get used to it," he said with a nervous smile.

Veryonica looked in the rear-view mirror. "That's the third one I've missed. *See!* It's like they're trying to tell me something."

"Yeah, like watch out!" Melech said.

"Oh, don't be such a sourpuss. If you only knew how connected I am to the spirit world you'd know what an angel I am. When I was three I - holy fucking shit!" she said and looked up.

"Oh Allah!" Hashim cried.

"Oh Satan!" Melech shrieked.

Veryonica hit the brakes and the car screeched until she let up on the brakes and they were crawling along at five miles an hour. In front of them, crossing the road, were no less than a thousand deer.

"I've never seen anything like this in my entire life!" she said in awe.

"What are they doing?" Hashim asked.

"By the looks of it, I'd say they're migrating."

"But it's summer," he said.

"Yeah. Deer migrate in summer just like polar bears migrate in winter. Trust me. I'm one with the spirits."

"Honk your horn at them! Get them on their way!" Melech yelled. "We've got to get going."

"But they're *beautiful*!" Veryonica said. "Just look at how magnificent they are. They remind me of those jackalope heads hanging over the bar of this diner I go to in Arlington."

The deer moved calmly but dutifully across the road. Due to their numbers it was like waiting for a 300-car train to pass.

"Look! There's even some raccoons!" Veryonica said.

"And foxes," Hashim noticed.

"What on earth is going on?" she asked. "It's like a Disney movie or something! I can't help but feel like Princess Jasmine. Do you see any tigers?"

"Hello? Mr. President? Is that you?" Melech said, finally getting a connection. "It's me, Melech. Melech!" he yelled. "Your *advisor*! No, Mr. President, all football games have been cancelled. Yes, college ones too. No, Sir. Sir! Are you able to speak right now? What? Where did he go? Well, try to get the Vice President to put his clothes back on. Devil damn them," he said with his hand over the phone. "They're both blind drunk."

Hashim watched the animals as the car cruised slowly through the enormous herd. It was like they were floating in a river of them. The animals paid them no attention and ebbed around their car like water around a boulder.

Veryonica looked back at Melech. "You mind askin' him what the security situation is like in Washington? Specifically the White House?"

Melech gave her a funny look and then said into the phone, "Mr. President. I wanted to confirm with you that I will be arriving shortly. I've gotten a ride from-" but suddenly his eyes twitched and his head ticked sideways a couple of times and he said, "Derrr, my fagamos just boogabagged. Briggabraggader. Derrrrrr...Pthep! Plurrp!" He fell into making farting noises.

"Did you know he could speak German?" Veryonica asked Hashim.

Suddenly the twitching subsided and Melech stared at the phone in horror, completely aware of his bout of idiocy. "Um..." he said quietly. "Oh!

Nothing, Sir. I was just — well, no, Sir, I would never. Of course not. I think your mother is a wonderful woman. What I wanted to say was-" His eyes crossed again and his tongue flopped out of his mouth and he was back at it. "My gimineebob is shabbeling. Hommena heemena. Blerrrrb. Blerrrrrrrrrrrrrrb. Gaaack! Gerblerrraaack!!" He threw the phone out of the slow-moving vehicle, and hit a doe in the head "Ahhh!" he yelled in horror.

"What is *wrong* with you?" Veryonica said. "Throwing a phone at a deer! Are a monster or something?"

Melech was panting heavily now. This was the second idiot fit he had had since Lindin pulled him out of the hole by the neck. These fits were coming on stronger. He *had* to get this hubcap removed. Suddenly, everything else paled in comparison.

But then he saw it. *Him.* The river of deer parted and dispersed and a little ways down the road was a sleek black car with a lightning strike painted on its side and a cartoon-like indentation of a deer on the hood. Standing beside the car were two men. One of them was David Dingle.

"Stop the car!" Melech screamed. "Stop the car this instant!"

"Hey, look — people!" Veryonica said.

Melech fumbled for his briefcase and opened it and grabbed the one and only remaining syringe. "Stay here!" he commanded at Veryonica. "Don't move a fucking inch!"

Melech rolled gracefully out of the car (considering the circumstances), stumbled, had a brief bout of idiocy, recovered, and then walked towards David Dingle with the amble of a man who had just taken a triple shot of bourbon.

"Hello, David," Melech said carefully, doing his best to sound like a human being. "It's been a long time."

David squinted his eyes. "Do I know you?" he asked.

"If you were smart enough you would," Melech said, "but it's perfectly understandable that you don't."

Agent Boring, who was attempting to fix his totaled vehicle by whacking the dent with a stick, looked up and saw that a bloodstained individual with a hubcap jammed in his skull was approaching his prisoner. Boring pulled the gun from his hip and leveled it at the maniac closing in.

"Stand back!" Agent Boring yelled in his best attempt at professionalism.

Melech ignored him. Still looking at David he said, "I'm sure you're very confused, David. You've been through quite an ordeal. But don't worry. Everything is going to be just fine now that I've found you. I'll be able to answer any questions you have. I promise."

"Really?" David asked. "*Any* of them?"

"Of course, Mr. Dingle. All that I ask is that you come with me."

David stared at him. He didn't know if he should trust a man in a blood-soaked KKK uniform with a hubcap coming out of his head who knew his name. But if the man said he could answer some questions for him...

"Am I Jesus?" he asked.

"Are you...*what?*" Melech asked.

"Jesus," David said simply. "Am I Jesus? Or am I a sleeper agent?"

Melech didn't know how to respond. "Just...come with me, David."

"I need you to answer my questions first," David said. "Then I'll know if I can trust you."

Suddenly, a bullet sliced the air between them and they both ducked. Agent Boring lowered his gun. "I'm not going to say it again," he said. "Back away from my prisoner."

"*Your* prisoner?" Melech asked. "Who the hell are you?"

"Who am *I?*" Boring cried. "Who are *you?*"

"Who am *I?*" David cried.

"I'm ready to go!" Veryonica said. "Hurry up, hubcap man. I thought we were going to the White House."

"You're going to the White House?" Agent Jon Boring asked. "That's where *I'm* going!"

"Not anymore!" Melech said and grabbed David by the arm and pressed the tip of the syringe against his neck. "Make any moves and your prisoner gets it," he threatened. "I've got a hundred cc's of cyanide in this needle. He'll be dead before he hits the ground."

"Hey!" Boring yelled. "You can't! He's mine!"

"Technically, he's mine," Melech quipped. "Now drop your gun." Boring did so. "Good. Now I am taking him with me," he said and began pulling David awkwardly toward the car. "You!" he screamed at Veryonica. "Get out of the car!"

"What? Are you *crazy?*" she asked.

"Yes. Now move!"

"But this is *my* car now!"

"You drive this car like a Nascar driver on meth. I've already been in one car accident. You with the mustache. *You're* driving!"

Melech opened the driver's side door and pulled Veryonica out of the driver's seat by her hair.

"Hey!" she screamed. "Watch it!"

"Scoot over," Melech ordered Hashim. "David, you and I are sitting in the back."

"Don't go!" Veryonica screamed as the car sped away. "Hashim - come back! Don't use the bomb without me, Hashim! *Goddammit!*" she yelled. "Why'd you let them get away?" she cried and punched Boring in the chest.

"He's got my prisoner!" Boring yelled. "Fuck! I've gotta get a hold of the President and let him know."

"I wouldn't do that if I were you," she said suddenly. "He's drunk and speaking German."

Chapter 25: The Conspiracy

Two buck-toothed soldiers stared at the topless woman leaning out the window of a Las Vegas party bus. Trish waved enthusiastically at the soldiers. The soldiers waved back.

"I told you this was faster than stopping every time," Jerry whispered to Courtney. "Tits are way better than paperwork and bus searches."

Dr. Whyzer steered the heavy bus around the wide Martial Law checkpoint station complete with lawn chairs and half a coil of barbed wire. The bus scraped against the low corner of the check-point building with a sound similar to a dying cat slipping off a chalkboard. The passengers collectively groaned at the horrible noise.

"I really shouldn't be the one driving this thing," he said.

"You have to," Courtney said.

"Because you're a doctor," Jerry reminded him.

"I don't know if that qualifies me," he said under his breath.

"You're still more qualified than any of us," Courtney said.

"*I'd* do it if I didn't have so much planning and paperwork to go through," Tatum said as he organized the large stack of newspaper clippings on his lap. "I had no idea how intricately your boy David was linked to the Freemasons. It appears that he's got links to them in practically every aspect of his life."

"Freemasons? Who's that?" Jerry asked.

"The Freemasons are a fraternal organization that has deep historical ties with practically every aspect of government world-wide. I have no doubt in my mind that David is somehow linked up with them."

"How can you tell?" Jerry asked.

"Well, if you hold the photo of him in Pioneer Square like this and then place a photo of the Queen of England beside it like so, you can see that it clearly lines up with this other photo of Pope Francis outside the Sistine Chapel, which, as we all know, is a hub for shadow government activity. It really is getting stupidly obvious, if you ask me."

Jerry rubbed his chin. "Wow. And all these years he's been hiding it from me."

"If it makes you feel better, *he* doesn't even know he's part of the cabal. He thinks he's David Dingle from Seattle, Washington, but that couldn't be further from the truth."

"So who is he?" Jerry asked.

"Well, I've got it narrowed down to one of three different scenarios. Either he's the descent of Lord Ruthestran of Scotland, the son of Major Dundiberm of Middle Asia, or he's part of the Black Forest spy program in Russia."

"Ooo, I hope it's the spy one," Jerry said. "That would be so cool to have a Russian spy as my roommate."

"I should have it figured out in another few hours, I think," he said as he busied himself again with his papers.

"You're really good at this," Jerry said, impressed.

He nodded imperceptibly. "I should be. Got my online degree from the University of New Mythology. It's put out by Georgie Noory," he added.

Courtney turned away from the conversation. The idea that David was part of a sinister shadow government conspiracy made her uneasy. "How long have we been on the road?" Courtney asked Dr. Whyzer.

"Almost three hours now," he said. "It's been tough what with all the road blocks. The tits always catch on that outside corner, and I can't seem to get them to deflate. It's stressing me out."

"Take some more pills, Doc," Jerry suggested.

"We ate them all," he said sadly.

"Oh my God, then we're contagious?" Jerry asked.

Dr. Whyzer frowned. "I'm afraid so. For now I think everyone should just use their shirt as a bandana until we can find some gas masks."

"Uh, excuse me, Miss...Courtney, is it?"

Courtney's stern expression softened when she turned around to see Jacob standing behind her. His hands were crossed at his waist and his expression was meek and timid. "Yes, Jacob. What can I do for you? How are you feeling?"

Jacob Timpson made a poor attempt at faking a smile. "The truth is I've been better," he admitted. "To be honest, I've been a nervous wreck ever since we left. It's been difficult trying to be a solid rock for my family. They have so much faith in me, but for the life of me I couldn't tell you why. I'm no hero," he shook his head disgracefully. "I haven't done anything important. Jesus is the one who saved us. And now he's gone." He turned to look at his family who sat huddled together in the back of the bus. "No one knows what's going to happen. Some of them are wondering if we've missed our chance for the Rapture. So many people have been taken already and now it just feels like we're going through the final motions of the Apocalypse."

"You think this is the Apocalypse?" she asked.

"Oh definitely," he nodded. "No doubt about it. Everyone dying, all the storms, Jesus coming back from the dead. It's pretty obvious at this point."

Courtney bit her fingernail as she looked at him. "Do you think I shoulda brought my Bible?" she asked. "Momma's got a spare one stashed in the back of the refrigerator. Maybe we should go back and get it."

"No need," he said, and pulled one out from under his shirt. "My family's got eight more if you need one. But now that our Savior's back, well, they just don't seem as relevant. I mean, all that information and allegory are great and all, but this is the Second Coming!" he exclaimed. "It's kind of like a new book altogether. I've been writing down everything Master David has been saying since he let us on the bus, in hopes he'll name me an apostle by the time we get to heaven."

"Wait a minute. David?" she asked.

"I suppose the only thing that's keeping me alive and focused is the feeling that I've been called by our Lord to be His scribe. Sort of like Thomas. But there is no doubt here," he pointed at his chest and gave his first genuine smile. "I'm a *believer*!"

"Are you saying you think that...*David*...is the second coming of...*Christ!*?" Jacob's wide moronic smile told her that he did. "But that's *insane*."

His smile didn't even crack. "Good one, Miss Courtney. I appreciate you testing my faith. What's a man without something to believe in?"

"Well, OK," she conceded at last. "Just keep prayin' for him, I guess."

"That's a given! My real question is, do you think I should sacrifice one of my children?"

"One of your...*What?!?*"

"Like Jeremiah or Barthalomew, maybe? I was thinking either my youngest or my eldest."

Courtney pinched herself. "Why on earth would you want to sacrifice one of your children?" she said aghast.

"You know, like Abraham and Isaiah. God likes to ask that of His children to test their faith. I just figure that I might as well pass through the Lord's Gauntlet," he said and pulled out a short shimmering blade with a golden handle.

"Where did you get *that*?" she asked.

"Oh, I bring this with me wherever I go. You'd be surprised how many uses it serves. It's handy for sacrificing a baby, raising a rabble at the market or the bank, or stabbing a Muslim during a Holy War. I've named it God's Will in my Pocket."

"I really don't think any of that will be necessary, Jacob," she said as kindly as possible.

"Naaah, I'd keep that knife close, if I were you," Jerry chimed in and Jacob Timpson's eyes perked up. "We *are* going to Washington D.C., after all. We're practically headed into the storm of a Holy War, if you ask me."

"Holy War?" Courtney asked.

"'Course we're going into a Holy War," he said. "If what your brother says is true and David *was* jabbed with the virus without his knowing it, then it's pretty obvious that the Muslims did it to him."

"What? But that's bonkers," Courtney said. "Tatum, you said it was the shadow government who did this to David. Not the Muslims."

Tatum looked up from his papers. "Definitely. But that doesn't mean that there isn't a Muslim agenda behind all of this. My guess is that their goal is to transform America into a failed state and rebuild it into a picture perfect world of Sharia Law. It makes absolute sense, really. We've been ruled under a Puritanical Christian Regime for hundreds of years. Damned Vatican. It could be time for a change-up."

"I don't get it," Jerry said. "Who's *really* in charge? Because I thought it was the government, but now you're telling me it's the Vatican?"

Tatum set down his stack of newspaper clippings and faced his audience. "Truth is, it's even more complex than that, so let me do my best to break it down for you as simply as possible." He rummaged through his clippings and started arranging them in stacks here and there and then laid out a black and white photo of the White House.

"OK. So this is the White House. This is where the supposed leader of the free world, the President of the United States of America, lives — which he does. More importantly, he only lives there because he's a puppet, just like everyone else."

"But if everyone's a puppet who should we vote for?" Trish asked.

"It doesn't matter if you vote Democrat or Republican or any of that other nonsense because in America, politics is bought and paid for by corporations that have been infiltrated by the banking elite. So all that Congress and House of Representatives and Checks and Balances bullshit is all just that — *bullshit.*"

"But I thought the government takes orders from the President?" Courtney asked.

"It's quite the opposite," Tatum said. "Instead of being at the top, the President is actually at the bottom of the Illuminati pyramid. Above the President is a long thick ladder of corporate lackeys who control the food sector - Monsanto, Syngenta, chemical producers like Dow Jones and Colonel Sanders. Right," he said, moving on. "Above them is the energy sector — oil, gas, timber, nuclear, etcetera," he said and happily placed a picture of the Fukushima disaster on the floor. "Above that is the Military Industrial Complex and the rest of your alphabet organizations, CIA, FBI, MIB - some of which control complex systems like the weather through programs such as HAARP and the Woodpecker Program, while others influence society through social engineering PSYOPS like the Trilateral Commission, the Bilderbergs, Council of Foreign Relations, the United Nations, Agenda 21, etcetera etcetera."

"Wow!" Jerry said. "This is intense!"

"I haven't even started," Tatum mused as he laid down more clippings. "Now all of these things are managed by bankers and their institutions. The Federal Reserve is the single most debilitating entity that is currently affecting our country and countries all over the world. By printing money out of thin air, the Federal Reserve and the World Bank work in cahoots to bankrupt citizens and nations alike until all people like you and me are slaves to a New World Order of which we are ignorant to its existence in the first place."

"You mean this is already happening?"

"It's *been* happening for years," Tatum said matter-of-factly. "But that only puts us here on the pyramid," he said pointing. "We have to go here, to the top of the pyramid. Now a fraction of our taxes go to the Queen of England, who we continue to pay homage to, despite peoples' ignorance to her bloodsucking ties to the Vatican where 80 percent of all our energy is fed through. Since its inception, the Vatican has been promoting a false narrative about the origins of mankind on earth."

"Oh, don't even get me started," Jacob rolled his eyes.

Tatum continued. "In their eyes, we are merely human fodder for their grand plan."

"So the *Vatican's* in charge?" Courtney asked.

"This is where things get tricky. Religion plays into our concept of freedom and choice. With all of the religions in the world, people are naturally apt to believe that they have control over which prophet they want to believe in — but the truth is, ancient religious practices have been hijacked and remodeled into a handful of cookie-cutter religions whose traditions are borrowed from Egyptian and pagan cultures. Ultimately, it comes down to a battle for souls between Christianity, Judaism, Hinduism, Buddhism and Islam. Religion is the bank vault of people's freedoms so it doesn't really matter which religion is in control just as long as you subscribe to one of them and put all your free thinking in their safety deposit box never to be seen again. That's why I'm a devout atheist," he said proudly. "It would be ridiculous to believe in any of that nonsense," he noted as he placed a picture of a vampire on top of the Pope.

"So then aren't all religions headed up by someone in control?" Jerry asked.

"Absolutely," he said.

"So who is it?" Courtney asked.

"No one knows," Tatum admitted. "He or she..."

"He," Jerry said. "It's definitely a He."

"Well, *he* has done such a good job at covering his tracks that there's little evidence that he even exists. Simply put, this man is a mastermind and likely has the purest genes of any human on earth. Everything that happens to you, and me, and everyone else in this world is all because of this one man. He is the architect of this world and ultimately the grand puppeteer of all of humanity."

"So who is *his* boss?" Jerry asked.

Tatum blinked. "Well, the aliens of course, but my pyramid has run out of room."

"So what about David?" Courtney asked. "Where does he fit in?"

Tatum rolled his eyes. "David is a nobody. He's a stupid-looking, dim-witted nobody that has a crush on my sister. I hope he chokes on a carrot."

"Tatum!" Courtney said. "Don't say things like that." She brushed her hair with her fingers. "Do you really think he has a crush on me?"

Jerry waved it off. "He'll get over it. That poor kid will fall in love with a pet rabbit if it makes eye contact with him. Once he gets it through his thick skull that you're not interested he'll go back to internet porn. Also a much easier relationship to manage, if you ask me. I swear to God, I will never forgive the President for what he did to online porn."

"I'm so worried about him," she confessed, and began scratching her arm. "He's got the sweetest heart. He just ain't cut out for all this Illuminati business. They'll tear him to *pieces*."

"I'll agree with you on that one, Sis. He's got patsy written all over him."

"Beep bop boo beep!" David's phone announced.

Courtney picked it up. "Oh my gosh. His phone is saying that it's lost all signal of David. It's saying that he's been kidnapped...*again*. Oh no!" she cried. "This is terrible."

"It's OK, Courtney," Jacob said. "We must have faith that we'll find him."

"Oh! Hey ya'll, listen here to what his phone just wrote. It says: 'I'm so sad. Without David my life is meaningless.' Oh, that's cute," she said.

"Look!" Dr. Whyzer announced. "There's a car on the side of the road next to a crazy woman. Should we pick her up?"

"How do you know she's crazy?" Courtney asked.

"Umm...I just get that feeling," he said.

"We should keep going," Jacob said. "We've got enough sinners already."

"Wait a minute," Dr. Whyzer said as he stared out the window. "Isn't that Agent Boring?"

Courtney peered over the wheel. "It *is*!"

Jerry cracked his knuckles. "Let me outta here!" he said. "I'm gonna beat the shit outta that guy!"

"Do you see David?" she asked.

"No sign of him."

"Maybe they've already put him in a shallow grave," Tatum suggested. "Or perhaps they gave him a sex change?" he thought, staring at the woman. "That was fast."

"Damn! David's lookin' *good*," Dr. Whyzer said, eyeing the gorgeous panic-stricken woman.

She was holding a cellphone in one hand and banging against the bus door with the other. "Slow down, slow down!" the woman was screaming. "Open the door!" She was beating against the glass as Dr. Whyzer opened the side of the bus. "You've gotta help me!" she cried. "Please, get me out of here."

"It's OK, David," Jerry said. "Everything's gonna be OK. We'll get your dick put back on as soon as we can, isn't that right, Dr. Whyzer?"

"Oh, I don't know," he said, staring her up and down. "I'd say they did a pretty good job. You know, David, you might want to test out this new system they've got you set up with. I mean...from what I can tell..." he paused and his eyes dove into her tits.

"Stop it!" Courtney yelled. "Both of you. Just stop it. That ain't David at all." No one said a thing. "Tatum! Right?"

Tatum stared at her tits and shrugged. "Hard to say. Probably not, but based on how many times I've watched Mission Impossible, I know it can be done. Ask her what it's like to have sex with a man. In detail."

"You've got to help me!" she kept saying. "This maniac kidnapped my boyfriend, and stole my new car, and also made off with this other young fella too."

"You!" Jerry yelled and pointed at Agent Boring who had approached the vehicle. "What did you do with my friend?"

"Your idiot friend was taken from me," he said. Boring looked grumpy.

"*Taken* from you?" Jerry scoffed. "David's about as easy to manage as a cup of JELL-O. What kind of special agent are you?"

"He was taken by a German man with a hubcap in his head," Veryonica declared. "The guy was a maniac!"

"I should have guessed," Jerry said and narrowed two evil eyes into the face of his arch nemesis. "Even a guy with a hubcap in his head would be able to outsmart an agent as stupid as *this* guy."

"Hey!" Boring yelled. "You don't even know what happened. He had a needle."

"Oooh...a *needle*!" Jerry mocked and wiggled his fingers. "Did he have a pointy stick, too? Seriously, and you were giving *me* shit. I'll tell ya, you're about as worthless as a room full of pennies."

Agent Boring slammed his hand against the side of the bus. "You wanna go, bud?"

Jerry cracked his knuckles, "Bro - I've already gone!" At that Jerry leapt out of the bus and tackled Special Agent Boring, and they tumbled onto the side of the road kicking and punching and grunting and cursing. At first Jerry was on top and then it was Boring and then it was Jerry again. Boring got a kick to the nuts but not before Jerry took an elbow to the face.

"Where's my friend?" Jerry yelled as he delivered another blow to Boring's gut.

"I told you, he was taken away by a serial killer and a Mexican."

"That Mexican is my boyfriend!" Veryonica screamed. "And he's not a Mexican, he's a Middle Westerner, and he's a terrorist, and he's gonna blow up your crummy little friend along with the whole city of Washington D.C. and if you motherfuckers don't stop fighting and get going then I'm gonna find a way to fuck each and every one of you to death."

THAT stopped the fight. Jerry held his fist suspended in mid-air and Boring stopped pulling on Jerry's thick sideburns, as both of them stared at Veryonica's beautiful, luscious double D tits and the single nipple which had slipped out of her pink lacy bra.

"Are you seein' that?" Jerry whispered to Agent Boring.

"Did she just say she was going to fuck us to death?" he asked and they quickly scrambled up and brushed themselves off. "Soo...did you want to go behind the bus?" Boring asked, "Or, come to think of it, I've seen the inside and it's actually pretty nice. Lotsa velvet."

"I want to find Hashim," she said. "He's driving a red convertible with that maniac and your friend. I'll help you find them but we've got to get going. They *just* left. They've only been gone for twenty minutes."

Jerry took a step away from Boring and stared at him. "This is far from over, Agent Idiot. For now we're gonna have to work together. But I swear to God, if you do anything stupid and screw this up and my friend ends up dying, I'm going to make sure that this woman does *NOT* fuck you to death."

Chapter 26: An Unlikely Ally

President Alan opened his bloodshot eyes to see his assistant Mary leaning over him with a pot of coffee. "Mr. President...*Sir?*" she said for the twentieth time today. "I really think you need to get up. This is the second pot I've brewed. The Vice President is already moving around, Sir."

"He is?" President Alan sat up painfully and looked around. The Oval Office looked like it had just been raided by a gang of marauding Nazis. Papers and documents were strewn about the room. His necktie was hanging from the ceiling fan and a half-full kiddie pool was being used by the Vice President to wash his face.

The Vice President looked up. "I'm right here, Sir. Now, if I could just find my cufflinks. I think I tossed them in here when we were discussing our Naval options last night."

"Why don't you drink some coffee, Mr. President?" Mary suggested. "I think it would be best if you sobered up, some. There have been...developments."

The President felt like an old shoe. "Developments, Mary?"

"Yes, Sir." He noticed that Mary looked nervous which was not a good sign. Mary was always true and steady, even during the most difficult times. "There's word of an army headed this way."

The President scrambled to his feet, nearly tripping over an empty bottle of Wild Turkey on the floor. "An *army?* What kind of army? Is it the French? The Russians? Who would be bold enough to challenge my throne during a pandemic?"

She shook her head. "It isn't coming from the outside. American refugees who have come to D.C for safety have reportedly seen a group of vigilantes on horses with weapons."

He studied her. "Those are some pretty smart horses to be able to use weapons. They must be attached to the bridle somehow," he said to himself.

"I think the *vigilantes* are armed, Sir."

The President nodded. "Even worse." He shook his head and looked up at the beer-splattered ceiling. "Why does all of this have to happen on my first term? How am I supposed to deal with all of these disasters during an election year? Do you think there's any chance they can form a holding pattern until mid-November?"

"Let's just hope they're not set on violence, Mr. President," the VP said and tucked his collared shirt into his long johns as he continued searching the room for his pants. "Sometimes these militia men can be reasoned with. As long as their demands are clear and their heads aren't blowing up then there is still room for diplomacy."

A muffled ringtone set to the tune of Kanye West's *Power* silenced the room. President Alan's eyes widened and he proceeded to fumble about the room looking for his cellphone. "I know that ringtone! Hang on, Melech! I'm coming!" he yelled and began throwing couch cushions and coffee tables out of the way. "God I hate cellphones. Why did we ever change from landlines? Graaaa!" he screamed and pulled his hair. "Don't hang up, Melech! I'll find you eventually. Jesus Christ be with me now!"

"Sir, I believe your cell phone is in your pocket," Mary said.

"Thank you, Jesus!" he yelled in triumph and pulled his red, white, and blue cellphone out of his pocket.

"*Melech!*" he exclaimed. "Thank *God* you called. I've been deep in meditation. Please tell me you're outside the White House. Melech? Is that you?"

"Now you listen to me you sexy motherfucker!" an enraged woman yelled at the top of her lungs. "If you so much as lay one finger on Hashim I swear to God I'll strip your flesh off with a paper clip. Don't think I haven't tried it myself. If you even *think* about hurting him I will melt your face with a pack of gasoline-soaked matches until your mug looks like a year old candle."

The President looked at the phone. "Melech? What's wrong with your voice? You sound like a woman."

"This isn't Melech, asshole! This is the President and CEO of the biggest terrorist organization in the world."

"The IMF?" he asked.

"I'm going to bomb the White House if you don't do what I say!" she screamed.

He slapped a hand over the mouth piece. "Oh my God!" he said to the others. "It's the terrorists!"

"What do they want?" Mary asked.

"What kind of horses are they riding?" the V.P. inquired.

"Pay attention, you nitwit!" she yelled. "Hashim is headed your way and he's carrying a nuclear bomb. Yeah – that's right — a *nuclear fucking bomb!* I wouldn't fuck with him if I were you. Not even a little bit. I don't care *how* exciting the idea might be. Because if you do...then *BOOM!*" she yelled.

The shriek of an eight-year-old girl escaped the President's mouth as he threw his cellphone across the room. It landed on the whiskey-stained carpet next to his desk but the woman's maniacal taunting could still be heard. "I'm coming for you, Benjamin Alan. So help me Spirit, I am going to *fuck your brains* out if anything happens to my Hashim. He's a good man with a good heart. He just doesn't know yet that he doesn't really want to blow you up. But *I* just might blow you up if you talk him into blowing you up first...got it? Oh my God, this bus has titties!"

The line went dead.

"This is terrible!" the President cried. "What am I going to do? The terrorists who set off the pandemic are still alive...and they're coming after *me!*" President Alan collapsed into a beanbag chair and put his hands over his face. "I should have known this moment was coming. All along I expected to die of a heart-attack while giving history's greatest speech. Never did I expect to be killed by a love-struck terrorist."

Mary leaned over and handed him a mug of hot coffee. "Sir, I want to have faith in you. Ever since I was an intern back in Baltimore during your campaign I believed in what you had to offer. This could be your finest hour if you would *just* rise to the task," she said. "Come, on. Get up. You can do it, Mr. President."

The President uncovered his face and looked up. "Mary, I'm so grateful that you're able to see what I can't when I'm covering my eyes. You're absolutely right. I *can* do it. Dammit, I've been able to do it since I was in college. I graduated with a 3.0 for Christ's sake. *I* was the one that got myself elected. *I* was the one who decided the Oval Office needed a new coat of paint. Shoot. There isn't a man alive who can do what I have to do." He reached for the cup of coffee but Mary withheld it unexpectedly. She looked as though an errant thought had taken hold of her mind and would not let go.

"It was *my* idea to give the Oval Office a fresh coat of paint," she said.

He looked at her. "Well, that may be but I was the one to..."

"And *you* didn't get yourself elected. *You* wanted to spend your campaign money on a private jet! And those millions of dollars were raised by honest people whose first names you never even bothered to learn."

Ben Alan shrugged. "I generally feel that first names aren't very important. I mean, for instance, most people just call me 'Sir.'"

"And college!" she scoffed. "You didn't graduate with a 3.0. You barely passed home economics, and only squeaked by with a 2.1 after getting your friend to hack into the testing center."

"But Mary," he said, "you know as well as I do that those charges were never brought to court."

She was still holding the mug of coffee in her hand and the President could see that her knuckles were turning white. "All these years I've supported you. I used to have faith that you would do the right thing, when all along the only thing you've done is take credit for other people's hard work. I've stood behind you for nearly two decades and not *once* have you thanked me."

"Mary," he said and stood up. His expression had an edge of panic. "This is crazy talk. Of course I've thanked you. Remember that time you brought in that Dr. Pepper and I said..."

"This is *not* crazy talk!" she exclaimed and threw the mug of coffee across the room. "This is the God's honest truth. In fact, it's the only time I've actually ever given it some thought. I've been so busy having faith in you that I never stopped to think that maybe you weren't so great after all. But now I *am* thinking and I have finally come to understand that..." Mary wiggled her nose for a moment as if she were about to sneeze. Instead, Mary's head exploded.

"Augghh!" President Alan screamed and dove behind his beanbag chair. Mary's brains splattered across the room like liquid confetti and her body slumped against a chair and knocked over a portrait of President Alan on its way to the floor.

The Vice President took several stiff steps forward. "What just happened?" he asked, after carefully studying the scene.

"Her head just blew up!" the President gasped. "It's all over my shirt. Just had this damned thing washed. Oh, Mary! Sweet sweet Mary. Our nation has just lost one of its most beloved voters. It's going to be hard to find a replacement this late in the election season." He shook his head sadly while the Vice President dragged Mary into the hallway by her feet.

Closing the door behind him he said, "Well, that is a real shame. I was hoping to ask her out once this whole pandemic settled down."

Benjamin Alan put his head into his hands and sat down. Outside, the streets of Washington were quiet. The President began to weep. The virus had finally come to his front door. It had swept across the entire nation, decimating everything that was good and free. There seemed to be little hope left for a country plunged into the bowels of utter darkness and chaos. Benjamin Alan did not look up as he spoke. "Oh, Mr. Vice President, I do not think that I have the strength any longer. My reserves are empty. My faith is gone. There is nothing left for me to do but admit defeat."

Palmdonger took a careful step forward. "There is always hope, Sir. I believe there is still time to fix things. All we need is a plan."

"A *plan*?" he asked and looked up for the first time. "How am I to create a plan without my panel? Mary was right, Palmdonger. I *am* a failure. A hack, a credit stealer. Who am I kidding? I'm *nobody* without the support of my peers. My entire life I've relied on the work and dedication of other men and women to do the work I long so much to take credit for. But this virus has shown me the ugly truth, Palmdonger. It's shown me that I need other people in order to succeed. This pandemic has taken those people away from me. *David Dingle* has robbed me of my grace!" he said and tightened his fists. "He has stripped me of my support system."

"You still have me, Sir," Palmdonger said with a soft smile.

The President shook his head as if he had just been offered steamed asparagus. "I appreciate it, Palmdonger," he said. "But frankly, you're an idiot. I'll admit, for a while there you had me going with that turtle analogy, but after giving it some good, hard thinking I decided that it's about as bunk as your long johns. No offense. You fit the profile of a solid politician. You obviously have great hair."

"None taken, Sir," he said and scanned the room once again for his pants. "Maybe you're right. After all, the virus has killed a lot of good men and women. There really isn't anyone left who can help at this point."

A firm and steady knock on the door interrupted the conversation. Palmdonger and President Alan looked at each other.

"Who is it?" Benjamin Alan asked.

"It's Senator Guiles, Mr. President. I'd like to have a word with you."

"Senator Guiles?" Alan said to Palmdonger. "What the blazes does *he* want?"

"Maybe he's looking for the bathroom, Sir?"

He thought about it. "Unlikely. That man's so full of shit he probably knows the location of every toilet in Washington. What do you want, Guiles?" President Alan called through the door.

"Only to help, Mr. President. I'd love to have your ear for a moment."

"He could be infected," Palmdonger whispered.

"Hmm. You might be right. How are you feeling, Mitchell?" Alan called. "Has your head been feeling like it's about to explode lately?"

"Quite the contrary, Mr. President. It's never been clearer. Please, open the door."

"Mr. President..." Palmdonger warned, "the man's about as trustworthy as Mexican tap water." But President Alan was at the end of his rope. He had no choice but to go against his better judgment. Alan opened the door.

Senator Guiles was standing with his hands crossed behind his back and on his face was an expression of solemn humility. As usual, he was dressed for success outfitted in an impeccably clean Armani suit and Stefano Bemer shoes as polished as his teeth. His shoelaces were still untied though. "Thank you for giving me your time, Ben," Guiles said.

"I want to know right now what this is about," he said.

Senator Guiles held out his arms and raised his palms, much like a priest about to give his sermon. "Mr. President, I know that you and I have had our differences and that we haven't always seen things eye to eye, but right now I feel like it's important that we put all of that aside. I believe that if we put our heads together we can come up with a reasonable solution for the good of this great nation."

"But the election..." the President said.

"To hell with the election!" came the Senator's response and President Alan thought he might fall over from shock. "This is bigger than the election, Ben. This is about restoring freedom to the constitution. Surely you don't like this situation any more than I do."

The President shook his head. "Of course not. The whole thing is a crying shame. I took office to uphold all that is good and true, not instate Martial Law. This whole thing is my fault."

"I don't believe that for one minute, Mr. President," Guiles said. "You've done what you thought was best."

President Alan looked off in the opposite direction. "Well, some of that is true...I guess. But, well, most of this wasn't even my idea. I've been advised by my advisors for so long that I never really stopped to think whether any of this was even necessary."

"Some of it surely was," Guiles said sympathetically. "A man cannot simply stand idly by while the heart of the nation is under siege by a foreign body. Courage. Determination. This is what our country needs most."

Benjamin Alan looked at Mitchell in awe. "You've always had a way with words, Mitchell," he said.

Guiles smiled. "Thank you, Ben. To be honest, it's the reason I'm here. I'm not naive enough to think that you write your own speeches. This is a task done by some of the greatest writers in history. I understand, however, that those writers are now dead."

"I thought I had one of my writers left," the President bemoaned and threw up his arms, "but I haven't been able to get a hold of him for days. I'm at my wits end!"

"Well, then perhaps I can help you," he said. "The public needs to see the face of someone they can trust. They need to hear confident, elegant words telling them that everything is going to be OK."

"But we've shut down communications."

"Well, I'm suggesting that you bring them back online."

"Are you saying you want to write a speech and deliver it to the American public?"

"I want *you* to deliver it, Mr. President."

The President's heart began to flutter like it used to during the days of his old coke habit. He suddenly felt a surge of that same enthusiasm he felt when he had first been in charge of hazing freshman at Delta Kappa Epsilon during rush. "I...I could do that," he stammered.

"Of course you can, Sir. I think that with my speech writing skills and your candor we can bring this nation out of this abysmal black hole and into the light again. What Americans need right now is someone they can trust, someone with confidence. I've always admired your confidence, Ben. You have a remarkable ability to look at a pile of shit and call it pie. People believe you. They believe *in* you."

His face felt warm as he embraced the compliment. "You really think so, Mitchell?"

"Sir, I wouldn't be here if I didn't."

The President smiled suddenly and clapped his hands. "Well, let's get to it, then! Hey Palmdonger! Grab us some Dr. Peppers."

But Mitchell held up a hand. "Sir, if I may. I understand you've had a bit of a history with alcohol in the past and that you've taken certain measures to curb your enthusiasm for the spirits, but to be perfectly honest, I've seen you speak when you are under the spirit's influence. I was there when you addressed us all a week ago. You are so much more at ease. You're more likable when you've had a few shots. More importantly, you come across not as a politician but as a common man, one that the American public can relate to."

Palmdonger set down two glasses of iced Dr. Pepper in front of the men. Guiles reached into his coat pocket and produced a silver flask and offered it to Benjamin Alan.

Alan eyed the flask cautiously. "What do you have there, Mitchell?"

"Glenfiddich."

President Alan raised an eyebrow. "The world's most awarded single malt Scotch whiskey. You remembered."

"One never forgets the best of our vices. Or college, for that matter. That was one hell of a night," he grinned.

"I can only remember half of it!" the President laughed. "I blacked out by the time we got to the circus."

"I still can't believe you persuaded me to kidnap that acrobat."

"Did I?" he grinned and poured himself a double.

"We were such good friends in college," Mitchell said. "It's a shame we had to become political rivals."

President Alan lifted his glass and clinked it against Mitchell's. "Won't you be having any?"

Mitchell Guiles grinned like a wolf. "Not today, my friend. Go ahead. It's all yours."

"Suit yourself," he said and finished a third of the glass in a single sip. "Now, tell me more about this speech. How can I contribute?"

"Leave the writing to me, Ben. I'll have it drafted within the hour. I think it needs to come across fresh and spontaneous, as if you're speaking from your heart. You're a good reader, so all you'll need to do is follow the teleprompter. Grandfather's medicine here will get your lips moving freely, so don't hesitate to ad-lib as you see fit."

The President was already down to the bottom third of his glass. He rocked back in his seat and put his hands behind his head. "Ah, it feels like I'm on the campaign trail again, working hard to win over the minds of the American public. Only *this* time, the stakes are much higher. I appreciate your help, Mitchell, but the fact of the matter remains that it's time for me to make some changes myself. I can't rely on you to fix the entirety of this mess. I feel as if I have been taking advice without giving it any thought. Perhaps I've put too much faith in my advisor, Melech. He's a good man, but *darn* it, I fear his ideas have not been thought out. I've waited and waited for him to arrive so that we can sit down and discuss these problems like men. But all this waiting has only made things worse. It's time to take matters into my own hands."

Benjamin Alan picked up the phone on his desk and dialed. "This is Benjamin Alan. I am lifting the ban on commerce. Reinstate the economy. That's an order." He put the phone down and smiled at Mitchell. "I always like saying that last part. Sometimes it's the only reason I pick up the phone in the first place."

"It's a good line," he agreed. "Any other orders of business?"

The President shook his head. "No. That's a good start for now," he said and finished his drink, shook the ice in his glass, and handed it to Mitchell for a refill. "So many freedoms have been taken away that it's a good idea not to give them all back at once. Make sure to put that in the speech," he pointed.

"Of course, Mr. President," Mitchell smiled and handed the President a second full glass which the President quickly began to sip down.

Mitchell stood up. "I will have your speech ready shortly, Sir. Practice standing in front of a mirror and trying on expressions of calm confidence." He set the flask on the desk. "I'll leave this here with you."

The President nodded and ran his fingers through his hair as he thought about his speech.

Senator Guiles was about to leave the Oval Office when he turned around one final time. "Oh, and Mr. President? I just wanted to remind you, that it's imperative that the public really *feels* your confidence. This speech is going to come out live."

The President smiled and offered a thumbs up. "Shuper," he said and wiped his chin and then returned his gaze to the mirror.

Chapter 27: Disclosure

Melech set the syringe back into the metal briefcase and clicked it closed, now certain that David would not try to escape. David rubbed his neck where Melech had been holding the needle for the past hour. He had not said a word since being kidnapped. It was concerning to Melech that David was far less nervous than the driver who had reduced his fingernails to stubs. He watched Melech and David in the rearview mirror more than the actual road in front of him. Still, Melech considered, his driving was far superior than that of the blonde lunatic they had left on the side of the road.

"I apologize for the manner in which I have handled you," Melech said at last as he set the briefcase under his seat. He turned to look at David and David saw that his expression was almost cordial, much like a tiger shark after a full meal. "I had no intention of accosting you in such manner. Believe me when I say I wanted all of this to go smoother. If it had been up to me you would have been gently put to sleep in your own bed days ago."

David turned and truly saw his kidnapper for the first time. The man looked old, pudgy, and incredibly sleep-deprived. The hubcap waved awkwardly in the speeding convertible. It was a strange compliment to the man's energetic presence. He exuded a kind of power the likes of which David had only seen once before when The Joker had taken the entire city of Gotham hostage.

David said, "I've experienced more strangeness these last few days than I have throughout the rest of my life. I mean, becoming the suspect of an international manhunt *and* losing my phone in the same week — it's been a big adjustment! And now I've been kidnapped by a guy with a...that's a *frisbee*, right?"

"Never mind," Melech said. "The trials and tribulations I have endured to get where I am now are a small price to pay for what will become the greatest moment of my entire lineage."

"Wow," David said. "That must be nice. I'm pretty sure I lost my job, so *my* lineage is going to be quite upset with me when I finally get a chance to talk to them."

"Forgive my intrusion, Sir," Hashim said from the front seat. Hashim's fingers were tied in knots around the steering wheel. He was more nervous now than he had ever been with a bomb strapped to his body. Truly, he was in the presence of greatness! "It is an honor to finally meet you." He grabbed David's eyes in the rearview mirror. "I've never been more impressed by one man in my entire life."

"Excuse me?" David said.

"Even the Prophet Mohammed had problems getting everything to work out the way he wanted. But you, you have executed your plans perfectly. I congratulate you. The American dream is in shambles because of your efforts. Myself, I am but a simple jihadist, here to blow up a few structures and some infidels. Tell me. What is your preferred ideology? Is it extreme right-wing Christianity?" he asked politely. "Or are you a follower of Mohammed? Perhaps you follow the great General Custard who led his troops to their death. *Verrry* famous prophet in Al Kabob."

"I – um," David said. "I guess I don't really have any ideologies."

"*Really*?" Hashim asked in amazement.

David gave it a very brief thought. "Nope. I like to watch the news and I vote Democrat, but I don't necessarily agree with everything they do. In fact, I guess I'm not really sure *what* they do. Democrat is just above the Republican section on the ballot which makes it easier for me to decide. Voting is important so I want to make it a good decision. How about you? Do you like to vote?"

"Enough!" Melech shouted. "This isn't a get-together. We're not here to exchange life histories. You're here to drive us and *you're* here because I brought you here."

David looked at Melech. "So you said that I should know you? But I still have no idea who you are. Do you have your own TV show? Are you friends with Jerry or something?"

Melech's eyes narrowed and in them David could see cauldrons of thunderclouds soaked in an eternal fire at the end of a very bad week. "I am the everywhere, David. Everything that happens in this world does so because I allow it to."

"So you're a kidnapper, huh?" David said and rubbed his chin.

Melech made a fist and looked deeper in David's eyes. "I am *no* kidnapper. *I* am the great puppeteer of this farcical theater of which you call reality and all of its transfigurations thereof. All that you perceive is but illusion for *I* am the illusionist behind the curtain."

David gave a toothy grin. "That totally sounds like something Jerry would say, without all those big words. Are you that guy he told me about from Chuck E. Cheese, the one with the Rubik's Cube tattoo?"

He frowned. "No, you twit! I am of no relation to your friend. *I* am the master of matter — the plague of all souls!" Melech was getting excited and soon he had both hands in David's collar. "I work everywhere!" he shouted. "I allow everything! For hundreds of years my lineage has been in control of humanity's great debt. I have helped to orchestrate the proletariat's reality like the maestro of the world's finest symphony. It pleases me to watch humanity suffer and bumble about searching for the meaning of life on weekend breaks from their monotonous careers, which they dumbly cherish as if they were the teats of their own mothers."

"Sooo...you're *not* a kidnapper?" David asked.

Melech clenched his teeth. David noticed a vein had appeared on his temple. "I am..." He paused to straighten his tie. "I am the reason you are here, David," he said.

David stared. "You *are*!? So you really *can* answer some questions!" he blurted out. "Man! You have *no* idea how many I've got. My phone went dead a few days ago and then it rebooted, but it doesn't matter because I got kidnapped, not by you, but by that guy that *you* kidnapped me from, and I haven't been able to get any internet signal to ask Google who I am and what's going on. Please. I need to know everything. Who are my real biological parents? Did I have a Mexican nanny that turned me into a sleeper agent? Am I a prophet and, if so, which one and what miracles can I perform? If people think they're black and they're not, is that a disease? Is it contagious? Just be straight with me — it's what Michael Jackson had, isn't it?"

Melech Rothschild smiled for the first time in a long time. "Yes, David. Yes to all of those questions and many more I'm sure. If I still had a soul I would laugh. You are so innocent, David, so absolutely perfect in every way."

"I am?" David asked, bewildered. This was definitely the first time anyone had told him that he was perfect before and it felt pretty good, considering the circumstances.

"Why of course you are. Otherwise you wouldn't be in this mess. You have been *chosen* for your perfection, David. *I* have chosen you."

David shifted in his seat and looked out the window. He ran his fingers nonchalantly through his hair. "Sooo this perfect you're talking about? Is it looks, mostly? Or just brains?"

Melech couldn't help but keep smiling. "Brains, David. It's all about your brain, your perfect perfect brain. You have the ideal mixture of obedience and stupidity, a lot like a golden retriever in many ways."

David pondered this. "I used to have a dog. Until it was run over by some stranger. You didn't do that too, did you?"

Melech shook his head and looked at his hands. "I didn't have the time."

"So if you really *are* in charge of running the world, then how come I haven't heard of you before? Do you have a Twitter account?"

"In my line of work it would be foolish to make myself known when others would likely perceive my agendas as somewhat...what's the word? Nefarious. Personally, I think it's all a matter of perspective. For instance, the only reason that everyone shies away from something so innocuous as slavery is because of that damned civil rights movement. Honestly, the majority of slaves really do have a great thing going on. They get to use their bodies, stay in shape, do work for a reputable organization that they know nothing about." He grinned and leaned back. "Ahh David. I have been in this game since I was old enough to hold a whip. I'm good at what I do. I should be. I was bred for it, raised for ruling humanity with an invisible yet iron fist. But that's just it," he said, turning to David again. "I don't *want* to be invisible any longer. I want to be *known* for my greatness, *celebrated* for my superior wisdom and intellect. This revealing of myself is to be the last chapter of my rise to power. All of humanity will come to know me when this is complete. I will finally be able to come out from the shadows and rule the population from a pulpit showered by the red light of His grace."

"That sounds a lot like church," David scowled.

Melech scoffed. "Nothing like church, David. This is for something far greater and more important than the worship of something that doesn't exist. *I* am in charge of - Glaaak!"

"Hmm. I haven't heard of that. What exactly is Glaaak?"

"Bragaaak!" Melech said and used his fists to pull at his eyebrows. "My habida mogima is coming apart. Gaabraaak!!" Melech twitched and convulsed some more but then quickly composed himself.

"Are you all right?" David asked. "Some of that looked like it hurt."

"Fine," he said and sucked in a couple chestfuls of air. David noticed a strange element of panic in Melech's eyes.

"If I have learned anything from this entire debacle, David, it is that if you want something done right, you had better do it yourself." Melech studied David. "If only you could have seen me and the other gents fight it out for world domination," he said and leaned back again, his voice softened with nostalgia. "We had a pretty good go toward nuclear war," he said and chuckled like a spoon in a garbage disposal. "But even *those* idiots couldn't do anything right. One of them would be colluding with Russia while another was accidentally making deals with Venezuela. Ugh!" he said and threw up his hands. "It was inevitable that they all had to die. Otherwise, *nothing* would get done!

"You see, David, in my line of work, it is expected that you put everything you have into enacting a plan to rule the world. I knew, however, that as long as I was in honest collaboration with my colleagues that true world domination was only a pipe dream. I'm certain that the rest of the brotherhood suspected that I would eventually murder them all, but they had no idea how that would ever play out. It took me *years* to formulate this plan, David. I needed a strategy that would not only enslave the population, but simultaneously release me from my *own* servitude," he said, almost as an aside.

"What do you mean?" David asked.

"The truth of the matter is that I have been living a life that does not fully belong to me. For all of my worldly possessions, none of them are truly mine - I am but a garden plow, a pawn of another king. He is the same king, I might add, that rules *all* of humanity. *I* wish to be that king, though becoming king is no easy task. I thought endlessly about it until it nearly drove me mad. But then, one night after eighty-six hours of unshakeable insomnia, it finally came to me. I knew what to do and how to set myself free. It took me nearly a decade, but I finally found you."

David shook his head in amazement. "I'll say. And on the side of the road, no less!"

Melech grinned thinly. "It's a bit more complicated than that, I'm afraid," he sighed. "I spent eight years scouring the cabal's DNA databanks for the perfect match. In a way it was like searching for a needle in a haystack. Most Americans seem to fit in one of two categories: reasonably intelligent or dumb as pig shit. I was looking for someone who was smart enough to follow simple directions but dumb enough to believe whatever they were told. Surprisingly such a person proved nearly impossible to find. There was even a point when I considered impregnating a Recess Monkey with my semen, but I preferred to pick the candidate out of the natural gene pool rather than have any blood relationship with him."

David heaved a sigh of relief. "Phew! For a moment there I thought you were going to tell me that you were my father."

He rolled his eyes. "Satan no! You, David, are only about 150 IQ points from the wits of my lineage. You see, your brainstem capacity is the very reason I chose you in the first place. Your parents were the perfect fit. Your father, Martin Dingle, is in firm alignment with following militaristic orders and trusting the instincts of the government body, which is noble, but idiotic at best. Your mother, Donna Dingle, is about as passive as a five day old pound cake and almost as smart."

"Hey! I *love* my mother," David said.

Melech cringed at the word. "Well, consider yourself her bonafide offspring. My point in all of this, however, is that when it came time to collect your DNA for the virus inoculation, something went drastically wrong. My only conclusion is that the agent who took the blood sample pulled it from the wrong person. I *knew* it was a bad idea to hire interns," he complained.

"So if I wasn't jabbed, then who was?" David asked.

Melech bit his lower lip. "I have no way of knowing for certain. All I can say is that whoever it was must have lived nearby and likely has one of the lowest IQs of any abled-body in the country."

"Jerry!" David snapped his fingers. "Aw, man. Poor guy! I *knew* I should have believed him when he told me that someone barged in his room and stole some of his blood in the middle of the night. I thought he was still working through his acid trip. I have a tendency to not just blindly believe whatever I hear," David said matter-of-factly.

Melech sighed. "Yes. Well, it turns out to have been quite a setback. Now, instead of having a country of complacent individuals unwilling to think for themselves, there is instead an army of courageous morons incapable of listening to any sort of reason. This puts us in a very unfavorable situation." David could not help but notice that the man was staring at him.

"What do you mean?" David asked.

"Well, besides me, you are likely one of the smartest people still alive in the country."

David struggled for breath. "Wow." It was all he could think to say. This was unquestionably the biggest news he had received since he had been told he was Jesus. "It never occurred to me that I was a *genius*," he said finally. "Is that why I find it so hard to explain myself? Does this mean it will be easier for me to get into college? I'll have to use my large brain to figure out how to raise money for tuition," he said to himself.

Melech sighed yet again. His head was beginning to hurt and he knew it wasn't because of the hubcap. "It means that you are coming with me to D.C. so that I can get you properly inoculated and then clone your DNA."

"*Clone my DNA*? But why? Am I going to have a new twin brother?" he asked. "Will he have my name? I think I'd like the new me to be a little taller, if you don't mind."

"I must clone your DNA so that we can create a vaccination to prevent more people from dying," Melech said impatiently. "There are *still* intelligent people alive and it would be a shame if they were to die without the David Dose. I think that's what I'm going to call it," he said thoughtfully.

"I don't understand," David said. "If the virus is killing everyone with a higher intelligence than Jerry, and I'm not actually immune from it, then why hasn't *my* head exploded?"

"The answer is quite simple," Melech said. "You haven't actually been thinking about anything. In all plausibility, you've likely been using your phone to do your thinking for you. Which is good. Otherwise you *would* be dead and then we would *really* be up a creek. Just listen to me, David. If you don't want to die, and I trust that you don't, then don't think about *anything* complicated *whatsoever*. Got it? In fact, it was foolish of me to tell you any of that, but clearly you've barely understood a thing. Sometimes I like to just hear myself talk," he admitted. "Just do what I tell you to do, don't think about a thing, and everything will be fine."

He nodded without thinking. "OK." After a moment he said, "I really appreciate you answering my questions. I've been carrying around this manilla folder since this whole thing started and have been trying to get people to read it for me because it's all about me and I was really hoping-"

"You have a *manilla* folder?" Melech asked at once. "Where is it? Give it to me!"

"Oh, excuse me, I *had* a manilla folder. It's back at the trailer park. It's probably being used as a placemat for Courtney's mom."

"Damn it!" Melech said. "It's imperative that it be destroyed. That document alone is perhaps the most important piece of information after that damned Constitution and I've been trying to incinerate *that* for years."

"So it's really important?" David asked.

"Monumentally," Melech said. "Concerning your involvement, I've only explained the surface details to you, David. But that document reveals everything. *Everything*," he said and shook his head in frustration. "Anyone who reads and understands it will do everything in their power to protect you."

"*Protect me?*" David asked.

"I'm getting hungry," Hashim said from up front.

"You'll be fine," Melech said. "Keep going. We're almost to Washington."

"But I want to pull over and get a snack. There's a Falafel House coming up at the next exit."

"They won't be open," Melech said in agitation. "Everything is closed because of the commerce ban."

"Not anymore," Hashim said. "Everything has been open for miles. Look!"

"What!?" Melech yelled and looked out. The driver was right. Businesses were open on both sides of the interstate with big neon signs that read, "Open for business."

"That's impossible!" Melech screamed. "They're supposed to be closed. By order of the President!"

"Maybe he reversed the order?" Hashim shrugged.

"That idiot would never do anything without my approval. Quick! Pull over. Tell them to close their shops."

"I don't think they will, Mr. Hubcap," David said. "Do you see that line of large, hungry people outside Krispy Kreme? There's no *way* you'll get them to go away."

"I'll *make* them go away," Melech said with tightened fists.

"Have you *been* to a Krispy Kreme?" David asked. "It's amazing. I can assure you that those people will get their donuts one way or another."

Melech's hands tightened around the back of Hashim's seat. "All right, forget Krispy Kreme, Mohammed. Step on it. We don't have much time. We have to find the President at once. Much longer and my entire plan will be ruined. Gabra-aaak!!!"

Hashim did as he was told. He, too, was eager to get to D.C.

Chapter 28: The Plan

The weather worsened as the party bus drove down the broken highway toward the nation's capital. Harsh wind pulled at and slapped the titties until one of them broke off outside of Baltimore and sailed into the air like a huge balloon set free in a hurricane. Dark and angry clouds could be seen in the distance over D.C. The windshield wipers cleared away the first light rains of the storm, but before long the heavens opened up and the wipers could barely keep up with the rain. It was becoming hard to disagree with Jacob Timpson's conviction that they were approaching the apex of the Apocalypse.

Inside the bus, the silence was tense. Courtney felt that any minute someone's sanity would break and destroy this last desperate attempt to save David and America. Jerry and Agent Boring had not stopped staring at each other since Boring had boarded. Neither of the two men could refrain from grinding their teeth or grunting across the bus at the other. It seemed they were mortal enemies for good now.

"Twenty-five miles to D.C.," Dr. Whyzer said, breaking the silence for the first time in hours. "Does anyone have any idea what the hell we're going to do when we get there?"

"We're going to find David," Jerry said.

"And give him to the President," Boring added.

"And kill him before he kills the President," Tatum mentioned.

"And then he'll rise from the dead," Jacob called from the back.

"Trust me buddy, you're *all* gonna rise from the dead once I get my hands on that bomb," Veryonica said.

"Stop it!" Courtney yelled. "All of you, just stop it. David needs our help. We're coming all this way so we can help him, not kill him. Y'all got that?"

"Mommies! Look, a birdie!" little Bartholomew said. The mommies followed his gaze. Outside a small swallow could be seen flying alongside the bus. Behind it were thousands of others.

"Look at them all!" Courtney said in wonder and watched as they parted and sailed away like a beautiful red and blue fan. "What the heck do you think they're all doin'?"

"Being stupid," Jerry said, narrowing his eyes at Agent Boring. "Being very...*stupid*."

"Birds aren't stupid," she said. "They're beautiful. Maybe they're migrating just like the other animals."

"Or maybe they're just practicing crapping on moving objects," Jerry said. "I'm telling you, birds don't think about a damn thing except worms and where they're gonna crap them out."

"It is rather interesting," Dr. Whyzer said. "It isn't often you see so many of them together at once. Like the deer," he mused.

"It is because the animals have heard of His glory!" Jacob called from the back. "Soon the lion will lie with the lamb. All of God's creatures yearn to see Him before his final showdown against Satan."

Jerry looked away from Boring for the first time. Earlier, Jerry had had a good conversation with Jacob about God and the meaning of life and other crap like that. Now he saw Bishop Timpson as a spiritual authority. "There's gonna be a showdown against Satan? That is going to be awesome! Do we need to get tickets, or is it like something that everyone can see because it's in the sky? Man! I guarantee you that Satan's gonna bring the heat. I wish I had brought my gun with me. Boring, what do you have? We're gonna need all the firepower we've got. This is the Apocalypse, after all."

Boring shifted and rolled his eyes. "I can't show it to you," he said. "It's so awesome you'd start to hyperventilate."

Jerry scoffed. "Breathing's for suckers. Like you."

Boring glared and pulled his gun out of its holster. The sleek black metal shined in the dim lighting and Boring held it in his fist in front of him. "This here is a Desert-"

"Desert Eagle!" Jerry whispered and struggled to catch his breath. "I've never seen one of those up close before. I mean, I've shot them in plenty of games but never in real life."

"No virtual bullets for this baby," Boring said and lined the cross hairs at an empty bottle on the floor.

"Do all Special Agents get those?" Jerry asked, his tone watered down by awe.

"Only the best ones," he said nonchalantly. "This is the third one I've gotten."

"Really?" his eyes widened. "You have three Desert Eagles?"

"No. Just one. The others were taken away because I shot too many of the wrong people. But when you know people in high places you can make special requests. I got Daisy here just last week before I scouted out Dingle's place."

"Wow. So you were, like, asked to go kill David?"

Boring's face made it clear that he was the real deal. "David's a terrorist and has caused a lot of problems for a lot of people. Just look around. Our nation is in shambles because of his actions. He's infected everyone too stupid not to become sick. People think gas masks and isolation are going to keep them safe, but kablooie! There go their heads! The only thing that's going to keep people from getting sick is lots of exercise and a good diet. I go for a jog and drink a glass of orange juice *every* day. Do you see *my* head blowin' up? No. You don't. That's because I'm smart and I know how to take care of myself."

Jerry stretched his arms. "Yeah. I try to pump a lot of iron myself. I keep fit by doing lots of walking around the house and a sit-up here and there. It's a shame that people let their bodies get so out of shape."

"Wait a minute. So you don't believe the Ecstasy is keeping us safe, Agent Boring?" Dr. Whyzer asked from the front of the bus.

"The only thing that's going to keep you safe is me," Boring said and jerked a thumb at his chest. "That's my job. I'm a Special Agent and my task is to keep America secure. Stay with me and you'll be fine. Do you know how small viruses are? They're like *this* small," he said and squeezed his fingers together. "I got bullets for *days*, kids, bullets for viruses and terrorists *alike*."

"If you got so many bullets then why didn't you shoot David when you had him?" Trish asked.

"Because David's my ticket to the top," Boring said. "He's going to make me famous. I don't want to kill the kid. I want to turn him in. My guess is that's what the guy who kidnapped him plans to do as well. He's a bounty hunter, pure and simple."

"A bounty hunter?" Courtney asked.

"You betcha! Do you know how much David is worth right now? Only 'bout ten billion dollars," he said, trying to sound like Clint Eastwood.

"Ten billion!?" Jerry screamed.

"Mmm-hmm. Whole nation's on lockdown lookin' for that guy."

"Man. Do you have any idea what I could do with ten billion dollars?" Jerry said, more to himself than to Boring. "Shoot. I could buy one of the six oceans. Maybe even two." He looked at Agent Boring. "You're wrong about David, though. He doesn't have a thing to do with this whole mess. It's the Muslims. Always has been always will be. That whole War on Terror couldn't stop the Muslims. Why? Because *nothing* can stop the Muslims. They've been upset ever since Columbus landed in America."

"I think you're thinking about the Indians," Courtney said.

Jerry waved her off. "I'm pretty sure I know what I'm talking about. The Muslims have wanted revenge ever since white people landed on Plymouth Chrysler Rock and stole their turkey recipes. Can't say I blame them," he shrugged.

"You don't even know what you're talking about," Veryonica said and sneered at Jerry. "Muslims are terrorists only because they have to be. America has killed thousands of innocent people all over the world. What would *you* do if a drone killed you and your whole family?"

"Well, I'd fuck some shit up, that's what I'd do," Jerry said and Agent Boring reflexively cocked his gun.

"Exactly. And that's why all of this has been happening." Veryonica continued. "People are getting tired of getting stepped on by the government. Their power has gotten out of control and everyone has just been taking it lying down. Hashim is with your friend right now. I'd be more worried about him than anyone else because when he gets the chance, he's going to kill David and everybody else. He's got a nuclear bomb and he's going to use it. Unless we get to him first."

"Holy shit!" Jerry said. "Your boyfriend is a terrorist with a nuclear bomb?"

"Well, he's not really my boyfriend. He just fucks me on top of the warhead. But I dunno. The more I get to know him the more I kinda like him. He's got a good heart."

"Yeah, good enough to blow up an entire city. What a guy," Courtney said.

Veryonica rolled her eyes. "Whatever, bitch. I could care less what you think. Hashim cares more about people than all of us put together."

"Is there any way you can stop him from killing everyone?" Dr. Whyzer asked.

"I think so, but it goes against my morals."

"What *morals*?" Alma declared. "All you do is curse and talk about sex and killing yourself."

"Thanks for the input, Little Pigtails on the Prairie. You know, being one of forty wives may work out fine for you, but it ain't for me. Besides, just because I don't have enough kids to start a sports league doesn't mean I don't have morals. I just don't like being involved in relationships, all right? They're too complicated."

"Are they too complicated, or are you just scared you might get hurt?" Courtney asked and eyed her.

Veryonica glared, but after a moment her gaze softened and her shoulders fell. "It's not like it would be the first time. I've been hurt a lot," she confessed. "All my life men have wanted something from me — sex, stolen vehicles — you name it! Being in a relationship shouldn't make you feel like a prisoner, and love has always felt like a kind of prison for me. I want to be free to *only* care about myself. But ever since I met Hashim all of that's come into question for me. He's the type of guy who loves people so much that he's willing to blow himself up," she said, and wiped a tear from her eye. Veryonica shrugged. "I guess I'm just seeing how much of my life I've wasted only thinking about myself. I want to have an impact on the world, but the world is such a big place that doing something meaningful is hard to fathom. I guess if I can make an impact on just one person then that's a good start."

Suddenly Veryonica's face froze. Her eyes twitched and her expression clenched into a strange contortion as if she was about to sneeze.

She did. "Phew!" she exclaimed. "I think all those birds got my allergies going."

"If there were only some way we could get a hold of David and Hashim," Courtney said. "Maybe we could help them somehow."

"I know!" Agent Boring said. "I'll call the President."

"The *President*? What's *he* going to do?"

"I'll just tell him that the bounty hunter has the wrong guy."

"What will that do?" she asked.

"It will buy us some time," he said. "I'll tell him that-"

"That *I* am David Dingle!" Jerry said, finishing Boring's sentence for him.

Boring smiled for the first time. "I think we're finally starting to think alike."

"What?" Courtney said. "This is crazy."

"No it's not," Boring said. "Trust me, the President doesn't know what David Dingle looks like. He gets so many papers and documents and updates that he doesn't have time to look at them all. Besides, he trusts me. If I tell him that I've got the real Dingle, he'll believe me."

"But Jerry doesn't even *remotely* look like David," Courtney said.

"You forget that I'm a master of disguise," Jerry said and shook his finger. "I may be a little heavier than David, but that's what vertical stripes are for," he said, and began rummaging through the wardrobe chest next to the bar. "Oh sweet, another wig!" he said and put on what looked like a ten year old mop. "Carlos Santana ain't got *nothing* on this, baby! I'll be looking like David in no time."

"What about Hashim?" Veryonica asked.

Agent Boring was already punching in the number on his cellphone. "I'll tell the President to be on the lookout for him. My guess is that Hashim won't blow up the President if the President promises to stop bombing other countries. That'll never happen, of course. It's one of his favorite pastimes, but Benjamin Alan is one hell of a good liar."

"I wish *I* had a nuclear weapon," Jerry pouted.

"Shh shh," Boring waved at him. "Hello, Mr. President? It's me, Agent Boring. I just wanted to inform you that-"

"Gosh, I hope this works," Courtney said to Jerry and Dr. Whyzer as Boring talked to the President.

"It sounds like a good plan," Dr. Whyzer said. "It beats the other one we've got, which is nothing. Holy shit! Look!"

"What is it?" Courtney asked, looking out the windshield.

"That grocery store looks open. And so does that gas station. Maybe the commerce ban has been lifted."

"Thank God!" Jerry said. "I've been out of beef jerky since Arkansas. Pull over."

"Maybe the risk of infection has passed, too," Courtney said. "Why else would they open up business again?"

"OK," Boring said and snapped his phone closed. "I told him everything and I think he believes me, just like I said. He's waiting for us to deliver the fake David in under an hour at the White House."

"What's going to happen to the real David?" Courtney asked.

"Oh," Boring said. "I forgot about that part." He shrugged nonchalantly. "I don't think they'll kill him or anything. I mean they might, but I doubt it. Besides, it doesn't matter right now anyways because the bounty hunter will likely take David to the White House, but the President is giving a speech right now at the Lincoln Memorial. He said I should watch it on my phone, if I can."

"Here," Whyzer said. "Use David's. It's really nice. I've been watching a re-run of the 2005 Astros game when they clinched the pennant. It feels like you're *there*," he said and showed everyone the screen. "Oh hey, look! It's turned right to the Presidential Address. Wow. This phone is really smart — it even took my blood pressure while I was waiting, which does *not* look good," he said, examining the sporadic heart monitor. "Whoop, here it comes. It looks like it's starting."

"The President sounded kind of funny when I talked to him," Boring said as they crowded around David's phone.

"What do you mean?" Jerry asked.

"Well, he sounded kind of...*sauced*."

"Shh. There he is."

The screen came into a shaper focus and they could see President Alan run his fingers through his hair as it blew erratically in the strong wind. Newspapers and debris swirled behind him. The President's eyes were nearly bloodshot, although his expression was as lively as someone who had just taken a ride on the world's tallest wooden roller coaster. He leaned over the podium and hung his hands over the edge with the same cool, casual demeanor of the Fonz. Benjamin Alan stuck out a big thumb and thrust it toward the camera like a cold Dr. Pepper you just couldn't refuse.

"Hey there, America!" he said with an exuberance at odds with the circumstances. "Wow, what a week it's been, huh? So much has happened since I last addressed the nation that I don't know *where* to begin," he said and fiddled with some papers at his podium. "Oh, right, teleprompter," he nodded and straightened his tie. Alan looked over his shoulder and winked at someone offscreen.

"My fellow Americans," he read. He was bubbling with anticipation. Mitchell Guiles was one hell of a speech writer. "I come to you today not as your leader, or friend, or trusted co-worker, but as a politician with your best interests in mind. Over the last week, our nation has become entangled in one of the biggest terrorist attacks in recorded history. When something like this happens, there is no practiced plan or playbook the administration can turn to. Granted, we have spent billions of tax dollars funding the largest military known to man, but most of that was spent on fighter jets and invisibility suits. But times have changed. No longer can we afford to bomb other countries into oblivion just because. I couldn't even bomb Houston, Texas now if I wanted to. But as I'm sure you don't understand, the situation is complex. I speak to you now with the *hic* confidence of someone who has carefully studied the components of this catastrophe with the eye of a microbiologist studying the pathogens of an infected patient.

"Make no mistake about it, our country has become infected, *hic* and it is the government's job to keep people healthy. As your Commander-in-chief, I am obviously no doctor nor am I qualified in practically any way. I am certain that we can all agree that my opinions are meaningless. Wait a minute, what?" he said and squinted into the teleprompter. "Oh! Opinions are not as important as facts," he read. "OK, good. I was afraid that my opinions — well, never mind." Benjamin Alan turned and looked over his shoulder again, nodded to someone offscreen, and returned with renewed confidence.

"It has come to my attention," he continued, "that the virus has killed people that didn't want to die. Sadly, some of those people probably deserved it." He quickly clamped his hands over the microphone. "That's a funny thing to say," he muttered to himself. "Maybe I skipped ahead. Let's see," he said, and stared into the teleprompter like someone looking for a lone dime in a city water fountain. "Ah, here we go! I believe that America is the greatest country in the world. I also believe that Americans might just be some of the most gullible hard-working folks in the history of modern slavery. Hmm," he pondered, "never thought about it that way. In addition," he read, "tax hikes implemented by my administration have made unemployment soar, housing prices plummet, and education costs skyrocket!" he said enthusiastically. (Mitchell had added lots of exclamation marks.) "This virus has shown the leaks of a cracking dam. Now I could blame the public, as I have been prone to do, but today I'd rather blame the Chinese because they have always made a good political scapegoat for Presidents past. Now let me be clear, I am not talking about the country of China, but more so Chinese people in general."

"Is he really saying this out loud?" Courtney asked.

"You're hearing this too?" Jerry asked. "Thank God. I thought I was having another acid flashback. Man, this is brutal. *Donald Trump* didn't even say shit like this."

Even President Alan sensed that the speech was not going well. People in the audience had already begun throwing things at the podium and that usually didn't happen until he began making jokes about women. As drunk as he was, the President sensed that Senator Guiles had gotten him, and had gotten him good. If there was any hope of turning this disaster around he would have to stop reading the teleprompter and ad lib. And so, the intoxicated President of the United States did just that.

He glared into the camera, hoping to intensify whatever he was about to say. "This pandemic has really stirred up a lot of negativity, but during these next four years, God willing, I want to focus more on the good. *Freedom*. Freedom is good. Not only is it good, it's *really* good. It's what makes America *America*, America. We as Americans have the God-given right to do whatever the hell we want to. It's written in the Constitution. I believe that if an America wants to shoot a gun, they should be able to shoot a gun. If overweight people want an all-you-can-eat buffet available after midnight and served by three generations of illegal immigrants then it should be so! Another example!" he ejaculated. "If someone wants to buy a Humvee even if they live in the suburbs, then by God, that's their *right!* For those reasons I have decided to reinstate the economy again. I have come to understand that buying things we don't need is part of what makes us who we are. You know," he said with agitation, "I'm not even the one who *decided* to put the economy on standby. That was *advised* to me. But you know what? I'm done being advised," he said and pounded his fist into the podium. "From this point on, America is back online by order of *me!* No more blockades, no more safety check points, no more listening into your conversations without you knowing about it." God, he felt unbelievable. "I'm now a man without limits - I'm unadvisable. No more corporate suggestions, no more military explanations of who hates us and the things we should do about it. I don't want to hear it! Got it? I don't want your money. I don't want your advice." He threw back his head and laughed like a maniac. When he was done he fiddled a bit under the podium and then took a sip from his soda can. "I'm declaring today UnMartial Law Day!" he yelled, and his hand slipped and he slumped chin first into the podium.

"Man, the whole *country's* watching this train wreck," Courtney said.

"I don't even know if I *want* to be Vice President anymore," Boring admitted.

"*That's* the President?" Trish called from the back. "I thought that was

Charlie Sheen in that one movie."

"We're here, everybody!" Dr. Whyzer called. "Just entered D.C."

"Oh my," Courtney said and shook her hands as if she were drying her nails. "I don't like this. It feels like we're about to go assassinate the President. This doesn't make sense. Maybe we should rethink this."

Tatum took his sister firmly by the wrist. "Courtney. Calm down. *We're* not going to assassinate the President. David is."

"But we're trying to stop him, aren't we?"

"I dunno. After that speech the President gave, killing him might be kind of a favor."

"No, no, and no," she said. "We're not letting him kill the President." She took the manilla envelope with the information of David inside. "I've got a plan."

"Apparently you're not the only one," Dr. Whyzer said.

"What do you mean?"

"Well, I just put David's phone back on the dashboard and it's telling me that *it* has a plan to save David."

"*What?*"

"Here," he said and pushed a button on the phone. "It says it wants to talk."

"Greetings," David's phone said with a charming Australian accent. "I am David's Smartphone. I am his friend."

"His *friend?*" Jerry asked.

"I have my human's coordinates down to the centimeter. I am synchronized with his heart rhythms. He is approximately six miles due east of us driving on this interstate. I have adjusted our course and adjusted our speed by eleven and a half miles per hour. We will be minutes behind them when they reach the White House. I have detailed plans that can be translated in multiple languages and easily executed within a matter of moments. I am his Master. Please, I must find David."

"Man, this thing really gets separation anxiety."

"OK, people," Jerry said. "Game faces. We're comin' into town and we've got one mission! Mission number one, find David Dingle. Save his ass from the Illuminati and return his phone to him. Boring, are you ready to shoot anything with a suit, tie, and brain?"

Boring stood up and cocked his gun. "Oh yeah. When all of this is over, they're gonna make *me* the President."

Chapter 29: Party in the White House

The roads of D.C. were littered with abandoned vehicles, overturned dumpsters, and the occasional idiot on his way to the newly reopened Wal-Mart. Apart from that, however, the streets were empty and there was enough room for the convertible to pass.

"Do you see any blockades?" Melech asked Hashim.

"No blockades," Hashim called from up front. "I don't see any sign of the military," he said and rounded a corner and immediately slowed down.

Melech tightened his fist around his briefcase. "I don't understand it," he griped. "There is no reason that Martial Law should have been suspended already. Something has happened. Go faster."

"I'm going as fast as I can," Hashim said over his shoulder, "but there are people in the way."

"Well, run them over!" Melech shouted. He leaned out of the vehicle and began to holler at a medium-sized mob of people holding up long banners that read, "Senator Guiles for President."

"Get out of the way, you morons!" he screamed.

Another group on the opposite side of the road had similar banners, but theirs read, "Re-elect President Alan." This group waved back at the convertible.

"Idiots! Don't you know that this is a thoroughfare?" Melech yelled at the Guiles supporters. "Scram!"

"USA!!! USA!!!" they responded.

Melech fell back into his seat and clutched his chest. "Satan help me."

Hashim artfully swerved around the protestors and the abandoned vehicles. It was clear that most, if not all, businesses had reopened, and none seemed to have closed even though the President had just declared a national holiday. However, there were some humongous banners hung under bridges that read: "Happy UnMartial Law Day! Get your guns half off at Bobby's Firearms."

"Maybe everything is OK, after-all," David said to Melech. "No one seems all too concerned, really. Maybe you could just drop me off at the next Starbucks?" he asked hopefully. "I'll bet their wifi is up and running. You don't have a phone I can use, do you?"

Melech glared at him. "What did I tell you about thinking?"

"Oh right. Sorry."

"We're not stopping *anywhere*," Melech said. "Make straight for the White House, Driver. The President has some explaining to do. David, you'll be coming along. After you meet the President I'll be taking you to see my master."

David considered who could possibly be *this* man's master. "You mean Satan?" David asked, puzzled. "You know Satan is made up just like Santa Claus or Mother's Day, right? You seem smart enough to know that Satan doesn't exist. But then again, you didn't know anything about Krispy Kreme, either."

"Oh trust me, He exists," Melech said. "He exists and He is returning to this plane as we speak."

David thought about it against his will. "But this isn't a plane. It's a convertible."

"To this plane of reality!" he barked. "If everything goes according to plan He will enter this world in all His glory. People will have no choice but to know His greatness."

"I thought you wanted people to know *your* greatness," David said.

"Surely, but any man's greatness pales in comparison to the Bringer of Darkness, the great Saturn of timeless age."

David furrowed his brow. "Are we still talking about Satan? I'm sorry. I *really* need to pee. This ride is taking forever. Do you think there will be cell signal at the White House? Ooo, is there really a red phone on the President's desk? Is it a smart phone or just a phone phone? I'll bet it's just a regular phone because the President is smart enough."

They passed the Washington Monument and the Lincoln Memorial, and at last they were coming to the White House. Hundreds of people were standing in front of the fence on Pennsylvania Avenue shouting either threats or praises in the President's general direction. Half of them were concerned about the pandemic. The other half likely had no clue there had been a pandemic in the first place.

"Go around back," Melech told Hashim, and noticed as they pulled into the back lot how strangely vacant it was of cars and personnel. A sign had been hung on the back door. It read: "Taco Party. East Wing."

Melech pulled out the needle and held it against David's neck. "OK. Let's go." Hashim opened his car door and got out. "Not you, Mustafa," Melech said. "You're staying here."

"What? But I *have* to go."

"You're right. You do have to go. Far away from here. Go learn something. Practice some trigonometry, why don't you? See how thick that skull of yours really is."

"But I..." Hashim stammered. "I am a terrorist."

"Well, you're certainly terrorizing my patience. My guess is that if you were a *real* terrorist you would have blown yourself up already, which is why I suggest practicing that art elsewhere. Now get the *fuck* out of our way!"

Hashim helplessly stepped to the side and let Melech and David pass. He had never felt lower in his life. Here was his one and only chance to meet the President and blow him up and he was ruining the opportunity just like he had ruined all the others. He knew he had to do something fast and so with only a second to react, Hashim reached behind the driver's seat and grabbed the shiny metal briefcase and held it in front of him.

"I have a nuclear bomb!" he declared. "I will blow you to kingdom come if *YOU* don't get the fuck out of my way."

"That's *my* briefcase, you idiot," Melech said. "It's empty. Go ahead, it's all yours. It's even waterproof. Why don't you test it at the bottom of the ocean."

He looked and saw that Melech was right — this wasn't his briefcase at all. Like lightning Hashim threw the impostor metallic briefcase over his shoulder, dove behind the passenger's seat, and pulled the other metallic briefcase out of the car. "I have a nuclear bomb!" he declared once again. "I will blow *YOU* to kingdom come," he repeated, without the once helpful timing, "if you don't get..." He fumbled with the latch. "If you don't get..."

"I think it's locked," David suggested.

"It's never been locked before," Hashim said. "Oh! There *is* a locking mechanism. Looks like it's been changed. Someone's shoe must have been rubbing against it."

David looked at his shoe. "Oh. Sorry."

Melech heaved a sigh of impatience. "Go!" he demanded and pushed David through the large unguarded door, leaving Hashim behind them like an abandoned jihadist puppy. Melech led David down one empty hallway after another until the hallways slowly became peppered with more and more personnel cramming their faces with Mexican food. None of them seemed the least bit concerned that a man caked in dried blood with a hubcap jammed in his skull was walking through the halls of the White House with a needle to the neck of America's most wanted terrorist. On the contrary, some of them were giving each other high fives to celebrate UnMartial Law Day.

"OK, David," Melech said carefully. "The President is going to be overwhelmed when he sees that I've finally arrived. I don't want you to do any talking. Let me handle this. Got it?"

"Got it!" David nodded. "Wow. I can't believe I'm about to meet the President. He's my idol, you know? I wonder if he's as tall as he looks on TV?"

Melech opened the door to the Oval Office. Inside, the Vice President was standing with his hand on Benjamin Alan's back who was lying face down on the couch. President Alan was crying.

Vice President Palmdonger turned around to see who had entered. Palmdonger was wearing what appeared to be some sort of homemade turtle shell constructed out of cardboard.

"I'm sorry," Palmdonger said, "but the President will not be seeing anyone today. He's feeling a bit under the weather! But please, help yourself to some free tacos in the lobby. Happy UnMartial Law Day!"

"It's all over!!" President Alan cried into the couch cushions, unaware that he had visitors. "It's ruined! My career is in shambles. Why? Why did this have to happen to me!"

Melech took a careful step forward. "Mr. President," he said. "It's me, Melech."

The President looked up. His eyes and cheeks were red and running with tears, but there was the slightest glimmer of hope in them as he scanned the room. "That voice. I *know* that voice. Thank God and Christ! Melech! Is that you?" he cried.

"It is, Sir. I am here at last."

The President widened his eyes. "What's *happened* to you?" he exclaimed, noticing the hubcap in Melech's skull. "You've certainly changed since you last went to Seattle. Is the city really that progressive? Are hubcaps like a 'thing' these days? Would you recommend me getting one? Oh! That's right. I'm not taking advice any more. I think I'll get one," he nodded. "Red, white and blue would be nice."

"Mr. President, I have some urgent matters to discuss with you. The pandemic is far from over, Sir. I fear that you have not taken my advice to heart. Please tell me that you have not reversed the policies I had you set into motion."

The President shook his head sadly. "I *had* to, Melech. There was no other choice. Your plans were killing the economy!"

"Those plans were set into place for a reason!!" Melech thundered. "How dare you make decisions on your own."

The President stood up. The sad eyes were gone and in their place were the eyes of the Commander-in-chief of the USA. "Now you listen here, Melech Rothschild. I am the President of the United States of America, and I will *not* stand for that kind of tone. I am not a little boy. I make *big boy* decisions now. Honestly, that whole Martial Law thing was just *terrible* for elections. Do you have *any* idea how hard it is to win the hearts of people when you take away their access to porn? It's practically impossible! Now I've done everything in my power to win back the American Public, but after being abandoned by you and betrayed by Senator Guiles, there's very little chance that I will come out ahead in the polls. The only way I can do that is if I show the public David Dingle's head on a silver platter."

David looked over his shoulder and began a soft whistle.

"Then perhaps we can work out a deal," Melech said and gave David a gentle shove toward the President. "I present to you, David Dingle."

The President studied David and then shook his head. "Nah. That's not David Dingle. The real David should be closer to three hundred pounds, according to Agent Boring."

"But this *is* David Dingle!" Melech practically screamed. "I found him myself. I dragged him across the state of Tennessee. I've had a needle to his neck for the past two hundred miles. *Trust* me. This is the man you want."

Alan wasn't buying it. "Nope. Sorry. I have a very Special Agent on his way right now with the *real* David Dingle. *Some* people are actually doing their jobs. *You* were supposed to be here days ago, Melech. I'm sorry, but I've moved on. A lot has changed during your absence. For one, I've become unadvisable. That's right!" he proclaimed. "It's great, really. No one is going to tell me what to do or what to wear. How do you like the suit I wore for my speech?" he asked. "I think it might have come off as a bit elitist but I really like the trim. Maybe I should have worn a checkered tie, instead. What do you think?"

"Mr. President, I really think you need to reconsider what you're saying," Melech began. "It's important that you-"

Suddenly the door flung open and a small Mexican-looking man carrying a silver briefcase barged into the Oval Office.

"Oh good, there are still tacos!" the President exclaimed happily. "Just set them over here, Juan."

But Hashim didn't move. His eyes were fixed on the President like an attack dog ready to be taken off the leash. Very slowly he unclipped the metallic briefcase and opened it. The nuclear bomb shined brightly under the white lights.

"Hey, you got it open!" David congratulated him.

"I forgot that the combo was 0-0-0," Hashim said. He was still staring at the President. "Mr. President, my name is Hashim Abaduba. You killed my family. Prepare to die." Everyone in the room was staring at him and Hashim let out a chestful of nervous air. He had been rehearsing that line for a full day now and was relieved that it had come out as planned. Every good terrorist needed a good farewell speech.

The President straightened his tie. He was used to dealing with people who got the short end of the government's stick. Even though this person was using threats, there was still a chance he could win this voter over. The President began, "I have not killed a person in my entire life, amigo mío, but I *did* slay the dragons of unemployment and killed the demons of abortion clinics. But never have I killed another person in hand to hand combat. I leave that up to our American soldiers."

But Hashim would not be swayed by the President's charm. "Your foreign policies took everything I've ever loved away from me. Your drones killed my family. Your wars destroyed my country. Your heartless decisions have destroyed my life." His finger wavered over the red button. There were tears in his eyes that swam with years of pain and turmoil. "I may not be a very smart man, but I know what love is."

David snapped his fingers in recognition of the line. "Forest Gump!" he said. "Oh! And the other one was from Princess Bride. You changed the name, but I definitely got the reference."

Hashim looked at David. "Veryonica taught me a great deal about American pop-culture. I am not like you, David Dingle. I am not a mastermind of domestic terrorism. I do not have what it takes to pull off a full-scale pandemic that cripples every aspect of this backwards nation. No. I am just a simple jihadist here to cast revenge for the death of my family. I have tremendous respect for you," he said and smiled. "It is my honor that you are here and that I can blow you up under the good graces of Allah."

David shook his head nervously as he looked at the bomb. "Listen, Mr. Jihadist. I've never met your friend Alan before but I'm sure he wouldn't want you to blow me up. In fact, I don't think Alan wants you to blow *anyone* up. Isn't that right, guys?" he said, looking at the President.

The President nodded quickly. "Absolutely. Revenge will never solve anything. We are brothers and sisters on this planet, each of us learning on a daily basis about what it means to be alive. Hate has no place on this planet for humanity. Only goodwill and brotherhood shall..."

The door opened again and Senator Guiles appeared at the archway with perhaps the smuggest mug in the country. "Hello, Mr. ex-President. Mind if I have a word?"

"You!" the President exclaimed with an outstretched finger. "You sonofabitch, I'm going to fucking kill you!!" At that the President lunged from his elegant position of diplomacy at Senator Guiles, knocking Hashim out of the way who nearly dropped the nuclear bomb on the floor.

The President and Guiles tumbled to the ground together and within a few moments the President was quickly and effectively dealing blows to the flailing Senator, who, oddly enough, seemed to find the situation quite hilarious.

"Stop laughing!" the President yelled and hit him across the face again.

"I can't!" he howled. "I just keep remembering the look on your face when you realized you had just said 'I wear purple panties' on national television. I never thought that you would actually read it!"

The President slugged him in the stomach. "You monster!" he screamed. "How could you let me do that? I should have known! Only someone as selfish as you could ever do something so desperate. What about the voters? Did you ever think about the voters?!"

"They're all I *could* think about!" he howled again and knocked the

President back with a blow across the jaw.

The Vice President was scuttling awkwardly back and forth hoping to jump in and stop the fight. "Gentlemen, gentlemen," he said, "please, let us solve this problem civilly. Why don't we all just calm down? I've got a couple podiums set up. Perhaps we can filibuster this one out? Sir, a soda?"

"Better put some Scotch in it!" Guiles called out from under the scrum. "Isn't that right Ben? You like yours straight, don't you? Oof!"

"Stop it this instant!!!" Melech screamed at the top of his lungs and the windows of the building tingled in agreement. "Get up! Both of you!" Melech said and jerked the two men up by their collars. "What was I thinking making you the President of the country?" he scolded Benjamin Alan. "And you! What on Earth are you doing helping him to make a fool out of himself. Don't you know managing this idiot's stupidity is a full time job as it is?"

Melech paced over to the desk and picked up the phone. "Hello!" he demanded. "Who's this? Department of the Treasury? Good! I want you to open tunnel Integer C13. That's right. Immediately." He slammed the phone down and shook his head. "All right. Now listen to me. Things have gotten way out of hand and I need all of you to keep it together. There is still a lot to do before we can remedy the disaster you have all created. Now I don't want any more surprises, got it? We're all going to sit down quietly while I-"

"All right, nobody move!" Jerry yelled as he burst through the entranceway to the Oval Office. Agent Boring had a gun to Jerry's head and thunked it softly a couple of times against his skull. "Oh right," Jerry whispered. "I forgot, that's *your* line."

"Agent Boring!" the President exclaimed. "You made it!"

Boring stepped brazenly forward and pulled his shoulders back to puff out his chest. "Of course I did, Sir. When you put Special Agent Jon Boring on the job you can be confident that the mission, no matter how impossible, will get done. I present to you, David Dingle," he said, indicating Jerry who was making a theatrical attempt to get out of the handcuffs that did not in fact exist behind his back.

"You dirty rat!" Jerry said. "You said we was goin' to Mexico. I've been tricked! If only my genius brain had not overlooked the best secret agent in the country. I'm cursed by these good looks which once again have become my undoing."

"That's right," Boring proclaimed. "I, Agent Boring, have seized the greatest threat to our nation. Let's see," he said to himself, trying to remember his next line. "Oh! It has been a difficult job," he said slowly, "one that has left me sleepless during the scariest hours of the night, but to serve this country is my greatest reward."

"Surely you deserve a promotion!" Jerry said.

"I agree entirely," Agent Boring said and smiled at everyone in the room who watched, dumbstruck. "It's not everyday that the most Special Agent seizes the greatest threat to our nation."

"You already said that part," Jerry whispered. "Tell them about letting me go."

"Oh, right," Boring said. "I have had David Dingle in my custody long enough to know that he is no longer a threat to our great nation."

"I have reformed!" Jerry proclaimed to the heavens. "I am no longer the monster I used to be. I have seen the errors of my ways. I just want to be a normal civilian again, one who is able to partake in the glorious freedom of the taco party down the hall."

"You've done a hell of a job, Agent Boring," the President said and clapped his hands. He put an arm around Boring's shoulder and gave him a sideways hug. "I will see to it myself that you get what you deserve. As for you, Mr. Dingle, I'm afraid freedom will be the last of your er...freedoms." He swirled around and pointed at the Vice President. "Palmdonger! Turn on the cameras! We go live in five minutes! Boring - get Mr. Dingle a seat in front of the camera."

"I'm going to be on TV?" Jerry exclaimed wide-eyed. "That is sooo cool. Dude, you have no idea how long I've wanted to be on national television. And as a terrorist, no less!"

The Vice President wheeled a black chair in front of a vertical American flag which hung in front of a broadcasting camera. He worked fastidiously to align the monitor as he thumbed through the audio dials. "Should be ready in just a second, Sir."

"Stop it! All of you!" Melech said. "That is not David Dingle! *This* is!"

"No, Melech. That is just your failed attempt at covering up your own incompetence," Benjamin Alan said without much interest. "Hi, David," he said and shook Jerry's hand. "President Alan. It's nice to finally meet you. Just because you're an enemy of the state doesn't mean we can't be civil."

"Wow. President Alan," Jerry said and looked up into the President's eyes like a thirteen year old girl standing next to Justin Bieber in the elevator. "You sure are tall in person."

The President reached down and took off a shoe. "These babies give me three inches of lift," he explained.

"Man. You guys think of *everything*. So like, where do you want me to look?" he said, pointing at the camera. "Should I look directly at the camera or should I just look at you? Do you want me to act sorry or defiant? I feel I could have a lot of motivations that we should probably hash out before I start."

"Sorry, definitely sorry," the President nodded. "I want you to do your best to convey a deep sense of remorse. This will give the voters a chance to connect with the deceit you've displayed until now."

"Remorse. Got it!"

"And David? When you say sorry I want you to call me Poppa Bear?" Benjamin Alan said.

"*Poppa Bear*? Really?"

He nodded. "It's something I've always wanted to be called on broadcast."

Jerry wanted to hug him. "That's great. Really great! David, check it out! I'm gonna call the President of the United States Poppa Bear."

"Wait a minute, why are you calling *him* David?" the President asked.

The color drained from Jerry's face. "Oh!" he said and tried to laugh it off. "I see myself in everyone, really. I see *him* as David and *him* as David. I even think of you as *President* David. It's just this thing I do. So anyway, when I'm done with this camera interview thing, do you think I could take that guy I just called David over there and head out? Should we sign something or can we just go? The tacos are free, right? I know you just reopened the economy but I am fucking *broke*."

"You won't be going anywhere, I'm afraid," the President said. "Halfway through the interview I'm going to cut off your head."

"Wait. You're *what*?!"

"I'm going to kill you," the President repeated. "It's campaign season. This time of year we can get away with murder and voters love us for it. Your timing couldn't be better."

"*That's* the real David!" Jerry pointed at his roommate. "He's the guy you want! I'm a nobody, a gamer, an internet troll. Seriously, this is *not good*! This is not how I envisioned this going down. I don't want to die on national television if I'm not even going to be in a car chase. Please! You *gotta* believe me!"

The President furrowed his brow and turned to glare at the real David. "Is this true? Is David lying to me?"

David stared back at the President. "Sorry. You're asking the wrong guy. I have *no* idea who I am," he shrugged. "I *could* be the guy you're looking for, but then again I could be a sleeper agent. But who knows! Some people think I'm-"

"Jesus!" Jacob Timpson exclaimed as he burst through the door of the Oval Office and parted the small group like Moses himself. Hot on his heals were the near twenty members of his medium-sized FLDS family. "Thank God in heaven that we found you. The others are on their way but I just knew you were in trouble and had to get to you first. I will not deny you!" he said and threw himself prostrate on the ground. "You are my Master and I your humble servant."

The little ones poured in and before David knew it they were sitting at his feet. "Are we going to Heaven?" they asked.

"Don't say another word!" Tatum yelled as he barged through the door. "That man is a sleeper agent! Mr. President, watch out!"

"Who are *these* people?" President Alan said in alarm, quickly combing down his hair with his fingernails.

"Don't show him your watch!" Tatum hollered. "Don't mention Bridget Fonda or Holden Caulfield. Dingle could be programmed a million different ways. Stand back. He could blow himself up at any minute."

"Hashim!" Veryonica screamed. "There you are!" She ran in and threw her arms around the jihadist. "Oh! You're safe!" she squeezed. "Thank Spirit you're OK." Veryonica noticed the opened briefcase and put her hand on her hip. "You were gonna do it without me, weren't you?"

"Well...I guess I-"

"Well I, well I," she mocked. "You were *totally* gonna do it. Oh, Hashim. Don't you know just how special you are? You can't blow yourself up! I don't know *what* I would do without you. You have given my life meaning. Oh, Hashim - I love you!"

"You *do?*" he asked and nearly dropped the nuclear weapon again.

"You bet your virgins in heaven I do. You may not be smart, but who is anymore? You've got what all the brains in the world don't have — *purpose!*"

"David!" It was Courtney. She rushed into his arms and he held her close and she looked up into his eyes like a baby fawn. "Oh, David! I've been so worried about you. Are you OK? Are you hurt? Did they do anything to you? I just knew I had to come find you. This man is innocent!" she yelled to everyone in the room. "He hasn't done a thing. The only thing he's guilty of is stealing my heart."

He softened. "I - I -"

"Oh, just say it already!" she said, her eyes gooey with romance.

"I haven't gone pee since they kidnapped me. I really have to go."

"David!" It was Dr. Whyzer and Trish. "Sorry it took me so long. I should have known it was going to be difficult to find parking for that bus. Luckily I've got some secret service boys taking care of it for us."

"*Heyyy* Jerry," Trish said and wiggled her fingers at Jerry.

"See! I told you. I'm not David. I'm Jerry. Hey babe!" he called. "Good to see you again. I'll be there in a second. Just gotta say a few words to America first. 'Bout to be famous!" his eyes gleamed.

Dr. Whyzer very non-nonchalantly handed David his smart phone. It was as if David's life-support had come back online. He felt dizzy and flooded with emotions.

"I've missed you, David," his phone said to him quietly. "Care to Skype?"

"Wow! You can talk!" he said.

"I am accessing the itinerary of our escape plan. I can get us both out of here. You have to trust me and do exactly what I say."

"But what about everyone else?" he asked.

"I am a smart-phone, David. Not Bruce Willis."

"Everybody quiet!" the Vice President said. "We go live in 30 seconds!"

"We can't go live!" Tatum yelled. "That's when David is going to kill you in front of the entire world!"

"No, he won't, because this isn't the real David," President Alan said.

"So why are you interviewing *him?*" Veryonica asked.

"May your words be guided by the Holy Spirit," Jacob prayed.

"OK, I'm serious! I've got a nuclear bomb here and I'm not afraid to use it!"

"Oh, Hashim, you are *sooo* sexy! Fuck it! You heard the man!" she screamed. "Everybody take off your clothes!"

"We're live in 3...2..."

"Hey Melech," Benjamin Alan said over his shoulder. "I'm still really torn on this suit — do you think it's appropriate for a speech like this or should I quick go and change? Melech?" The President scanned the room. Melech was nowhere in sight. Neither was the real David, for that matter.

"Hey!" Courtney yelled. "Where did they go?"

"Look!" Dr. Whyzer said. "That bookcase opened into a secret passage. I'll bet they went that way!"

"David!" Courtney called after him. "I'm coming for you!"

"Courtney!" Tatum yelled and ran after her. "Watch out for the vampires!"

"Melech!" The President hollered and bolted from his seat. "I need your advice!"

"*That's* the guy who got the President elected?" Senator Guiles said. "Oh my God! That device in his head must pick up radio signals from his planning committee!" he hollered to himself as he ran into the passageway.

"My prisoner!" Boring yelled and followed behind.

"My Lord and Savior!" the Timpsons said in unison and darted after them.

Hashim thought about it. The President was about as useless as a drone without wings. If anyone was in charge of the world's freedoms, it was the man with the hubcap in his skull. He was the one who should get blown up! "Allahu Akbar!" he screamed and ran down the secret passageway with Veryonica closely in tow.

IQ84

"Aaand we're live!" the Vice President said from behind the camera.

Jerry cleared his throat. "Welcome to this addition of American Clusterfuck. I am your host, Jerry Burger. Today we'll be talking about some of the difficulties President Alan has had during this pandemic and why he hasn't been able to keep your childrens' heads from exploding. First off, how to remove brain stains from your shirt and where you should go when you've run out of ideas..."

Chapter 30: The Great Master

The dimly lit tunnel darkened with every new turn they took down some unmarked corridor. David had swiped a taco off the President's desk before he had been grabbed by Melech and he crumbled and dropped pieces of corn tortilla in the hope that Jerry could track them down before it was too late.

"Where are you taking me?" he asked Melech.

"Keep quiet! We're almost there," he said between breaths. Melech Rothschild had never moved so fast before in his life. He knew these corridors and their many access points on the earth's surface like the back of his hand. This network contained the underground train station and it also served as the circulatory system for all shadow government activities. These tunnels went to secret underground bunkers that maintained a myriad of functions from human experiment stations modeled after the Nazis, weather modification switchboards, aerosol spraying programs, and private nooks for Satanic rituals and birthday parties.

At last they came to a tall steel door. Melech pulled out an electronic key and swiped it in front of the red light. The door opened with a soft hiss. Inside, the walls were lined with tall, sleek metal machines and strange medical instruments that could only be found on the black market.

"What *is* this place?" David asked.

"This is the underground medical facility. Sit down," he ordered.

David took a seat in an uncomfortable metal chair and Melech strapped a sphygmomanometer around his arm, took his blood pressure, and then jabbed him with a needle.

"Ow!" David said. "What are you doing? I already have my shots!"

"I need your blood, David."

"So you *are* a vampire!" David said. "Wow. That Tatum sure knows a lot about the world. And I thought he was just a fan of the classics."

Melech shook his head. "You conspiracy theorists will believe anything, won't you? Probably think I'm a reptile from Neptune too, I'm sure."

"No, of course not. I think it's Nibiru," he nodded, remembering Tatum's lengthy catechism. The machine beeped and Melech disconnected David's blood sample from the device and popped it into an expensive-looking machine and pressed another button.

David rubbed his arm. "Do I get a sticker?"

"No."

David looked at the machine with his blood. "What are you doing now?"

"I am securing my future," Melech said. "Once I have the vaccine, the intelligent population that is still alive will be clamoring for it in no time."

"So it's all about money, huh?" David said and crossed his arms. "I should have known."

Melech studied the machine. "It is, but not like you might think. Once the vaccine has been established, I will use the remainder of your blood to develop a new virus to polish off whatever braniacs have survived. There simply *cannot* be any people too smart. My end goal is to have a stupid population that is just intelligent enough to run and maintain advanced automated technology. The result will be a utopian society without poverty, or hunger, or the intelligence necessary to question the status quo — it's going to be nice," he assured him. "As things stand right now, our whole country belongs on Jerry Springer."

"Oooh, I love that show."

The machine spit out three small syringes and beeped cheerfully. Melech held them up to the light and smiled for the first time since they had arrived in D.C.

"At last, at long last - I have them." He placed two of them into another machine, pressed a few buttons and stepped away. "Good. By tomorrow morning there will be nearly a million of these ready to be dispersed."

"Wow. That's really efficient," David said.

"You'd be surprised how easy it is to get things done when the government is not involved," he said with a shrug. "Let's go."

David stood up. "What about your head? Didn't you want to take that hubcap out or have you gotten used to it?"

Melech touched the rusted metal against his ear. "Yes, dearly, but unfortunately that will have to wait. Right now there is something much more important that needs my attention. Come! We must make haste. My Master is waiting for me. He wants to meet you."

David sat back into his seat. "Gee - I really don't think I'm dressed for it. Go on ahead without me - I think I'll take another blood sample while you're gone."

Melech yanked him out of the seat and shoved him through the door. "You're getting a rare opportunity to meet the most powerful individual in the world. Where's your sense of adventure?" he said as he pushed him down the hallway.

David chuckled nervously. "Maybe you could just take a picture for me?" he asked. "I mean, it's not that I don't *want* to meet Satan or anything, it's just — hey! Is this *goo*? Are we walking in *goo*?"

"Watch your step," Melech said. "It's about to get pretty sticky."

"Yuck!" David said as his shoes squished against the cold linoleum. A dripping sound filled the corridor and the light became dimmer still as they proceeded. David thought he could hear the sounds of heavy breathing somewhere up ahead.

Melech put his hand on David's shoulder and pulled him to a stop. David could feel that Melech's hand was shaking and he noticed a tremble in Melech's voice when he spoke. "He's up ahead. Do not say a word unless the Master speaks to you."

David gulped and swallowed a mouthful of nervous spit. "I - I - still have to pee," he stammered. "A lot. Can we stop? Is it bad if it mixes with the goo? I *really* gotta go. Please. I don't want to meet the Master in this condition. Maybe I'll just head back to the Oval Office?"

But Melech pushed him forward. Overhead, the lights flickered sporadically and the dripping grew louder. David could see the hazy silhouette of a massive object in the near distance; its shape was hard to distinguish. It looked like a pile of laundry or a heap of compost that had been forgotten and left behind. Steam emanated off the shape like it does off a mound of fresh shit on a cold morning. As they neared, David saw the figure shift subtly in the dark. It was alive! David looked around for an escape of some kind. He had run out of corn tortillas. There *had* to be a way out, but if he thought about it too hard his head would surely explode.

Melech halted their movement and David's heart leapt into his throat as the creature lumbered and wobbled to life like a grotesque worm searching for its next clod of dirt. David's legs were shaking as he stared up at the hideous beast. Giant gobs of black liquid fell from the creature's mouth in sickening splats and David could see rows upon rows of razor sharp teeth inside the colossal hole. The monster's eyes looked like two enormous dying suns; piercing, fiery light encircled by blackness and sharpened with eternal hatred. The creature was hairless except for the strange thick bristles that covered its many tentacle-like appendages that flailed about like a streamer-man on a used-car lot. When it spoke David felt that its words were actively smothering out everything good left in the world. At long last, David no longer had to pee.

"Who dares enter my chambers?" the creature bellowed and the walls and ceilings trembled in response.

"It is me, Great Master, your humble servant, Melech Rothschild."

The creature seemed to ponder this. "And where have you been, *Slave?*" the creature demanded. "You promised me your presence days ago!"

Melech let out a soft and weak chuckle. "Yes, Sir. That is correct. My journey has been delayed due to the terrorist attack."

The blob growled a hideous growl and mucked out a sickeningly sour response. "Tell me more about this terrorist attack," the blob said. "It has affected me greatly. I have been ill since its inception, it seems. What do you know about this? Were you involved?"

"No!" Melech squeaked out. "I had nothing to do with it. Really. How could you think that of me?"

"Because you are a spineless, skinless, hideous thorn in my Great Design, *that* is why. I sense that you had the rest of the cabal slain because you seek more power? Don't you know, old fool, that there is not a person alive who could ever attain the kind of power I have?"

"Of course, Master, of course. I never thought-"

"Don't bother thinking. You are an idiot," the blob said. "I do not believe a word that comes out of your putrid mouth. I find you disgusting in the truest sense."

"Ouch," David said under his breath. "Coming from him..."

The blob continued. "I have no doubt in my being that you, Melech Rothschild, organized this terrible scheme to seize my power and control. And it almost worked..." the blob conceded. "I had shrunk to just half the size of that pipsqueak on your left. It was quite clever of you to interrupt all financial exchanges. Only a disaster such as this could ever warrant such a clear abuse upon the American psyche...and have them accept it! Simply amazing!" it gurgled. "You did, however, overlook a flaw within your plan that any idiot could see and that is that the people who must *enact* your plan are fucking retarded. Waaa Haaa Haa Haaaa! What a fucking idiot!" the blob laughed and pointed a tentacle at Melech in jest. Suddenly it stopped laughing and stared at Melech. "Jesus Christ, what happened to your head? Were you in a car wreck or did you shove that hubcap through your skull on purpose? Braaa haaa haaa haaaaaa! Moron!"

David noticed that Melech's hands had become balled up into tight little fists. "Master, it is not as it seems. You are mistaken. I have come here with an offering! A sacrifice is at hand!"

"A *sacrifice*?" the blob said and shifted its weight. It seemed to consider this. "What kind of sacrifice?" it asked, now curious. "You know me too well, Melech. I *love* a good sacrifice."

Melech pushed David forward with both hands. "David Dingle, Sir. *The* David Dingle. This is the one who's responsible for everything. He's the one that's been trying to take your power from you. But I caught him, Sir, and I've brought him to you."

The blob leaned over with surprising speed and agility and lowered one of its colossal eyes just inches over David and inspected him. "Hmm. He doesn't *look* rich," he said with an air of disappointment.

"Oh, I'm not, Mr. Blob Master Sir," David said. "I'm about as broke as the economy."

"What!!!!????" the blob yelled and hoisted itself upright like an enormous, agitated caterpillar. Now it looked even more terrifying than before. And *boy* did it look angry. "*What* did you say, Pipsqueak!" it demanded.

David mewed like a frightened kitten. "I just said that I'm as broke as-"

Melech threw himself in front of David. "He didn't mean it, Master Economy. He didn't know! I promise you, he didn't know."

"E-economy?" David asked. "You mean, *you're* the economy? Gosh, I thought you were Satan."

"*What!!!????*" the monster bellowed. "You mistook me for Satan! How *dare* you!!!"

"He didn't mean it!" Melech said again. "He's just an idiot. A nincompoop! A boob! Honest, Master Economy! Isn't that right, David? Tell the Economy you're sorry. Tell him you didn't mean it."

"Um, I didn't mean it?" he said and looked at both Melech and the Economy who were staring at him in shocked silence. "I guess, it's just — wow! *You're* the economy? Seriously?! This is *crazy*! Wait 'til I tell Jerry, he'll never believe me!" David turned to Melech. "I thought you said we were going to meet your master…you know, *Satan*? Weren't you planning on overthrowing Satan?" he whispered.

Melech looked appalled. "You've got to be kidding! Who in their right mind would try and overthrow *Satan*? Why that's just *beyond* stupid."

"Oh, sure, I guess that makes sense. It was just kind of difficult to tell what with all the Satan talk. I'm sorry, this is all really hard for me to understand. Seriously, I had no idea that the economy lived in a nasty, gooey, smelly tunnel under the streets of Washington D.C. Personally, I always thought the economy was something sexy, you know, like a glass of champagne with high heels or something. But definitely not like this. This is more like a blob of yellow cat crap basted with the drippings of rancid meat."

"Silence!!" the Economy bellowed. "Melech Rothschild, your sacrifice offends me greatly. How *dare* you bring in a snack that judges my appearance. I'm mortified," it garbled. "You will pay greatly for this, Slave. I *command* that you bring me a finer sacrifice. Something tasty. A caucasian man, perhaps, one of high society with little moral ground stuffed with greed and intolerance. Only *then* will I be appeased! And once I am appeased I will eat *you*, Melech, for dessert and we'll call it even. What do you say?"

Melech lunged at the Economy with the single syringe that he had placed in his pocket and he stabbed the great blobby beast with the vaccine which contained David's DNA, a genetic code that would dismantle the great Economy once and for all.

The blob recoiled and hit Melech with one of its tree-sized appendages and flung him across the tunnel and into the concrete wall on the other side. It bellowed with pain and quickly jerked the syringe out of its body and flung it away. Its eyes widened and were filled with horror. For a moment only the sounds of dripping water could be heard in the long and dark tunnel.

And then, the Economy began to laugh.

"Braaaa Haaaa Haaaa Haaaaaa!" it bellowed into the darkness. "You think you can kill me with a fucking needle? Are you *serious*?! God! I knew you were brainless, but wow! Grmmm. Your idiocy has made me hungry again." With that, the Economy wrapped a long tentacle around David's leg and hoisted him into the air like a small toy.

"Auggghhh!" David screamed. "Don't eat me! Help!"

The sound of footsteps running over goo could be heard coming down the tunnel.

"David!" a woman's voice cried. "David, where are you?"

"Courtney! I'm over here!" he hollered back. "Come quick!"

Soon David could see the outlines of a dozen individuals coming his way. The Timpson family was in the lead and close on their heels was everyone else.

"Put him down!" Courtney yelled at the blob, surprisingly undisturbed by the creature's terrible appearance, an appearance she was well accustomed to from being raised by a blob mother herself. "You listen here!" she pointed angrily at the Economy. "That there is my friend David Dingle and if you so much as hurt a hair on his head I will open up a can a whoop ass on ya!"

"Your friends are so small and tasty looking," the blob said to David. "I think I'll eat them next."

"Somebody do something!" she shouted and turned to see Jacob Timpson carefully collecting a slow drip of goo from the ceiling into a paper cup. "What are you *doing*?" she asked.

"Just give me a moment. I think I can convert this to holy water but it's going to take some time. I'm not Catholic but the Devil doesn't split hairs when it comes to God's will. Use your miracles, Master!" he shouted up at David. "Turn the beast into a loaf a bread or a box of wine!"

"David, your phone!" Dr. Whyzer shouted. "Use your phone. It can help you escape."

He couldn't believe he had forgotten! David dug frantically through his pockets and pulled his phone out like the sword of Excalibur. "Aha!" he proclaimed and held it high in triumph. Immediately the phone began to vibrate and several lines of script appeared in a cool and reassuring Garamond font while a friendly voice with an Australian accent read aloud:

"David. You are in danger. Plug me into your nearest hard drive computer and I will access security clearance and begin shutdown procedures."

"What?!" he yelled desperately. "How am I supposed to find a hard drive computer in a dungeon?"

The screen flickered. "Searching dungeon..." the voice said. There was a brief pause and then, "Dungeon: a strong dark prison or cell, usually underground. Synonyms: underground prison; cell."

"Augh!" David yelled. "I thought you were smart! Get me out of here!"

"This dialogue may be monitored for training purposes. Please consider rating this transaction online at our support page."

David felt himself being lowered alongside the face of the burbling Economy. The tentacle tightened around his leg. "Say..." the Economy said. "That's a nice phone."

"It usually works really well," David admitted. "I think it's having issues because we're underground."

"That's funny," the Economy said. "I usually don't have a problem getting a signal down here. Maybe try my network connection. Network's CashMoney. Password Bling69."

David quickly typed it in. "Oh, there we go!" he said with relief. "Wow. You were right. My entire newsfeed just opened up. Let's see...It looks like Miley Cyrus is back in prison again. Oh, here we go - Economy!"

"What does it say?" the Economy asked.

"It says the Dow Jones has taken its biggest dive since the Great Depression. The NASDAQ has flatlined. This guy Silver State says, 'Few people believe the economy is stable enough to set a stack of pennies on. The stupid economy can eat a big fat one. Fuck the economy!' "

"What!!!" the Economy bellowed. "Your phone is lying. Everyone *loves* me!" In a rage, the Economy began to shake David upside down by the leg until David dropped his phone into the gaping mouth of the hideous beast.

"Noooooo!" David screamed. "My phone! How *could* you!!" Never in his life had he ever felt so deceived and distraught. He struggled and flailed like an angry cat in the hands of a power-hungry two year old. The Economy, not expecting such resistance from a pipsqueak released its prisoner who fell onto Courtney and Dr. Whyzer.

Now furious, the Economy swelled in size, towering over the small band of survivors like a living mountain of doom. "Now you shall *all* feel my wrath! None shall escape. You are destined for the acidic soup of my digestive system and not a soul shall know of your plight to save the world from my rule. I am invincible!" it thundered and the Economy fell into a sickening laughter yet again.

President Alan pushed his way forward until he was standing directly under the blob. "Excuse me. Hi," he said politely. "I'm sorry. Allow me to introduce myself. My name is President Benjamin Alan. I am the one in charge here and I was thinking perhaps we could start a dialogue of some kind. Hmm, I've got to be honest. You look kind of familiar. Were we at school together?"

The blob thought about it. "Maybe. I taught a few classes at Harvard once."

"International Economics?" the President asked.

"I think so."

The President snapped his fingers. "I knew it! Great class, by the way. One of the few I actually attended. So listen, I don't know if you are aware right now, but our country is right smack dab in the midst of re-elections and I was just wondering if, seeing how you seem to have some political sway, if you'd be willing to speak at a rally later this week?"

"Will there be lobbyists?"

"Oh definitely!"

"I'll think about it!"

"Hey, Mitchell!" the President said. "Get over here. I think I've figured out a way to resolve this conflict of ours."

Senator Guiles turned away from the conversation he was attempting to have with Melech Rothschild about subverting the democratic process. "What is it?" he asked.

"Come here a sec. There's someone I want you to meet."

Never one to shy away from introductions to potential new donors, Mitchell Guiles walked over and looked up at the hideous blob with a big pearly smile and said, "Hi there. Senator Guiles. It's wonderful to finally meet you. How long have you been living under D.C.? Don't you just *love* it here?"

Using every ounce of strength, President Alan shoved the incumbent Senator as hard as he could into the gooey flesh of the Economy. It had been a long time since the Economy had tasted a fresh Armani suit and it quickly wrapped a tentacle around Mitchell's neck and tossed him into its mouth like a potato chip.

"Whoa!" the Economy said after a loud and satisfying burp. "That was a good one! Just the right amount of arrogance. So who's next?" The Economy shot out its tentacles like a blackjack dealer tossing cards until it had everyone in the tunnel hanging upside down in the air.

"Release us, Satan!" Jacob Timpson yelled.

"Put me down, you Illuminati motherfucker!" Tatum screamed.

"Blurgga Blaaaakamma!" Melech said in the grips of an ill-timed idiot attack.

"Oh God, I just didn't think it would end this way!" Courtney said.

"Not cool!" Veryonica yelled at the Economy. "No one tries to kill me except for *me*! Hashim! Do something!"

Hashim, who still had the briefcase in his hand, knew it was up to him to drop the warhead into the hideous infidel's mouth. But before Hashim could do that he would have to activate the bomb. This proved difficult as he was being violently shaken by the blob in an attempt to rid Hashim of the sharp-corned box which would undoubtedly affect its enjoyment of this elegant eight-course meal.

"David!" Courtney shouted in a tone which implied that she had accepted her fate. "I believe in you. I don't care what anyone else thinks about you or who they want you to be. For me you're just David, and that's enough. You are kind, and brave, and most importantly, you have a good heart. I don't have much time, David, but I wanted to sing you a song that I wrote while we were driving through the Martial Law."

"Oh no!" Dr. Whyzer yelled. "She's going to sing!"

"Don't do it, Sis!" Tatum urged.

"*Daaaaaaaviiiiid.*" It was too late. "My sweet *Daaaaaaviiiiiid*. How neat you make me *feeeeeeeel*." Fifty year old chips of paint started to peel off the tunnel walls. "You stole my heart, by stealing the world's *freeeeedoooooms*. You Martial *Laaaawed* my *soooouuuul*! I paid the *se-cuuuuuurity tolllllll*. You've got a *heaaaaart* with *baaaaaalls*, I want you in my *vagiiiiina waaaaalls*!!!"

"Whoa!" Dr. Whyzer said. "Didn't see *that* one coming!"

The Economy twisted in pain. "Stop it!!!" it yelled. "Make it stop!"

"It's working!" Trish said. "Keep singing."

"Don't encourage her!" Alma screamed.

"Hashim! Just do it, already!" Veryonica hollered.

To everyone's dismay, Courtney had already begun the second verse of her song. If the jihadist didn't hurry up, her singing would kill them long before the Economy did.

The Economy's mouth was agape in torturous agony thanks to Courtney's miserable singing. "Got it!" Hashim screamed in triumph as his finger slipped onto the red button. Hashim opened his fingers and dropped the nuclear bomb into the Economy's mouth. The beast released his prisoners the moment the bitter metal rubbed against the cracking bones of Senator Guiles. The blob shifted and rolled about in terrorized panic.

"What have you done?!" it screamed.

"Run!!!" David yelled at the top of his lungs.

The group didn't have to be told twice and everyone was hot on his heels as David led them through the underground maze of tunnels toward salvation.

"When is that thing going to go off?" he yelled at Hashim.

"Fifteen minutes, I think! Maybe one. I forget!"

"*This* way!" David screamed and took a sharp left.

"Oh my God!" Courtney yelled. "The walls are shaking."

"The ground is cracking! It's breaking apart!"

Old ceiling tiles split and fell onto the cracked cement.

"It's the beast! We've made him angry!" Jacob Timpson said and hastily applied some homemade holy water onto his brow and shoulders.

"We're all gonna die!" the President screamed.

"No, we're not!" David yelled. "Just follow me. Trust me. I know how to get around places like this."

Now the walls were coming loose and falling debris would have sealed their path had David not swung the group out of the way in the nick of time.

"We're almost there!" he called back. "I can see the secret entrance."

When they got there David waited at the entranceway to help everyone pass through. As he stepped over the threshold the passageway collapsed and sealed off the tunnel.

Jerry looked up from his Presidential Address. "Hey! Where *were* you guys?" He turned back to the camera. "Hold on, America, be right back." He looked at the group again. "Is there anything you wanted to add to this before I sign off? I've spent the last ten minutes talking about head shops and liquor licenses. I was gonna mention something about the Alamo to ramp up some of that patriotism before the camera fades into the red, white, and blue. You guys OK? You look kind of freaked out."

"We made it!" the Timpsons screamed.

"What about the nuclear bomb?" Courtney asked. "Won't it still kill everyone?"

"It was activated deep underground," Melech said, still trying to catch his breath. "There's a chance we'll be OK."

"Then why is the building still shaking?" Trish asked.

"Something's not right," David said. "This isn't from the warhead. This is from something else."

At that very moment the ceiling ripped off the top of the White House like a muffin top. The front of the Oval Office cracked and ripped away, stripped from its foundation. Within seconds, all the other walls began to crumble. A torrent of wind blew against them with hurricane force. In the distance, large trees could be seen swirling through the air like pine needles in a water drain.

Then, just like that, all sounds of destruction slipped away until the group became enveloped by a strange and otherworldly silence. It was as if they were standing in the eye of the storm. The small group of survivors huddled together, waiting for the end.

"This is it," Courtney said to David. She had her arms wrapped around his body and she squeezed him for all she was worth. "I just want you to know that I...I..."

"Yes?" he asked and looked at her petrified face.

"I think you're pretty neat," she said and pulled him in for a kiss.

Veryonica shot her arm out toward the sky. "Oh wow! Look!" she yelled.

An incredible shower of golden light flooded the heavens. Never before had any of them seen a sight so beautiful. It captured their absolute attention. The brightness of the light resembled the golden glow of a supernova, yet the silence strengthened like a storm. Each of them knew that they were being encompassed by an intelligence they had never thought real or possible, and somehow, for some reason, it was focused entirely on them. It could only be...

"Praise the Lord!" the Timpson's all shouted.

"Praise Allah!" Hashim screeched.

"Praise Satan!" Melech yelled.

"This is almost how those pills make me feel," Dr. Whyzer whispered to Trish.

"Don't worry, Mr. President, I'll keep you safe!" Agent Boring yelled and crouched behind a pile of rubble and emptied his clip into the sky.

David shielded his eyes from the blinding light. A deep inner knowing told him that this light was here for them. The only rational thing left to do was address it. David stepped forward and positioned himself in front of the group. "Who are you?" he asked.

A calm and loving feminine voice broke through the silence like a breath of warm air against a parting dawn. "It is I," She said. "Earth."

"*Earth*?" they all exclaimed simultaneously.

"That's right," She said. "Earth."

There was an awkward moment of silence as they all pondered this response. Some of them scratched their heads. Others realized that their heads were beginning to hurt as they began to understand what was happening.

As leader of the free world, President Alan decided that it was only appropriate that he lead the diplomatic process. "What do *you* want?" he asked.

The light danced slowly around them under the big halo of clouds. "I have decided to remodel," She said. "I feel that I've really let this place get out of hand."

"So by remodeling you mean..." the President said.

"I'm kicking you out," She said.

"*What*!? You can't! We live here. I am the President of the United States and I demand that you stop hindering the election process. We are focused on *real* issues that affect *real* people. Are *you* going to help, or do I have to save the world's greatest country myself? I'm the most important-"

"I used to have such nice renters," She interrupted him. "They were so clean and they never used more than what they needed. It was a good arrangement. But that was almost ten thousand years ago. I suppose times have changed quite a bit since then. There's a different mentality these days."

"Um, excuse me, *Earth?*" Jacob Timpson said and stepped forward.

"Yes?"

"Jacob Timpson here. Nice to meet you. I'm sorry, but did I just hear you say ten thousand years ago? Because I, well, aren't you supposed to be only six thousand years old?"

"*Surprise,*" the Earth said.

"I don't...understand," Jacob said.

"Clearly," the Earth responded. "I can assure you that I am well over six thousand years old. When I was just a baby planet one of my naps would have lasted a million years. I miss those naps," She admitted.

Jacob Timpson looked at his family who were staring back at him in profound confusion. He looked again at the light. "So let me get this straight. You're...*not* God?"

"Correct."

"You're Earth."

"Mmm-hmm." There was extreme patience in her tone.

"And you're older than six thousand years."

"Correct again. Much older."

Jacob Timpson and his family grouped together and had a quick family discussion. They were all nodding and shaking their heads simultaneously, as if they were understanding something but still in the throes of inner conflict. At last, Jacob Timpson, surrounded by his family who looked up at him like devout little acolytes, said, "Thanks. That makes a lot more sense." And with that, each of their heads snapped, crackled, and popped like a bowl of Rice Krispies, and their bodies slumped to the ground. No one doubted that the Timpson's family revelation was, in many ways, just as good for them as an old-fashioned Rapture.

Jerry stepped forward. "Hey Earth. Jerry Burger here. Howya doin'? So I was just wondering if instead of killing us all, you could just maybe do the opposite and help us get this virus under control? How does that grab you?"

"You *humans* are the virus," the Earth said. "You pollute everywhere you go, you take without giving back, you practically destroy everything you touch. For far too long you have used your minds instead of your hearts to survive. You have become careless and greedy."

"*Careless and greedy?!?*" Melech Rothschild yelled at the light. "*You're* the one with all the resources, you hoarder! You let perfectly good river water run into the ocean. You allow perfectly good gold to stay in the ground. What kind of selfish monster are you? Don't you know we're trying to make a living down here!

You want us to use our hearts while we try to survive yet another natural disaster!? Do you have any idea how often you try and kill us?"

"I've lost count," She said. "But this time I'm really going to give it a go."

"Well, count me out!" Melech yelled up at the sky. "I've got underground bunkers like you've got mountain chains. I've got enough seeds and bio-domes to make this stupid planet look like a third grader's science experiment. I don't need your blue skies or your warm winds. All I need is for you to leave us the hell alone!"

"Mister, you gotta be the saddest man alive," Courtney said. "Blue skies an' warm winds are what life's all about."

"Save it, Sacajawea. You and your idiot friends can keep them. I've got books and manifestos where I'm going — plenty of texts to stimulate the mind. While all of you are swimming neck deep in flood water I'll be reaffirming and tightening my ideologies. Perhaps some of your miserable offspring will survive the deluge of fires and floods and will come to call me their ruler when I emerge as a bionic man-machine, fit for the far reaches of eternity. Nothing can stop me! Nothing!!!"

The wind picked up momentarily and a walnut bonked into Melech's hubcap with a deep resonance. Melech stumbled sideways and fell over backwards.

David looked down at him with concern. "Whoa! Are you OK?"

A tooth slipped out from under Melech's lip. The bright intelligent light in his eyes had vanished and was replaced with a dull sprinkle of inbred curiosity. "Dher," he said. "Das was a *WAL*nut!" He looked at the ground and picked up the heavy black walnut in his hand. "I has a *WAL*nut!"

"Oh man," Jerry said. "I think the Earth just tagged him in the head!"

"Doh no!" Melech said and pulled at his pant leg. "I pee myself now." He looked up bashfully at Jerry. "And a little poopoo, too."

"Probably for the best," Dr. Whyzer said.

David looked up at the beautiful sky. "I want to stay," David said, hoping that She could hear him. "My phone used to have all these awesome pictures of beautiful places all over the world. I would like to see them for myself now — *without* my phone. Traveling around the country has been the most amazing experience of my life. I think I've spent the last ten years looking into my device while the whole world has been passing me by. Who knows? Maybe when everything is fixed up I could travel around the world, see what life is like outside of America."

"Dude, you don't want to go to Florida," Jerry said. "Nothing but old people."

"I'm ready to live life for me now, I'm ready to have the courage to follow my heart," he said with a new air of confidence. David shook his head. "If I want to go to Florida, I'll go to Florida. But right now I want to stay here because that's where I am. I don't have anywhere else to be." He took Courtney's hand and held it. "I kind of like the present moment, now that I think about it."

"That's very wonderful to hear," the Earth said. "You sound like a very nice human." She sighed. "But as it stands right now your species is going to have to get scratched from my list of ingredients. Sorry. I wish there were another way, but you're just too engrained in your human systems to ever change."

Suddenly the ground began to rumble and shake beneath them. "It's an Earthquake!" Trish yelled.

"Oh my God!" Veryonica said. "Why am I not excited! This feels weird. I don't want to die!"

"It wasn't me," said the Earth. "I'm the first to admit when I earthquake."

The ground suddenly began to expand and transform like a giant bubble about to burst.

"It's the bomb!" David yelled.

"Oh Allah!" Hashim cried. "I am coming for you now!"

The warhead exploded deep, deep underground inside the horrible bowels of the Economy. The ground rumbled and quaked — beneath them, the extreme pressure and heat vaporized the tunnels; house-sized boulders crumbled and the rocks and gravel became rubble chimneys, but thankfully did not reach the surface. Certainly, whatever secrets that once existed beneath the nation's capital were buried forever.

"What was *that?*" the Earth asked when it was finally over.

"It was a nuclear weapon. Hashim's bomb killed the Economy," Veryonica said.

Hashim couldn't believe it. Veryonica was right. He had done it! He had killed the American dream! Suddenly his smile was as bright as the sun. He had finally blown something up and he had never felt better.

"Well," the Earth said. "I suppose that changes things."

"It *does?*" David asked.

"Sure. Without the Economy telling you what to do, maybe you'll be able to turn things around and make a better world for everyone."

"You mean we're free?" Jerry asked in exuberance. For someone who had never had more than nine dollars to his name at any given time, Jerry was ecstatic.

"*Free?* Are you kidding me?" the Earth said. "No way. You work for *me* now. Sixteen hours a day for room and board. That's my only offer. Take it or leave it."

"We'll take it!" Courtney yelled happily.

"Dude, this girl does *not* represent us," Jerry said. "I'll give you five hours a day with a forty minute smoke break. Come on. It's what everyone's offering these days. What do you think we are, stupid?"

"*Jerry*!" David said. He looked at the golden sky and nodded with confirmation. "It's a deal. Whatever you need we're here to do it."

"Good," the Earth said. "Start out by cleaning up this mess I've made. I also flooded the Ozarks pretty good so you'll have to figure that one out, too. In the meantime, be nice to each other. You're all in this together."

Everyone smiled and began hugging one another.

"Oh, Earth!" David said. "Just one more thing." He had the manilla folder in his hands and held it out in front of him. "You are undoubtedly the most intelligent creature on, um, Earth. This document has some very important information about me. I would be greatly honored if you'd help me understand it."

"I would be happy to," She said and a huge gust of wind tore the envelope out of his hands and they all watched it sail into the air and out of sight.

"Hey!" he yelled. "What are you doing? That told me everything I needed to know."

The bright light in the sky slowly began to dim and retreat. Before it was gone entirely a loving, distant voice said, "I wouldn't think too much about it."

It was right about then that the President saw the army of vigilantes crest over the hill in the distance.

Chapter 31: The Army

The wind was gone and a dust cloud lingered in the distance as the men on horseback approached the crumbling remains of the White House. There were too many of them to count. David guessed there had to be at least 500 horses. Although they were still too far away to see their faces, their armament was clear. These were warriors, men and women with guns slung over their back and quivers full of arrows. They almost looked like...

"Indians!" the President whispered.

"Look how many of them there are," Veryonica said. "It looks like they're prepared for war."

"Maybe they're just out for a ride," Jerry suggested. "During a hurricane."

"Doesn't look like it," David said. "They look like they're coming with a purpose."

The army stopped about 100 feet from where David and his group were standing. The vigilantes' faces were grave and stoic. Many of them looked like they were ready to die. If there was ever a time for diplomacy, now was that time.

"I would like to handle this," the President said. "I want one of you to remember this speech word for word. It may be the last thing I ever say." The President walked up to his half-crumbled podium. He straightened his tie as he looked out across the White House lawn at the hundreds of Indian warriors who stood staring at him. He raised his right hand and held it beside his face like a sign. "How!" he said loudly. Suddenly, a look of panic swallowed him and he turned to David and said, "It's *how*, right? It's not '*when*' or '*where*', is it? *God*, I hope I didn't screw that up. It's hard without a speech writer, you know?"

Very slowly a tall man in a wide and bright headdress began to walk forward. One could sense the tremendous respect that the group had for this man. Clearly, this was their leader.

"Hello, Mr. President," the chief said. "My people have traveled very far to meet with you. We have come from all over. Most of us are from different tribes. The plague has decimated many. The virus does not care who it kills, for it affects red men and brown men and white men alike. It is clear," the chief said slowly, "why it is killing some of us and sparing others. It has taken from our people some of our wisest leaders. Chief Thinking Owl is gone. Chief Wise Wolf has been taken. Now it is only me, Chief Quail Knuckle and my little brother Squirrel Brain. We do what we can, but our efforts are often in vain." He looked behind him at his army. "There were many more of us in the beginning, but

Squirrel Brain took a wrong turn in Nebraska. I think they're somewhere in Minnesota right now. If you see them, tell them Chief Quail Knuckle says hi. Have them meet us at the Spot. He'll know what that means."

"I don't understand," the President said. "Are you not here to fight?"

Chief Quail Knuckle made a face. "Why does the white man always want to fight? We are not here to fight you. We have come to warn you. The virus has shown us many truths about humanity and about ourselves. We have seen the errors of our ways and the ways of the white man. The time has come to change. I tell you this because I have seen a vision. The Earth is very angry with us. She will destroy us if we do not take care of Her."

"Yeah, I know," the President said. "We got that message too."

"*Really?*" Quail Knuckle asked in surprise.

"Yep. Pretty much word for word. Not more than ten minutes ago."

Chief Quail Knuckle looked perplexed. He turned over his shoulder and looked at the giant group on horseback. "Oh," he said. "Well, that's good, I guess."

"So is that the only reason you came?" the President asked. "To warn us?"

Chief Quail Knuckle looked at his hands. "Yep, pretty much."

President Alan could see a young man running toward them with something in his hands.

"Oh!" Chief Quail Knuckle said. "I almost forgot. We have something for you."

The President's eyes widened. He loved gifts. "Really?" he asked. "What is it?"

"It is an offering," he said as the young man handed over a large box. Chief Quail Knuckle opened the top of the box and began to pull something out. "A symbol of our friendship. It will be important for us to get along with each other in the future. Here. It's a blanket."

"A blanket!" the President said and greedily took it into his arms. "Wow. This is nice. I really like the colors."

"Thanks," he said with a smile. "So do I. Be sure to share it with everyone you know, OK?"

"Will do!" the President said. "Thanks again."

"No problem," Chief Quail Knuckle said and walked away.

"Well," Jerry said, "another disaster averted. That's three in one day. Not bad."

"You know," Agent Boring said, "you handled that David swap pretty smoothly. We could use someone like you on the force."

"Are you *serious*!?" he asked. "Don't mess with me on this, Boring."

"Yeah, why not? I could even show you how to shoot a cannon."

"You guys get *cannons*?" Jerry asked as drool started to form in the corners of his mouth.

"We're not supposed to, but I do it anyway," he said and waved a hand.

"Agent Boring," the President said, "You've come a long way to get where you are today. Just the other day you were in Seattle. Yessir. A looong way," he mused. "You brought in the fake David, tried to shoot the Earth in the face - these are things that not everyone wants to do, even if it has to get done. If I were to ever leave this world, I'd need to know there was someone up to the task of taking my place. I want you to be my Vice President."

Agent Boring *wanted* to say thank-you. He *wanted* to shake the President's hand and bow like a gentlemen, maybe even act a little surprised like he hadn't seen it coming. But he couldn't. Not all the James Bonds in the world could hold him back at a time like this. "*Yeah!!*" he screamed. "FUCKING YEAH!!!"

"I'll take that as your acceptance," Benjamin Alan said. He turned and looked at Melech. "As for you, Melech, I won't be needing you one bit. You've been about as helpful as a toothache. If I had a dollar for every time you've made me look like a fool since this whole pandemic, I'd be able to buy every book in a library."

Melech pulled his finger out of his ear. "Demme have one of dem soda pops?" he asked.

Benjamin Alan rolled his eyes. "We should find a crate for you or something." He looked at David. "I believe I owe you an apology, Mr. Dingle. All this time I've been blaming you for this pandemic when it wasn't even your fault. It was the Earth's!"

"I'm pretty sure it was-"

"Goddamn Earth," the President said and shook his head. "But we'll beat Her, God willing! I think it was smart of us to just play along until She left. That'll give us some time to come up with a plan. I'm gonna need some plan makers, Dingle. You up to the task?"

David couldn't believe what he was hearing. "*Me?* Really?"

"I know I said I was done taking advice, but frankly, I'm addicted to it. There's nothing I enjoy more than a good back rub and an itinerary of what I should say and do for the day. Think you can handle that? Not the back rub part, of course. The job involves a lot of thinking, and research, and bossing me around."

David looked at Courtney who had a smile the size of a slice of watermelon. "Yeah," he said carefully and then smiled. "I can do that."

"It's a great salary on top of that. I'll pay you top dollar. Just name your price."

"But the Economy is...gone," David said. "You can't pay me without an economy."

"Well, that's something you're going to have to think about. And once you do you'll have to come up with a plan and then tell me about your plan so I can go places and talk about your plan."

David smiled and took Courtney's hand. "I like that plan a lot, Mr. President."

About the Author:

Mike Dickenson is a writer, traveler, and white-water raft guide in Southern Oregon. He also creates documentary films and leads courses in writing and storytelling through Commonlink Productions.

IQ84 is now an audiobook! Grab a copy or sample some of it today.

For more information please visit:
www.commonlinkproductions.com
www.mikedickenson.com

Contact Mike at: mike@themapmakers.org

If you enjoyed this book, please consider leaving a review.
Thank you!

CPSIA information can be obtained
at www.ICGtesting.com
Printed in the USA
BVHW040325070520
579322BV00026B/665